Restoration of Marriage

Karl Duff

WINEPRESS WP PUBLISHING

ISBN 1-57921-214-X
Library of Congress Catalog Card Number: 99-61133

Acknowledgements

Several persons have been involved in the review of this manuscript during its approximately 8-year gestation. Chief among those to whom I am indebted are Mr. Jimmie Sowder who reviewed it for biblical accuracy and application and Mrs. Sue Dowgiewicz who conducted a most painstaking and expert grammatical review.

Dr. Elizabeth Moberly was most helpful in assisting me in understanding her publication and views on homosexuality and in reviewing text which summarizes her work.

Most rewarding was the considerable time and patience many expended upon me for the testimonies within these pages to accurately reflect their stories, my daughter Suzy included among them. These are some of the precious brothers and sisters in Christ into whose lives I have been permitted to participate and see the work of God with great joy and satisfaction.

Contents

SECTION III: TEARING DOWN STRONGHOLDS

SECTION IV: APPLICATION AND TESTIMONIES

SECTION V: REPRODUCTION OF SEED

Section VI: Strength and Encouragement

Appendices

Preface

If you abide in my word, you are truly disciples of mine. (John 8:31)

We are a nation now writhing in the agonies of sexual immorality, seemingly entrapped in the age of unashamed "marrying and giving in marriage" which Jesus predicted in Matthew 24:38.[1] Most divorces (hence, the original marriages also) apply only secular definitions of marriage, not God's. We also see countless "informal" unions in adultery and fornication where sexual partners are sampled and even more quickly put aside. This is all at the expense of God's marriage covenant where man's seed is to be honored and protected in the same fashion as God protects His. God's Seed is the Word made flesh, Christ Jesus, who gives eternal life in His exact likeness and is never wasted. But we see human seed treated as sewage, wasted on the ground as "streams of water in the streets" (Prov. 5:15–17).

If the Bible has been set aside, can a mere book on the subject influence anything? This book's title, *Restoration of Marriage*, may seem overly ambitious. There is only One who saves and restores. "Unless the Lord builds the house, they labor in vain who built it" (Ps. 127:1).

There is even a danger. Despite best intentions to the contrary, we all have some tendency to attempt using "book learning" in one's own soulish strength rather than in response to the Holy Spirit. This will likely cause difficulties, as it has with me, in attempting to seek "postage stamp" solutions. We are suckers for information and may exhaust our flesh and mind attempting to follow ideas on our own strength rather than follow Christ. This does eventually bring us to our Deliverer but can also cause a lot of grief as long as we persist apart from Him. The only real Answer is Jesus Christ. He is, over and over, our only Life. He must be *living in us* or we die.

If one has Jesus, he has Everything. Apart from Him, we can do nothing (John 15:5). No extra books or formulas are needed if you have Christ. Loving obedience to Him will produce love for a spouse who somehow seems to have become impossible to love. So, if your marriage is suffering, know that your only help is in Jesus, not in this book.

Restoration of Men, which preceded this book, portrays God's basic design of men and women according to His own likeness. It is briefly reviewed in chapter 2. Understanding His design of gender is helpful in seeing how our sins against the opposite sex have broken the design and aided the enemy in building in us strongholds which war against our souls and soul mates. *Restoration of Men* does not by itself restore men but gives a basis upon which men can agree with the truth about their ruination, repent, and cooperate with God in His regeneration of new men in Christ.

This book is hopefully the same. It gives gender information that relates to the wars that take place in marriage. It provides a basis upon which husbands can take responsibility for their sins and rise to the occasion for which they were created, building a free woman and raising up godly seed.

Women can cooperate, too, but are held to no other standard than their morality before God and His command to respect their husbands. Possibly, if they know and obey Christ, some may renounce some of their strongholds that war against their husbands. But I view this as unlikely, perceiving that it is God's design and economy that a wife's sin be cleansed by Christ through her husband. It's unlikely, too, that wives will be able to turn aside from the type of help their souls so deeply crave for their husbands; i.e., their words, even deeply spiritual words, to which their husbands listen and respond. No, Scripture already says that husbands are "won without a word," flatly contrary to a wife's soulish desire (1 Pet. 3:1–6). Her true hope is in being peaceful, quiet, patient, and content in Christ while He works on her husband. Women can cooperate but can't lead husbands any more than they can lead Christ. It is God's grand design of gender and The Bridegroom's marriage to His Bride that the husband is head of the wife.

Many lessons of marriage are seen in Christ and His Bride. His own marriage and human marriage, as well, are upheld using the same precepts. What is needed to purify the Bride, He will suffer, not necessarily avoiding divorce (either human divorce or Israel or the Church, as we see in Scripture). But God is also eager to reveal His glory to a world sunk in sin— the miry clay of its appetites and methods (see Ps. 40:2). He puts many hopeless human marriages together again on a new foundation—Jesus, Himself. Nothing else will bring life to the dead.

So, caution rules. *Restoration of Marriage* offers insights, but it is not a cookie cutter. We should petition God for more of His beauty and glory in marriage. God may already be doing this. Out of His ageless provision for those caught in ruination and turning to the only One who can save, He has declared, "And the Law came in that the transgression might increase; but where sin increased, grace abounded all the more" (Rom. 5:20).

Section I: Review and Introduction to Design

1

The Gospel According to a Woman's Heart

He will exult over you with joy, He will be quiet in His love, He will rejoice over you with shouts of joy. (Zeph. 3:17)

Even young girls will read and understand the above scripture, whereas young boys will laugh at it if you try to get them to consider it seriously. These are the words of an exultant warrior who has been victorious in the winning of his bride. This can be confirmed by reading the immediately preceding sentence in Zephaniah 3:17. They are the words of God in our midst, the victorious warrior.

For reasons we can only dimly perceive, God has caused the entire gospel of salvation to be written into the hearts of girls, but not boys. Girls have a vision in full bloom by the time they are about ten or eleven years old, containing every essential detail of the gospel, usually as a personal dream or aspiration.

The vision is this: She is held prisoner in a castle or dungeon. It is protected by difficult and frightening defenses: castle walls, a moat, possibly a fire-breathing dragon or an evil giant. She is threatened by evil and cannot escape by herself. She needs a knight in shining armor, a man on a white horse!

The man exists for her. She somehow knows this, even if she has never met him. She knows that from somewhere this knight will appear and come to her rescue. In the process, she will see him overcome the defenses that hold her prisoner, facing danger and risking death on her behalf. He will prove his love for her to rescue her. She will belong to him for the rest of her life, marrying him and being wonderfully fulfilled in his love, in all sorts of romance, bearing his children and raising them with him.

Boys have only a tiny portion of the gospel in their hearts. That is, they have an aspiration to be heroic. They have an inkling that they are destined to do something "great." They desire to excel, to win regard of others, but it is so easily perverted it is hard to connect their inner motivation to their actions. They will compete in games, show off, tease, compete athletically, do pranks, joke, etc. to get attention. They can also easily be drawn into doing foolish things because of their desire to be recognized. Even as an undefined vision, it may even motivate to being the best at being bad.

Older boys and young men may have even more defined perceptions that they are destined for "greatness." But they have no idea as to what it is.

Beyond this, boys have no real comprehension of the gospel in terms of personal vision. They certainly do not have any idea that they have been marked by God to die on behalf of a girl. This is because they are still boys, and the pathway to manhood is a daunting experience!

Perhaps girls have been given more of a personal view of the truth because they, like Eve, are more easily deceived, and need more clarity in their hearts to motivate them away from deception. Possibly boys have lost what was originally understood because Adam sinned deliberately (without deception), perhaps knowing the outcome of his death (1 Tim. 2:14). Perhaps it is because women are *internal* and men are *external* in their design, internal comprehension being greater in the female, as discussed in later chapters. Perhaps because girls will become brides they possess the truth more clearly regarding their relation to the Bridegroom.

Possibly it is not given to boys to know the full vision and find satisfaction in it until they become men proven by fire; no boy could bear knowing what was required.

In any event, the fact remains; girls are given the gospel of Jesus Christ as a vision for their own lives. This vision, as well as the gospel, is God's provision working for good for those who believe. This is true at any age, at any level of sin's destruction, and at any stage of our restoration in Christ.

An outline of the situation might be as follows:

I. Girls have a motivational vision in all of the points described above.

II. This is a true vision of the gospel of Jesus Christ, containing all the following elements:

 A. The Bride's capture by evil.
 B. Satan's strong defenses and the risks in overcoming them.
 C. Her helplessness to do anything without a rescuer, a Savior.
 D. The existence of a Rescuer, Jesus Christ, the Son of God.
 E. The Rescuer's confrontation and overcoming of fear, evil, and death on her behalf, proving the love of the Rescuer, God Himself.
 F. Eternal security based on the proven love of God.
 G. Marriage, romance, intimacy, and fulfillment.
 H. The reproduction of the Hero Bridegroom's children through herself.

III. For women it is also a guide for their own lives. To the degree they are able to live in harmony with this vision, they will find fulfillment as women in relationship to men in marriage (if they aspire to marriage and a family). Certain elements are key. That is, girls are helpless to find and prove a husband's love. It cannot be manipulated. They must find a safe position of protection in order that the bridegroom find her and prove his love for her before marriage; i.e., *it is imperative that he do all the work, establishing the basis for the marriage covenant,* while she stays under protection. (Attempting to come down from the castle walls and help the knight slay the dragon brings disaster, but, unfortunately, this is where most girls go wrong.)

IV. Men must recognize that the bridegroom must be perfected by the Father (Heb. 2:14–18, 4:15–16, 5:7–9) before any marriage takes place. A man must submit to denying himself and submitting to the girl's father or other effective authority until he has proven his love and paid the ransom for the bride. He must become a true man, pay the ransom, and become bonded to the bride before the marriage covenant and before having sex with his beloved bride. (It is the violation of this by men seeking to satisfy their sexual desires outside of a marriage covenant that has brought men and our nation to ruin.)

V. Men and women must recognize that neither boys nor girls will ever easily submit to this process. Men are the agents of God in helping boys toward true manhood on behalf of a girl and in protecting a girl until the boy has been perfected. Women cannot apply fire to boys or make men out of boys.

We see that God has drastically different strategies for the transition of girls to womanhood compared to those that bring boys to manhood. For girls, it is a one-phase plan. A girl must remain a girl and stay under protection until the marriage covenant is established. She then becomes a woman by opening her body to her husband and bonding to him on the wedding bed. This takes place through receiving his seed. Until this takes place, any other "rescuer" is a false rescuer. Any actions taken out from under protection will work only to destroy her vision.

For boys, it is a two-phase plan. He must *first* be perfected as a man, passing through fire and paying the deliverance ransom, being bonded to the bride before the marriage covenant. His proof of love is the foundation for the bride's security and freedom to live as a free woman. When this is accomplished, *then* he may wed her and enjoy the fruits of his love.

What is the foundational truth of the gospel? Well, it is the proven fact that God loves us and has braved death to rescue us!

This chief truth must be established in our hearts before we can ever be saved. Once it has been established, the gospel applies to every area of our lives! *My* security and freedom to live to *my* full potential were established by God giving *me* the knowledge of His true and incredible love for *me*. Wow! This is such a personal gospel! God establishes it through each of us personally in Christ!

Then He enables each of us to live it personally on the face of the earth as a testimony to the glory of God! Isn't it wonderful that he has given to men and women to live out the gospel in their own lives and relationships in marriage!? The imprint of the gospel is placed on our lives. Every girl can live as the Bride of Christ and every man can live as the Bridegroom if they will live under the truth of the gospel.

These truths can be applied with great benefit to men and women who have been scarred by sin and who discover that God loves them! For those reconciled with God through Jesus Christ and willing to reorder their lives (Matt. 6:33), He will bring the gospel into living reality. The kingdom of God will reveal its beautiful fruit in earthly lives! God will provide covering for girls to help them find their true love. God will send bridegrooms who prove their love clearly once and for all, bonded men who will never abandon them because their commitment has been secured by fire. From this He builds women who are free, whose fruits go almost beyond comprehension (Prov. 31:10–31) and who do not need to go to war every day to get their husbands to prove again that they love them.

From boys of all ages God also produces men. Men who are free to love. Men who respond to the fire God provides them. Men who discover, sometimes in surprise, the great love they have for the women whom God has given them. They finally resolve it once and for all; the woman is worth it. At any price, yes, she is worth any ransom.

Once a man has this issue resolved in Christ, all things are resolved in his favor. God works on his behalf. When a man's ways become pleasing to God, the Lord makes even his enemies to be at peace with him (Prov. 16:7). God is looking for men willing to suffer pain as Jesus Christ did for His bride. The bride can never be free until she knows for sure that her bridegroom loves her. Everything depends upon that! God's plans intend to demonstrate that for her.

No man leaves the fire until the King calls him out (Dan. 3:26, 6:23), when the work is completed to the glory of God. Then God's promise is, "He will see His offspring, He will prolong His days, and the good pleasure of the LORD will prosper in His hand. As a result of the anguish of His soul He will see (the results) and be satisfied" (Isa. 53:10–11).

How many men have shattered the vision of so many women? How many women have run from the protection God has provided, only to see their aspirations turn to dust? How many girls and boys can now be protected through parents who have purposed their lives and marriages to produce godly seed?

These motivational words are of the Holy Spirit. In them are Spirit and life. "Groaning too deep for words. And He who searches the hearts knows what the mind of the Spirit is, because He intercedes for the saints according to the will of God" (Rom. 8:26–27). In the agonies of men and women seeking God, the counselor can touch upon what the Spirit is saying and confirm the Spirit's drawing of them to godliness in their marriages. Prayer and fasting, groaning, weeping, confession, and deep intercession, especially from men, are God's call to destruction of strongholds, to deliverance, healing, and reproduction of godly seed through the gospel of Jesus Christ.

2

Review of Restoration of Men

He sent His word and healed them. (Ps. 107:20)

This book is an extension of conclusions and precepts from *Restoration of Men*, which studies the origins of God's creation of man and the attributes He assigned to male and female. For the reader's convenience, these precepts are briefly summarized as follows:

(1) Although God declared His creation of Adam to be "good," God has an order of perfection that is greater than perfection of that which is merely singular or solitary. This greater state of perfection is through composite unity among those having separate identities and functions. The greatest example of this is in the Godhead, where Father, Son, and Holy Spirit have identical essence and nature, but different functions. The same precept applies to the separation of the male and female out of the original Adam into two creatures, man and woman.

(2) In the original foundational purpose of God's plan to reproduce all life "according to its kind," (or seed, Gen. 1:21, 24, 25) God divided His two chief attributes in the reproduction of life between male and female. These are derived from Genesis 15:1 and Genesis 17:1, the attributes given to the male being those of a "shield," and the attributes given to the female being "breast."

(3) Study of the detailed work of a shield reveals its nature of combat, mortal protection and covering over those protected, its damage through warfare, and its strict dependence upon an outside source of healing and restoration in order to retain its life-preserving power. Study of the detailed work of a breast reveals its nature of nurture, health and healing, and strict dependence upon an outside source of protection (a breastplate) in order to retain its health and life-giving power.

(4) The functions of godly men in the crucial areas of security to women are derived from the work of Boaz in the Book of Ruth; i.e., providing (a) physical security (b) economic security, and (c) emotional security.

(5) The breakdown of the basic functions of the shield and breast are seen in the fall of man in Genesis 3, through Eve's deception apart from protective covering and the fall of Adam through the prohibited nurture she offered him. These have great ramifications regarding the ravages of sin that have enveloped mankind since.

(6) God has provided for female soul bonding to a man through sexual intercourse and for male soul bonding to a woman through paying a "soul price" (i.e., a ransom) for securing her well-being, security, and freedom in the knowledge that she is loved. These precepts are also the same as those of Christ and His Church. Bonding of the male should take place prior to the marriage covenant and bonding of the female after the marriage covenant on the wedding bed.

(7) Much of the female weakness toward male seduction and harlotry is in failing to understand the complete difference between God's provisions for soul bonding between male and female and her misguided attempts to obtain a secure relationship with the male by submitting to him through sex. This has just the opposite effect that premarital celibacy and remaining under a strong covering until marriage would accomplish.

(8) The consequences of sexual immorality in destroying manhood and a man's ability to provide effectual covering for women are derived from Proverbs, chapter 5, and other like scriptures. These passages detail the "death" the comes to men who become so involved, a death that occurs in loss of wisdom, vitality, strength, and finances. The damage to women is in never knowing their true value and the reason their husbands married them. Their husbands cannot be entrusted with their security, and they never know beyond doubt if they are loved. They become crippled by insecurity and enslaved to continuously needing "proof of love" by their husband.

(9) Death comes to all relationships in which agreement/conspiracy takes place among the parties to commit sin. An evident symptom of such a conspiracy between two parties is role reversal where the subordinate party becomes ruler over the other person. Sexual sin prior to marriage is a particular example of this, nearly always resulting in the death of the marriage.

(10) God has means for producing true men from boys, both in perfecting from youth those not perverted by sexual immorality (Joseph) and in those corrupted by it (Judah). Both involve trial by fire and ultimate submittal to bond-slavery to God, even unto personal death. This is also the means by which men accomplish the work of God and find their greatest personal fulfillment.

(11) Apparently conflicting attributes given unevenly to the functions of shield and breast administer to the family and aid in preparing children to see the truth of the gospel. Chief of these is judgment versus mercy; the extraordinary conflict between being held accountable for actions and being totally released. These meet perfectly in the cross on Calvary. They also introduce us to the fact that the shield bears the consequences of any judgment brought on the family.

(12) The chief purpose of accountability is not to bring judgment upon others, but to find personal protection and extend it to the work of God, free of deception and destructive influences. Precepts of accountability and its protection apply to individuals, spirits, marriage and family relationships, and the Church.

This quick summary is helpful in providing reference for the commencement of this book. However, it does not necessarily persuade of truth. It is suggested that the reader review for himself or herself both the book and scriptural references upon which these assertions are made.

3

The Free Woman

As a result of the anguish of His soul, He will see it and be satisfied. (Isa. 53:11)

The secular world frequently captures images and trends that are amazing in their reflection of the truth, though there is little doubt that they do not understand the foundational truths that underlie their work. A good example is the rash of publications in the 1990's reflecting the search by men for "lost" manhood. Many techniques and solutions are being offered, but none by the secular world that recognize the roots of sexual immorality that have destroyed manhood.

Another example appears frequently in various types of advertising seeking to identify a spirit that will draw the attention of women. Although sometimes having sexual overtones, there are many which appeal instead to a deeper, foundational vision of women.

The ad generally shows a woman modestly dressed, perhaps in a casual dress or sports outfit, leaning back against the arm of a man who has all of his attention on her. She is smiling and may be moving, stopped by the camera at an instant that captures a carefree spirit of freedom and fulfillment. This is usually accentuated by a feeling of motion, the swirl of her dress or movement of her arms, as in a dance step but informal and free. The effect is somewhat that of a model demonstrating dresses, but where the dresses are not the center of attention. Neither is the man. It is the spirit of her freedom under his attentive care and strength that is the basis of the appeal for attention. The ad itself may be about anything. It is the spirit of the appeal for women's attention that is the significant thing. It is the appeal to be a "free woman," and the picture described has all of the critical elements to strike at what is *a central desire of every woman*.

It is the work of God to produce for the Son a bride who is a free woman. It is the work of men of God within their marriages to also produce women who are free indeed! Imagine that a secular advertising world could correctly identify and capture this spirit so precisely through a picture and exploit it for the purpose of creating a material desire to buy goods!

A free woman is a woman who is free from fear and insecurity, anything that prevents her from being a source of life to others. Her life is based on trusting God for her own needs and in serving others. The Bible is filled with pictures of this foundational work of God with mankind. This is a work of God of great beauty, "free of spot or wrinkle or any such thing," (Eph. 5:27) perfect and blameless, loved and cherished by her husband. From the stronghold of security that he provides, she is capable of prodigious feats of love. She is completely fulfilled in living her life for her bridegroom and others whom she loves, because within his protection she is free to truly love.

Paul explicitly introduces us to the free woman in the comparative pictures of Sarah, the wife of Abraham, and the slave Hagar, his maid, as well as in the comparison of Jerusalem and the Church. In the book of Galatians, he describes the "bond woman" Hagar as producing children who are slaves with her, while the "free woman" Sarah produces children who are heirs of promise, "born according to the Spirit" (see Gal. 4:25–29). A look at the spirit of Sarah is truly awesome.

Peter uses Sarah as the perfect model of a beautiful woman, having "the imperishable quality of a gentle and quiet spirit, which is precious in the sight of God" (1 Pet. 3:4). He likens her as capable of producing children in her same likeness, through Christ. In verse 6 following, Paul captures the *essential issue of the removal of fear*, appealing to women to submit to their husbands as Sarah did. "Thus Sarah obeyed Abraham, calling him lord, and you have become her children if you do what is right without being frightened by any fear" (1 Pet. 3:6). Sarah's submission to the periodic foolishness of her husband is really amazing since twice she submitted to being given away by Abraham to other men. Abraham was fearful of being killed by the men because of Sarah's beauty should they discover she was his wife (Pharaoh of Egypt, Gen. 12:11–20 and Abimelech of Gerar, Gen. 20). Both times God intervened to protect both her and Abraham.

The first incident took place when Sarah was about sixty-five years old and the second after she was ninety years old. Yet the Bible confirms that Sarah was "very beautiful" (Gen. 12:11, 14). Every woman should ask herself how Sarah portrayed such beauty far beyond the years in which temporal beauty is understood to prevail and should naturally seek this beauty for herself. It is in God's means to provide this beauty for women through a relationship with Jesus Christ, regardless of the wisdom or godliness of their husbands. He will provide it impartially to all whether they seek it or not as they learn to trust God and to "do what is right without being frightened by any fear."

However, it is more the purpose of this chapter to clarify further the tasks that are upon the husband in enabling his wife to become the free woman God intends. This is through the attitudes and acts that God portrays for him in obedience to Christ. These are difficult and deadly to the flesh. How are they portrayed by Scripture?

The most graphic and painful picture of a man suffering repeated dying and humiliation for his "many-membered" bride (1 Cor. 12:12) is Moses, a type of Christ who suffered as the husband of Israel while delivering her from the bondage of slavery to enter into the promised land of Canaan. Through forty years of almost unbroken suffering, misunderstandings, prayer and fasting, and all manner of trying circumstances, Moses shepherded Israel through the trials that produced a nation adequate in character and in the knowledge of God to obey Him. Reduced to utter dependence upon God, he was given guidance on how to prepare her to occupy the land God had designated for them. It is recorded that Moses fasted and prayed for Israel at least twice and possibly as many as three times for forty days and nights (see Exod. 34:28; Deut. 9:9, 9:18, 9:25, 10:10). He totally identified with Israel's success or failure and interceded for her with his own life, even asking that God remove his name out of the book of life if God would not forgive Israel for her sins (Gen. 32:32).

As a type of Christ and a portrait for husbands, Moses was given little fellowship or direct affirmation by anyone other than God during the time of his work. He did have a faithful (and nearly invisible) servant, Joshua, as a source of support, but he never received appreciation from the bride for whom his life was continually being laid down. At the end he was not even allowed to accompany her into the promised land but allowed only to see from afar (Note: with his *eyes!*) the place for which he had prepared her. His need for fulfillment from the work of his hands is earnestly recorded in Psalm 90 in which Moses' closing words are, "And do confirm for us the work of our hands; Yes, confirm the work of our hands" (Ps. 90:17). Yet at completion of his life on earth, the fulfillment of accompanying her into the promised land was denied. He died first. *He was required to see the results by faith, from a distance.* Although receiving approval from God for his faith, he, along with many other faithful men, "did not receive what was promised, because God had provided something better for us, so that apart from us they should not be made perfect" (Heb. 11:39–40).

It is difficult to convey this type of promise to carnal men as making a life of death and sacrifice all worthwhile. Yet God says it is. As stated in the previous chapter, He even records this for His Son, stating clearly in Isaiah 53 that this is the same form of gratification that is reserved for Jesus Christ. In the midst of His vivid descriptions of the suffering and intercession of Christ for His bride, He also states, "As a result of the anguish of His soul, He will see it (the results) and be satisfied" (Isa. 53:11).

Nature, actuarial tables, and the distribution of most private wealth to women record many of the same truths. Men die first; over 70% of our nation's wealth is in the hands of women. A successful man will leave his wife financially secure and blessed with godly children and satisfying relationships. Women do not have a great need for men once these things have been provided, and relatively few older women left under these circumstances are likely to remarry. This is quite in contrast to men who have experienced successful marriages and whose wives die first. Their needs for nurture and healing generally draw them quickly into remarriage. Thus the husband departs the scene with great importance attached to the *visible circumstances* in which he leaves his wife. He draws his satisfaction from how well he has accomplished his responsibilities to *secure and provide for his wife*. This is in sharp contrast to the factors from which the wife will draw her gratification. A free woman will be surrounded by fruitful life-giving relationships. It is the husband's job to see that the essentials to enable her gratification are the fruit of his life.

All the biblical types of Christ closely resemble this model. As a shepherd, Joseph was removed from his family and spent years as a prisoner in a foreign land before being elevated to kingship. After recognizing his brothers when they came to buy wheat, he was denied the immediate gratification of a family reunion and vindication of his earlier dreams until God's purposes of righteousness for the family of Jacob were fulfilled. He was without any sources of family affirmation. He was taught to deny himself and live according to the visions that God had given him as a youth. As a result, those he loved were delivered from famine into freedom and abundance. He did not see the vision fulfilled until after much anguish and suffering.

David also spent his youth as a shepherd, rejected and unaffirmed by his father and brothers (1 Sam. 16:11, 17:28). He faced his most difficult challenges from Goliath and fourteen years of persecution by Saul without any affirming support except for that of Jonathan. Through his faith in God, he defeated Goliath. Later, David constantly sacrificed his own safety and interests to refuse to take things into his own hands against Saul. God eventually placed him on the throne and delivered his nation from bondage to the Philistines.

There is also the portrait of Christ, Who gave Himself up as a sacrifice for His Church that "she should be holy and blameless" (Eph. 5:27). With no supporting affirmation, He went to the cross misunderstood, despised, and rejected, depending utterly on His faith and the promises of God for the results that were to take place. At the limits of His endurance, He found capacity to go forward purely on the basis of obedience to the Father. By His death, He brought His bride, the Church redeemed from sin, to a place of security and freedom. Oh, how like Him may we be in yielding our lives for the blessing of our wives!

There is surface similarity yet sharp contrast between the tasks of the man for his wife and the woman for her husband. The man is mysteriously drawn into "dying" alone for his wife, laying down fleshly things for the sake of her growth and freedom. He must continue to pay ransom, being forged by fire to undergird her doing the things in which God is drawing her under his protection. He is putting to death things in himself that interfere with her success. He is a bond slave in His search for wisdom in doing what is right and accomplishing her protection. He pursues new vision for her and her future, which was essentially nonexistent prior to marriage. In contrast, a wife is drawn to "live" for her husband, yielding the issues of control and headship to him and to God and fostering her motivation to support, encourage, and nurture him. She is led by her desire to meet his current needs according to the visions of her youth, which preceded the marriage. She finds fulfillment in freely living her life for him. He finds fulfillment in constraining and losing his life for her. The husband generally faces his task alone, without human affirmation, replacing forms of immediate gratification that satisfied him as a child (see 1 Cor. 13:11) for God's future provisions. The wife faces her tasks with more available resources in terms of sympathetic support relationships and continues to draw from more immediate sources of gratification through words. There is death and life in both individuals, but the husband is generally called to solitary "death" while the wife is called as a fountain of life in company with others.

Rahab was the woman of Jericho set "free" from the bondage of harlotry and the strongholds that had previously held her captive (while deceiving her that they were providing security.) She found true security in the Living God of Israel when she was persuaded by faith to place her security in Him. God's supporting agents were soldiers of Israel, men obeying God's call for a life-risking mission to spy out the city of Jericho. They provided her subsequent deliverance and set the stage for God to identify and fulfill His promises for all free women. It is one of the miracles of history that Rahab's offspring was the kinsman-redeemer, Boaz, who portrayed the Lord Jesus Christ in many ways and himself died several "deaths" to bring Ruth to a place of security and fulfillment as a woman.

Imagine the liberating power of God that was present in Rahab's life when she saw the glory of God on her behalf in rescuing her and then giving her Salmon as a husband. Imagine the joy when she gave birth to her own son, Boaz, blessed with the honor of his father's name and security, enabling his rearing and growing up! Imagine the beautiful relationships in a household that reared a man with the character of Boaz! Presumably Rahab may have still been alive to witness the marriage of her son to Ruth and to share in the joy of the birth of her grandson, Obed, together with the other women who surrounded Naomi and Ruth, saying:

> Blessed is the LORD who has not left you without a redeemer today, and may his name become famous in Israel. May he also be to you a restorer of life and a sustainer of your old age; for your daughter-in-law, who loves you and is better to you than seven sons, has given birth to (a son.) (Ruth 4:14–15)

Here is the fulfillment of the free woman. Listen to their mutual sharing of words of fulfillment!

Blessed be the eternal bride of Christ and our earthly wives He has brought so close alongside us!

4

Introduction to Marital War

I will open my mouth in a parable. (Ps. 78:2)

There is a painful war game that children play called "Paper-Scissors-Rock" in which each child attempts to outguess the other in choosing a weapon. Deciding simultaneously, each child must choose one of the above three instruments. If they happen to each choose the same item, a tie results and there is no outcome. However, if they each choose different items, there is always a winner and a loser according to the following rules: Rock crushes Scissors, Scissors cut Paper, and Paper covers Rock. The one choosing the prevailing weapon earns the right to hit the loser. The paradox of a weapon capable of being either victorious or defeated based purely upon the nature of the opposing weapon is probably not lost even on the young.

Marriage partners also have weapons, either of which can win. However, they each generally always use the same weapons. The weapon of choice for the husband is usually "hammer;" the choice for the wife is usually "nail." The hammer is heavy and blunt; the nail is light and sharp. The hammer crushes and smashes its resistance; the nail cuts and penetrates deeply with little exterior evidence of damage. Other sharp instruments could conceivably illustrate this point also, except that a nail is the only one that is driven by a hammer! Husbands fail to realize that they are generally the driving forces behind much of the pain of marriage inflicted upon themselves.

This somewhat crude illustration actually has more than passing resemblance to reality. Men generally continue to act out their blunt-edged boyhood temperament, never having really grown up. They take risks, contest, and seek sovereignty ("king of the hill") by nature. Wives discover after marriage that the masculine traits they admired before marriage were mostly outward symptoms of an inner boy. These superficial symptoms of boyhood depicting strength and protection are not what a woman really needs. What she really needs is *knowledge that she is loved by her husband unto death* and that he has *strength of character to do right* by her at his personal expense. Lacking this, she will promote her own views, driving her nails gently or not until they find their mark.

Boys are generally thoughtless with respect to risk-taking and relationships. They will squander resources and eagerly seek opportunity to contest. But risk-taking and compulsive boy-games of husbands jeopardize family safety and the security vital to women. If the boy is especially immature, he will pout, manipulate, or get angry when he loses or doesn't have his way. Broken relationships don't bother boys and are secondary to priorities of contesting.

But women suffer greatly in broken relationships. They need to relate closely with those who establish and confirm their value and standing. This is incompatible with angry confrontation, force, and heavy-handed efforts to prevail in contest. Confrontational threats quickly lead a woman into subterfuge and manipulation to avoid confrontation. Husbands easily discern this and typically react against it, thereby promoting more confrontation.

In this age, the battlefield upon which these issues are fought and lost has generally taken shape long before marriage by unconscious boys taking thoughtless risks with girls who foolishly think they can buy a permanent secure relationship in exchange for giving sex. By believing this lie, they irrevocably set their life's foundation upon harlotry, the exchange of sex for security. The disastrous consequences of this carry on into the repeated cycle of marriage, divorce, and repeated remarriage, all playing out the lusts, fantasies, and deceptions of harlotry. Men are permanently frozen into the impotence of boyhood and women who never know if they are truly loved become the heads of their husbands. Role reversal and constant contesting over sovereignty consume the adversaries. Enemy strongholds make war between spouses, each using their favorite weapons, until death prevails, though not in the form they contemplated when taking their wedding vows.

The husband's chief responsibility is to find his way in Christ out of the mess sin has created—both his own and his wife's.

What can we say to wives? Men need to be cautious in venturing into the vicinity of "strongholds" of wives who are not their own. Scripture teaches that primary responsibility for security, cleansing, and instruction of wives is in their own husbands. In general all such instruction to women should come through those whom God has placed in protection over them.[1] For wives, this is the husband. It is in this unique relationship that a man's experience with his wife can also be likened to that of receiving "nails." He must learn to respond as Christ to God's requirements for the purification of the bride. He must conform to crucifixion (See Eph. 5:25–33; Phil. 3:8–10).

A primary reason there are not more godly men is that there are so many women usurping God's rightful place as the heads over their husbands (1 Cor. 11:3). They do so in amazing clandestine strongholds of self-deception, which oppose the word of God and cause the most intense pain in their husbands. Wives might be greatly aided if they would trust God more with their husbands, recognizing that by so doing they will be helped toward their true goals, that of bringing blessings upon their families. But few there are who can discern and repudiate their evil behavior without convincing liberating evidence of God's love manifested through their husbands.

Unlike Adam, Eve's fall was rooted in deception (1 Tim. 2:14). Women are highly susceptible to the deception of Eve, a root stronghold that controls women even more strongly than it controls men. (Would any wife ever agree to this? Is this even *possible!?*) In addition, the hiding places of deception in a woman are so craftily hidden with the soft speaking, peace-seeking, and ingratiating natures of women that they generally escape all notice and accountability. To all, that is, *except the husband.*

Things no one else will perceive in a woman will pierce a husband's heart. The husband sees it all. He is accountable to God for his wife and is also the only one to whom she is accountable. He therefore is given eyes to see her nature and behavior. By design he bears her iniquities. He is pierced through by her transgressions. But he cannot righteously cry out. Being only a man, however, he cries out often enough to discover the further pangs of separation from God and men. A husband often finds himself alone while his wife is surrounded by her friends, children, and relatives. His soulish desire for sympathy is frustrated; there is no aid to a man being crucified. A husband's heavy-handed methods are evident to all, but seldom are the wife's subtle weapons even visible or consciously applied. Sympathizers will take up a wife's case against her husband, but seldom is the case the other way around.[2] This is by design, whether or not one is a believer. A shield is a shield. It is in the nature of the gender roles that the consequences of a woman's actions fall upon her husband.

She is free to take it for granted. If wise, she will also grant freedom to her husband to stumble along without reproach until God helps him to grow up more fully.

5

Contrast in Marriage Relationship

Your desire shall be for your husband, and he shall rule over you. (Gen. 3:16*b*)

One would think from a study of God's curse upon Adam in Genesis 3:17–19 that Adam wasn't even married. God defines to Adam the curse upon the earth, the toil he will expend procuring a living, and his impending death. These seem immense and painful, to be sure, but God says nothing to Adam regarding his relationship with his wife. Yet in the preceding verse dealing with the curse upon Eve, God speaks of her greatly increased pain of childbirth and pain in her relationship with her husband. This is not all. The difficulty of her relationship with her husband is defined as twofold. That is, Eve's attitude toward her husband and her husband's toward her are both contained in her curse. What do we make of this?

We might agree quickly that God seems to define the husband-wife relationship as having greater centrality to a woman's life than to that of her husband. Since this is directed at Eve, one could surmise the relationship aspects of the marriage to be more crucial to her well-being than to his and that the consequence of the curse on the relationship will be more painful to her as a result. One might extend the idea further that relationships with people in general are more important to women than to men. We might also deduce against the contrasting scripture of Adam's curse that the functions and success of a wife are keyed upon the *internal* life of the family rather than to the *external* business of extracting a living from the earth, generally assigned to the husband. Finally, there may be something in the contrast of the wife's "desire" for her husband and his "rule" over her that marks the true essence of the curse upon her. These two terms are in conflict. This curse may restrict her ability to relate well to her husband, painful because it is so crucial to her happiness.

Trusting in the righteous judgment of God and in the fact that He works all things for good, even that meant for evil (see Gen. 50:20; Rom. 8:28), we may consider there is appropriate justice as well as a propitiating blessing intended by God upon Eve. By providing her with severe travail and soul-bonding to her children ensuing from childbirth, we sense likely enhancement to her family faithfulness in child-rearing, perhaps even some protection to her corruption to further Satanic deceptions to "be as God." "Women shall be preserved through the bearing of children if they continue in faith and love and sanctity with self-restraint" (1 Tim. 2:15).

Eve's new difficulties with her husband may also harmonize to constrain her natural proclivities. As we will see soon in a study of the word *desire*, her desire for her husband is likened to "stretching out after" or "water flowing through." If righteously employed, it is evocative for good. If directed by evil, it is nothing less than the power of sin to occupy and control the object of its desire. This flowing through desire is gentle and subtle, but pervasive and powerful and defines her nature to her husband.   One of the aspects of the curse we surmised above is that she perhaps anticipates similar relational attitudes and responses from him. But this is not to be. He relates by employing rule over her.

As the later word study on *rule* also explores, a husband's rule contrasts with a woman's ways. Rule involves directness. Subtleties and hidden meanings are absent. Among men, government, and armies, direct statements reduce misunderstanding. A husband's style is to come straight to the point; words are explicit rather than implicit. *Rule* signifies relationship in which language is given and taken at face value and responses are measured the same way.

Rule may also be employed either for evil or good. But the focus is upon external results. Impact of rule on relationships, either through neglect or by necessity, is sometimes given less priority. A husband, initially at least, anticipates that his perspective will be shared by his wife. He is greatly perplexed when he discovers repeatedly that this isn't true. More forceful means of attempting to resolve word meanings only compound difficulties that to him are communicative and to her are relational.

More interesting gender contrasts await us. Let us consider some others before elaborating on *desire* and *rule*.

Other Design Contrasts Between Spouses

I have made a covenant with my eyes; how then could I gaze at a virgin? (Job 31:1)

Men, designed by God as a shield for their families and having tasks that have changed little until the most modern times, have an inherently different design than do their wives. Consider the work of shepherd, hunter, watchman, and soldier as typical examples of a shield, and consider the demands of these tasks upon their design.

All these professions require visual acuity and ability to interpret visual information. Defending against predators, tracking animals, aiming weapons, being alert for enemy activity, and engaging in active combat will penalize all those with poor vision. Also, information gained through observation must be inductively applied to determine likely outcomes, intentions of the quarry, army, or opposing soldier. Each task requires single-mindedness without distraction. Most are easily measured by a timely outcome.[1]

Furthermore, visual information which is kept to oneself is frequently useless. Men usually work in groups on such tasks. Therefore, critical information must be communicated in explicit words and using consistent rules of meaning and logic to enable other men to reach consensus, make decisions, and take common action. This places great emphasis upon men to live according to what their eyes see and use language effectual to communicate this information to others.

By similar analysis, men can also be seen to be results oriented; their tasks are urgent in securing life from a hostile world and cannot effectually be accomplished simultaneously with other major work. Men tend to focus totally on the single task at hand to the exclusion of other potential tasks, which indeed may follow, but sequentially rather than simultaneously. A man's fulfillment is therefore in completing an objective, not in merely participating in a process. When that completion is evident, men are enabled to go on to other things. Their gratification is in visually seeing the confirming results of the "work of their hands" (see Ps. 90:17). The deep need men have for visual confirmation and gratification is seen in this plea of Moses closing his prayer of Psalm 90 and in God's provision that Moses be allowed to see the promised land from Mt. Nebo, opposite Jericho. There "the LORD showed him all the land, Gilead as far as Dan, etc. . . . as far as Zoar." Then God concluded, "I have let you see it with your eyes, but you shall not go over there" (see Deut. 34:1–4).

This brief analysis leads us to sympathetic understanding as to the fact that men are creatures of the eyes. They deal with external, visually determined information and are constrained to simple rules of communications and logic enabling group goals and objectives. These conclusions are consistent with everything we know about men from observation as well as from Scripture. The ultimate gratification for the ultimate Bridegroom is "As a result of the anguish of His soul, He will see it (the results) and be satisfied" (Isa. 53:11).

Men are enticed and stimulated through their eyes. Their attraction to women is visual. They are put-off and impatient with process that does not evidence progress. They are prone to want to see convincing external evidence of objective truth and generally weak in discerning things not susceptible to visual determination. They don't do multiple tasks well nor work that doesn't produce a clear result.

A woman, however, is quite different. She, the breast of the family, is designed by God for the family's nurture and healing and, in contrast to her husband, is designed to network and assess needs for life-support from within the family. She is making assessments that are not based on logical external data but from internal data—the affairs of the heart and mind. She is designed to work in response to what she hears with her ears. Even before her children are able to speak in intelligible words, she gets her necessary information from their cries, laughter, sighs, or other forms of audio communications. She can tell in an instant what a particular tone of cry means, and when she gets up at night in response to the child (while the husband sleeps), it has been due to something she heard. She is activated by her ears.

The inflection of her husband's voice communicates much more information about his needs than do the surface meanings of his words. His words are only a loose framework in which she interprets her primary tasks to meet his needs and support their relationship. They may, in her opinion or in actuality, be totally different than what he is attempting to say.

A woman is generally not willing to sacrifice a relationship over a contentious issue. It is contrary to her nature. She will quite often duck confrontation just for the purpose of keeping a good relationship, whether with her own children, her husband, or someone outside the family. Her skills are great for nurturing and healing but not well suited for work in a confrontational environment.

She is primarily assessing *people* for the purpose of assisting those who are dependent on her. She is usually dealing with subjective information and applying intuition and her own emotions in evaluating a situation. These skills extend to aid her husband as well. She is better able than her husband at evaluating the character of others through what she hears them say.

In contrast to men and popular conception, a woman is not attracted nor sexually stimulated by visual input but rather through words. She internalizes words of esteem and love and, as Mary with the words of God through shepherds and angels, "treasures them and ponders them in her heart" (Luke 2:19). Evaluation of her worth and the reward for her work are provided to her through her ears (see Prov. 31).

These design features in a woman enable us to appreciate other attributes that may have caused us past amazement. How is it that a woman can do the same tasks over and over and still find fulfillment? The old adage "A man's work is from sun to sun, but a woman's work is never done" is really true. Food preparation, shopping, laundry, house cleaning, etc., are all tasks that seem to repeat themselves forever. How can a wife find enjoyment and fulfillment from work having no "bottom line?" The answer is that women are creatures of process. In stark contrast to men, they obtain gratification from all the tasks of nurture, despite their having no evident conclusion other than satisfying the needs of the ones they love.[2]

In addition, women have no difficulty at all carrying on multiple tasks and parallel thought processes, supporting the many simultaneous tasks on-going in the home and in attempting to anticipate other needs of her family.

Even sexual union portrays the same gender distinctions. The man is primarily involved in a result-oriented union with a "bottom line" of sexual climax. The woman is primarily involved in affirmation in the process of intimacy of relationship that frequently ends far too quickly for her.

The man may be stimulated and perverted by visual stimuli, the woman by enticing words.

Another distinction must be made. By nature, men are primarily oriented to *things* rather than people. Consider again their tasks. A hunter must know how his quarry behaves, where to find it, and how to attain (kill or capture) it. He must be able to track it, interpret its signs, and design strategies to overcome it. He must be able to observe complex behavior in a changing environment and to make logical decisions to minimize wasteful expenditure of his energies, time, and resources. Note that all of these efforts are related to assessing *things* for the purpose of obtaining *things* little related to people, relationships, and feelings.

In similar fashion, a soldier assesses the strength and intentions of his adversary. He must observe and logically process information to resolve decisions enabling him to prevail over the enemy. This includes whether or not even to engage in battle (see Luke 14:31–32). In confrontational matters, he is not concerned with preserving relationships. He is concerned with the efforts needed to make decisions that will overcome the adversary. Relationships and feelings are secondary, if considered at all.

For a soldier, as well as a hunter, there is also value in keeping his own intentions hidden from the enemy.

In summary, we see that a man is designed to procure and process objective information to support timely and logical decision making, and that he tends to deal with situations described by his eyes in the context of things, rather than people or relationships.

These characteristics of a man, which seemed very attractive to his wife in terms of her early projections of security (when they were single and courting), turn into a big liability when directed toward the wife after marriage. A man is poorly designed to sustain many of the processes and communications needs within a family, and he soon finds himself in constant difficulties with his wife. The wife, on the other hand, has totally different processes and communications that match up poorly with her husband. They are both hard pressed to know what to do. In even the discussion *process*, the two speak and listen at two different levels. He talks about things to which he thinks she is listening, but she possibly is not. She is attending to the process of building and maintaining relationships; he wants to resolve a "bottom line." She is speaking words which he does not understand and seems to repeatedly revisit the same points he thought had been resolved in yesterday's conversation.

It will become a source of amazement and irritation to her husband that she can track and converse in so many topics and considerations all at the same time, even changing subjects from one sentence to the next, occasionally even in midsentence, while he struggles to bring the previous thought to a conclusion. He will also resist interruption of work in progress to undertake a new "honey-do" request, which he views as a distraction and which his wife considers essential to affirmation of her home, hearth, and relationship with her husband.

The wife, in the meantime, struggles to find ways to enhance her position as helpmate and chief source of succor to her husband, not comprehending his single-minded fixation on certain things nor his frustration on failure to bring closure to many things. Avoiding confrontation and thereby avoiding resolution, the minds of husband and wife frequently remain on two different paths and conflicts remain unresolved.

God is working on both of them. The husband must become a creature of process and learn to appreciate and communicate with his wife in her exotic language. The wife must learn to aid in bringing closure to many topics which otherwise would go on forever.

Desire/Teshookaw

Yet your desire shall be for your husband. (Gen. 3:16)

Following the fall of man in the Garden of Eden, God pronounced a series of sentences on all parties involved, in chronological order of transgression. Starting with Satan, He gave a sentence which was at the same time God's promise of mercy for all mankind:

> Because you have done this, cursed are you more than all cattle and more than every beast of the field; On your belly you shall go, and dust shall you eat all the days of your life; And I will put enmity between you and the woman, and between your seed and her seed; He shall bruise you on the head and you shall bruise him on the heel. (Gen. 3:14–15)

In this promise of Messiah, the "seed" of the woman to be wounded yet to overcome Satan, the subsequent sentences on the man and the woman are placed in a context of affirmation and redemption. How wonderful!

To Eve He then said:

> I will greatly multiply your pain in childbirth, In pain you shall bring forth children; Yet your desire shall be for your husband, and he shall rule over you. (Gen. 3:16)

Then concluding with Adam He said:

> Because you have listened to the voice of your wife, and have
> eaten from the tree about which I commanded you, saying, 'You
> shall not eat from it;' cursed is the ground because of you; in toil
> you shall eat of it all the days of your life. Both thorns and thistles
> it shall grow for you; and you shall eat the plants of the field; by
> the sweat of your face you shall eat bread, till you return to the
> ground, because from it you were taken; for you are dust, and to
> dust you shall return. (Gen. 3:17–19)

We have raised the point that both rule of the husband over
the wife and the wife's desire for her husband are contained in
the curse on the woman. Why is this so? What is the true meaning of her desire for her husband and his rule that both are contained within the curse placed upon her? We saw earlier that both
of these involve only the marriage relationship, while the curse
placed upon the man seems to deal with other things not centered on the marriage relationship; i.e., his toil and relationship
with a cursed earth. Is it possible that the woman's curse identifies something particular to her female role, relationship, and
personal fulfillment in marriage?

We will look closely at these two curses in these next two
chapters.

Scripture is also clear that Eve was deceived while Adam was
not (see 1 Tim. 2:14). Eve believed a lie. Adam did not. She did not
believe she would die. Adam knew and apparently decided anyway to eat the forbidden fruit and experience death.[1] Eve's actions
produced the opposite of what Satan had falsely promised. By sub-
verting the relationship God had designed for her, she caused her
husband to fall from a position perfect for her true interests. Her
husband's headship and protection were first subverted, then perverted in all men. Husbands tend now to act as rulers over their
wives. A man's own perceptions, interests, and nature assert preeminence, placing his wife's opinions and wisdom in a secondary
role. The husband tends to decide for himself "what seems best"

and to impose his views through whatever means seem best to him. Eve's deception worked against her and generations of women by ruining husbands capable of giving themselves up in the manner of Christ for His Bride.

God's curse on Eve also set in women the perversion of her original sin; her own fallen nature has continued to work in subsequent generations of women. In the same unwitting and self-deceived nature, it draws a wife into actions that work against a husband and *against her true interests.* Indeed, her nature works against the ability of the husband to live his life on her behalf.

If Adam was not deceived, why did he "listen to his wife" (see Gen. 3:17)? What was in her voice and their relationship that made her offering so compelling?

Others have recognized that the "desire" of Eve's curse reflects neither romantic desire nor an unfallen condition.² What does it really mean?

There are twenty-two Hebrew words which may be translated into the English word *desire*, as contained in the King James translation of the Bible. The various meanings include a wide range of ideas, all included in the English word *desire.* These include "longing," "pining," "provocation [of desire]," "seeking or asking," "delight," "lust," "clinging to (joining)," "favor," "inquiry or demand," and others.*

However, the scripture above, taken from Genesis 3:16, contains only one of these many words and is not central to any of the above meanings. It is the Hebrew word *teshookaw.* This particular word is used only three times in the Bible and has a uniquely different meaning.

Teshookaw has a literal meaning of "to stretch out after." It is derived from the Hebrew root word *shook*, which means "running after or over," as in overflowing water. In its basic form it has no inherent implications of good or evil. However, the fact that it can have a perverse nature is evident in the fact that it is this same word, *teshookaw,* used in precisely the same fashion, that God uses

---

* Strong's Concordance

to describe the "desire" sin has for people when seeking to draw them into evil. In Genesis, chapter 4, Cain, after presenting an unacceptable sacrifice to God and suffering rebuke at its not being accepted, is admonished by God with the following words:

> Why are you angry? And why has your countenance fallen? If you do well, will not your countenance be lifted up? And if you do not do well, sin is crouching at the door; and its teshookaw [desire] is for you, but you must master it. (Gen. 4:6–7)

We see, therefore, that *teshookaw* has meaning that may be associated with the type of urging which sin brings to bear on one being tempted to accomplish its desires (see James 1:13–15). As sin seeks someone willing to yield to its urgings, so the woman has been given a power to "flow through and overflow" her husband. She has a basic desire to similarly project her own spirit and ideas of "what seems best" to her onto her husband, but in a dramatically different fashion than he does with her. Rather than project her views and desires overtly, she is more subtle. From an apparent position of submission, she employs more covert methods to reach into her husband's thoughts, emotions, and will. She pervades his body, soul, and spirit. She may utterly presume her own righteousness, not perceiving that she is acting just like Eve as she works her persuasion upon her husband. She may be totally unaware of self-deception.[3]

The pervasive nature of such projection of desire by the wife onto the husband is reflected in the root analogy in *teshookaw* of overflowing water that fills the entire vessel and flows over and through every passage in which water can pass. It suggests that the woman is gifted to communicate and influence at multiple and much deeper levels than the man is. There may be an apt analogy here to the spirit of man as well, inasmuch as it is water that is used by Jesus as the analogy of the Holy Spirit and all of its work in believers in Jesus Christ (see John 4:14, 7:38–39).

It is in such a righteous analogy as this that we see application of *teshookaw* in its third and last application in Scripture. This is where its use is evocative but not manipulative, given freely and righteously to bring about the yielding of a beloved to a lover's love. It is God's use of *teshookaw*.

In this final instance in which the word *teshookaw* is used in the Bible, we see more clearly how it conveys power *regarding the use of words;* in particular, the power of words to touch the whole person. In Song of Solomon, we are provided an allegory of the love of the Bridegroom, Jesus Christ, and His Bride. It is among the most evocative prose ever written to describe romantic love between bride and bridegroom, and the section in which *teshookaw* is used is among the most evocative of this entire book. Because of the intoxicating sensuality of these words, it has been said that the ancient Hebrews did not allow young men to read its words until they were eighteen years of age. Here we see the power of *teshookaw* desire in its most evocative and righteous form.

In the seventh chapter of the Song of Solomon, the bridegroom views his bride and describes her beauty. The reader will be attentive to the power of the words as they evoke our own images and responses. As we read, we are ourselves drawn into the vision-creating power of the bridegroom's words.

How beautiful are your feet in sandals, O prince's daughter! The curves of your hips are like jewels, the work of the hands of an artist. Your navel is like a round goblet which never lacks mixed wine; your belly is like a heap of wheat fenced about with lilies. (Song of Sol. 7:1–2)

The word he uses for "belly" is *behten*, describing her lower abdomen or womb. He is describing her naked, depicting her navel as something from which he desires to drink and describing the drink as something with an intoxicating effect.

Your two breasts are like two fawns, twins of a gazelle. Your neck is like a tower of ivory, Your eyes like the pools in Heshbon by the gates of Bath-rabbim; your nose is like the tower of Lebanon, which faces toward Damascus. Your head crowns you like Carmel, and the flowing locks of your head are like purple threads; the king is captivated by your tresses. How beautiful and how delightful you are my love, with all your charms! (Song of Sol. 7:3–6)

Yes, these are indeed evocative words that invade soul and spirit!

Having described her physical beauty and the delight she creates to his eyes, the bridegroom now further describes the passion he has for her:

Your stature is like a palm tree, and your breasts are like its clusters. I said, "I will climb the palm tree. I will take hold of its fruit stalks." Oh, may your breasts be like clusters of the vine, and the fragrance of your breath like apples, and your mouth like the best wine. (Song of Sol. 7:7–9)

Words of intimate love! One can feel the evocative force of these words on the mind, will, and emotions, clearly arousing a response in the whole person. This is the Bridegroom's *desire*. Now observe how his wooing purpose has its desired effect! The bride yields, expressing her own response to the pervasive intoxication of his words.

She speaks, "It goes down smoothly for my beloved, flowing gently through the lips of those who fall asleep" (Song of Sol. 7:9). Here is the poetic picture of a fully yielded woman: the peaceful, yielded, open lips of someone asleep. Then she says, "I am my beloved's, and his desire (teshookaw) is for me" (Song of Sol. 7:10).

Here we can grasp a sense of God's fullest meaning of *teshookaw*. The bride has expressed her response to what has been projected to her from the bridegroom. This is the effect of *teshookaw*: evocative power projected from one person to another. It is purposeful power directed at gaining favorable, yielded response in another person. It is *accomplished by means of words* that influence body, soul, and spirit to bring about a yielded, harmonious response of the whole person. It involves the stretching out of the spirit to reach, touch, and overflow another person.[4]

Note that in the bridegroom's words there is no attempt to get the bride to DO anything except yield to his intimate love. There is no ulterior motive, immorality, or manipulative goal to get her to do something for him except to respond to his love. His evocative words minister to the bride in a fashion that brings her to delightful, complete, yielded, peaceful, trusting joy in his love.

When righteously applied, *teshookaw* brings about such a loving response of the human spirit, producing life and harmony. When unrighteously applied, it is manipulative and coercive and, like all works of the flesh not of God, produces death (see Rom. 8:5–13). It is this type of desire and power that has been given to the wife for her husband.

Despite this power having been given to the wife, the husband is not relieved of the moral responsibility to discern righteous or unrighteous projections of *teshookaw* from her. Though the wife is provided as his chief counselor and helper (and God frequently speaks through wives to counsel and save husbands from error), husbands are nevertheless held accountable and judged by God for failure to discern unrighteous counsel. As God held Adam accountable in pronouncing his curse, "Because you have listened to the voice of your wife...", so He also held Abraham accountable to discern through Sarah whether or not she was giving godly counsel (see Gen. 16:2, 21:12). Men's lives alter dramatically by whether or not they successfully discern godly counsel through their wives' influence upon them.

Here we see the power given to women, the power to influence their husbands either for good or evil according to the power of *teshookaw*. Used righteously, within scriptural precepts of wise speech provided in Proverbs and the New Testament, a wife can serve as a powerful agent to harmonize with God's works of righteousness in her husband's and family's lives. Otherwise, her words can be a constant source of strife. We will see more of this in subsequent chapters.

8

Rule/Mawshal

...and he shall rule over you. (Gen. 3:16)

God's curse upon Eve went beyond her *desire/teshookaw* for her husband. He also spoke of the inverse relationship of Adam to his wife and said that Adam would "rule" over her. The Hebrew word used in Genesis 3:16 to describe "rule" is *mawshal*. It means "to have dominion, govern, have power, to reign." As with *teshookaw*, there is no inherent value judgment associated with use of this word. *Mawshal* is used in Scripture to describe the basic function of an office that governs. It is applied in a righteous sense, as in the Lord's rule (see Judg. 8:22–23; Isa. 63:19; Isa. 40:10; Zech. 6:13), and applied to rule which has been perverted because of God's curse upon the people (see Isa. 3:4, 3:12, 19:4). Its dependence upon context can be easily seen in Proverbs, where proper or improper use of rulership is used in teaching precepts of the consequences of character and behavior (see Prov. 12:24, 17:2, 19:10, 29:2).

There are other Hebrew words used to describe "rule" in which this is not true, such as in *rawdaw*, which means "to subjugate, to tread down," *mawlak*, denoting the beginning of rule, or *shawlat*, which means "to dominate, govern, or have premiership" without necessarily having office. *Mawshal* is therefore much like *teshookaw* in that the context of its use is necessary to determine whether it is being applied in a righteous or unrighteous sense. Yet it is part of the curse associated with the fall of man. We also know that natural man's perversion in his rule of his wife is a major source of difficulties in marriage.

Scripture sustains and it should be self-evident that the one upon whom the sword falls (i.e., the "shield" of the family) should also hold the office bearing ultimate responsibility for decisions, direction, and conduct of his family. This principle lies at the root of many of the precepts regarding the position in which God has placed husbands; i.e., their aloneness, the manner of their death on behalf of wives (as in death of their 'flesh'), and their fulfillment in conformance with Christ as discussed in forthcoming chapters. More difficult to grasp is the nature of how *rule/mawshal* (like *desire/teshookaw* in women) can be perverted by men according to their fallen nature. Pride, selfishness, and loss of wisdom cause the gift of rule to be used for evil. The power God gives men to bear responsibility for their wives instead produces war and death.

We saw in *Restoration of Men* that the temperament placed in men to contest, risk, confront threats, and bear blows is well suited to the difficulties of protecting and providing for a family. These traits enable men to father and husband the resources needed to raise godly seed. Righteous kings and governors have used them for the blessings of nations. However, characteristics useful for strength development and defense of a family do not adapt easily to internal administration of a family. Perversions are evident. Small boys use the same traits to cover up mistakes, hide weakness, assert superiority, or bully as weapons for conflict resolution. The same traits in tyrants have been used to amass power and destroy the innocent. A righteous man, on the contrary, finds that righteous self-discipline of rule (i.e., meekness) is the crux of a man's development toward godliness and *true rulership*. "Blessed are the meek, for *they shall inherit the earth*" (Matt. 5:5, emphasis added).

Much abuse of rulership among men can be attributed to failure of men to leave boyhood behind (see 1 Cor. 13:11) or wastage of their manhood through sexual immorality. Isaiah specifically connected loss of capacity to rule to the emasculation of men, prophesying that the nation of Judah's entire range of governing responsibilities (food, water, judicial, military, artistic work, and authority) would disentegrate and that God would "make mere lads their princes and capricious children will rule over them" (Isa. 3:2–4). A few verses later God laments:

> Oh, My people! Their oppressors are children, and women rule over them. Those who guide lead you astray, and confuse the direction of your paths. (Isa. 3:12)

These words accurately describe the impotence of fallen men over their families today. In God's judgment, *it is the natural inheritance of both men and entire nations* when men become sexually immoral; they lose potency in the direct sense of loss of power to raise up seed. As Proverbs, chapter 5 describes, an immoral man loses his "strength, vigor and hard-earned goods." We see the results in the United States of America today: 60% of its suicides come from fatherless children, and 70% of its long-term prison inmates have no fathers, nor do 80% of its murderers. It is a nation where males have indiscriminately wasted their sperm as "streams of water in the street," thereby losing capacity to reproduce life, in sharp contrast with those who have remained faithful to their wives and retained capacity to raise up godly offspring (see Mal. 2:15).

Kingdoms and households are similar. "In abundance of counsellors there is victory." (Prov. 11:14). A man's use of logic, reasoning, and words at face value are useful for measuring risks, teaching, persuading others, and giving orders but weak in discerning hidden dangers or emotional needs. Thus, male communications that may serve well outside the family may be effectual within a family only if combined with the gifts of wives. Some of the lessons God gave to the kings of Israel and Judah illustrate that kings must listen to other sources of counsel in order to hear from God. That is, many of God's warnings and directions to these kings were based upon unseen factors and either bore little evident surface logic or were contrary to reasoning. God's will therefore failed to penetrate the closed minds of these kings just as many wives' counsel fails to reach their husbands today.

Consider Scripture where counsel failed *and thus rulership failed.* The results were bad decisions for which the rulers were held responsible. Certain patterns in the books of Kings and Chronicles were repeated over and over:

- Unfaithfulness in carrying out assigned responsibilities (Saul, David, Uzziah);
- Failure to follow godly counsel (David, Rehoboam, Joash, Amaziah);
- Failure to remain free of ungodly alliances (Solomon, Asa, Jehoshophat);
- Involvement/alliance with many women (David, Solomon, Abijah);
- Idolatry (Jeroboam and all his successors);
- Complacency/Halfheartedness (Saul, Abijah).

The underlying wrong attitudes that caused these failures summarize even more briefly:

- *Fear*—of enemies or of the people when threatened (see Matt. 10:28);
- *Failure to fear God*—forgetting His past deliverances and becoming complacent in good times (see Prov. 1:7; Ps. 111:10);
- *Pride*—inability to accept correction (see Prov. 16:18, 29:23).

These wrong attitudes lay at the roots of men who claim to know God but don't seek, listen to, and obey Him. Confusion as to whom they should truly fear and refusal to humble themselves lead to destruction. Rulers must themselves also chose whom they will serve. Is it likely that a man who won't listen to his wife can hear God, or vice versa? In all cases in Scripture these wrong attitudes led to *failure to trust and obey God*, always the ultimate failure.

These failures extend precisely to those cited by our Lord Jesus Christ for His churches in Revelation, chapters 2 and 3. The issues for each problem church are as follows:

- Ephesus—Loss of first deeds and first love;
- Smyrna—Fear of death and suffering;
- Pergamum—Stumbling blocks of idolatry and immorality;
- Thyatira—Jezebel (gross witchcraft, idolatry, and immorality);
- Sardis—Incomplete/unfinished works;
- Laodicea—Lukewarmness.

It is the same today. The family represents the smallest "church" in the family of God and the smallest unit of rule beyond the individual. Godly rule in a family must therefore confront the same attitudes that God confronted in the Old Testament kings of Israel and the New Testament churches. Rule is given to husbands, but perverted dictatorial rule that doesn't seek and heed counsel leads to disaster.

Failure to trust and obey God is a life-threatening disability correctable only by exercising the Word of God. Men confronted by impotence in godly rule need to hunger and thirst to obey God's Word. Women who can easily "see" and applaud identification of obvious faults in men in these areas need to recognize that in *rule/mawshal* the man is being confronted in his most fundamental marriage relationship difficulty, one which is most difficult for him to discern and submit to God for correction. It is in the husband's very nature to employ rule without being conscious of it. It corresponds to the equally unconscious and elusive nature of *desire/teshookaw* which exists in wives, identified in the previous chapter.

Section II: Introduction to Strongholds

9

Strongholds

. . . for the weapons of our warfare are not of the flesh, but divinely powerful for the destruction of fortresses. (2 Cor. 10:4)

The Old Testament is full of the word *stronghold* (or, frequently, *fort* or *fortress*), but the New Testament makes little use of it. In the above scripture, the apostle Paul uses the Greek word *ochuroma* on its only occasion in the New Testament. Its meaning is that of "a fortification, a safe holding, a castle (or, figuratively, an argument) or a stronghold." The context of its use is that the children of God do not war according to the flesh but against powers and forces of the kingdom of Satan and are overcoming them through this warfare. Tearing down of these enemy strongholds is an aspect of our warfare. The same scripture goes on to say, "We are destroying speculations and every lofty thing raised up against the knowledge of God, and we are taking every thought captive to the obedience of Christ" (2 Cor. 10:5).

Gaining some understanding of the nature of Satan's defenses is helpful to the subsequent use of such words and our efforts in conducting spiritual warfare against him. What are these fortresses or strongholds we seek to destroy? What is their nature?

A number of Hebrew words used in the Old Testament interpreted in English as *fortress* or *stronghold* also contain other conceptual ideas worth noting. For example, the Hebrew word *metsuhdah* used in 2 Samuel 5:7, in addition to meaning "castle, defense, fort(ress) or stronghold," also means "a capture or a net:

also a fastness." The word *metsahdah* used in Judges 6:2 and 1 Samuel 23:14, 19, and 29 denotes fastness and wilderness strongholds, such as Masada, the famous Jewish mountain stronghold which fell to the Romans in the first century and which amply displays the fortress characteristics conveyed in its root Hebrew word. The word *mibtsarah*, used frequently in the Old Testament, also conveys the idea of man-made fortifications, walled cities, etc., devices men build to defend themselves (in contrast to defenses that may be offered by nature.)

An unusual insight into the nature of strongholds is given in 2 Samuel 5:7 in which the thoughts of those defending Jerusalem are recorded. Those who opposed the kingship of David over Jerusalem addressed him as follows: "...they said to David, 'You shall not come in here, but the blind and lame shall turn you away'; thinking, 'David shall not enter here'" (2 Sam. 5:6). Their futility in opposing the will of God in establishing David's kingship over Jerusalem and Judah is demonstrated in the results of the very next verse, "Nevertheless, David captured the stronghold of Zion, that is the *city of David*" (2 Sam. 5:7, emphasis added). This seems to reflect spirits of scorn, foolishness, and error working in those who trust in man-made strongholds as a defense, especially those that seek to work against the purposes of God.

It is also interesting that, with only the most minor exceptions, God reserves only certain other words in referral to the heavenly stronghold He offers to those seeking His shelter. The Hebrew word for "most fortified place" (as in "the fortified place of royalty") is *mauz* (maw-ooz). It is only used in regard to the strong fortifications of kings (Dan. 11:7, 10, 39) and in regard to the Lord Himself (Jer. 16:19). If applied to earthly kingdoms, it is identified as one which God can destroy (Isa. 17:9, 23:11). The other word reserved nearly exclusively for God Himself in the description of a heavenly stronghold is *metsudah*, defined above and used in 2 Samuel 22:2 and Psalm 18:2, 31:3, 71:3, 91:2 and 144:2. The only two exceptions to this are in its use to describe the holy city of Jerusalem (cited above in 2 Samuel 5:7) in resistance to the ascension of King David, and in the description of an eagle's stronghold in Job 39:28. Even these exceptions still retain strong implications of royalty and of the heavens, not present in other words used to describe earthly strongholds. These definitions help sharpen distinctions between God Himself, as a true stronghold, and earthly, man-made strongholds which oppose God.

In its New Testament application, the word for *fortress* or *stronghold* used in 2 Corinthians 10:4 clearly characterizes enemy strong places that argue against God and are being torn down in the life of a sanctified believer as he walks and grows in the likeness of Christ (Rom. 8:29; Eph. 2:10, 4:15–16). This war takes place within the flesh and mind of those who have received the Lord Jesus Christ. We hear the same author, Paul, describe this personal war.

Writing in the letter to the Romans, chapter 7, Paul said of the workings of sin:

> For we know that the Law is spiritual; but I am of flesh, sold into bondage to sin. For that which I am doing, I do not understand; for I am not practicing what I would like to do, but I am doing the very thing I hate. But if I do the very thing I do not wish to do, I agree with the Law, confessing that it is good. So now, no longer am I the one doing it, but sin which indwells me. For I know that nothing good dwells in me, that is, in my flesh; for the wishing is present in me, but the doing of the good is not. For the good that I wish, I do not do; but I practice the very evil that I do not wish. But if I am doing the very thing I do not wish, I am no longer the one doing it, but sin which dwells in me. I find then the principle that evil is present in me, the one who wishes to do good. (Rom. 7:14–21)

This testimony of the working of sin identifies both that (a) sin wages war in the flesh and (b) it does so against the spiritual knowledge of what is right. Evil is identified as actually present and working within the flesh of the believer. The war against sin "which so easily entangles us" (Heb. 12:1) continues after salvation during the growth and maturation of the believer.

This is evidenced in numerous other instructional scriptures as well. Peter urges believers as "aliens and strangers to abstain from fleshly lusts, which wage war against the soul" (1 Pet. 2:11). James provides an explicit account of how lust first entices, conceives, and then gives birth to sin, resulting in death (James 1:14–15). John identifies that the world and its lusts (the lust of the flesh and the lust of the eyes and the boastful pride of life), though passing away, are still a source of trial for those who love God (1 John 2:16–17). Paul cites the works of the flesh as "immorality, impurity, sensuality, idolatry, sorcery, enmities, strife, jealousy, outbursts of anger, disputes, dissensions, factions, envyings, drunkenness, carousings and things like these" (Gal. 5:19–21), which cannot enter the kingdom of God. The consistent theme of these and many other scriptures is that we are in a continual war between the love of God and opposing spiritual forces which inhabit our flesh and mind to work against us, producing death if they have their way.

These forces operate legally, according to the word of God and the curse of sin upon us, according to (1) the original curse of Adam (Gen. 3:16–19), (2) the law of generational curse (Exod. 20:5; Num. 14:18; Deut. 5:9), and (3) the law of God that all sin overtakes those who perform it, thereby producing death (Gen. 2:17; Num. 32:23; Rom. 6:23; James 1:15).

We observe also from history and especially Scripture, that strongholds exhibit two chief characteristics: external and internal. They make war on those outside while restricting those held within. As we shall see in the study of Rahab and Jericho, man-made strongholds produce prisonership, suffering, and death for the inhabitants trapped inside. *What was originally constructed and inhabited for purposes of protection eventually becomes an instrument of death when the enemy has control.* We become legal prisoners. As Jesus said in the judgment of Jerusalem, "For the days shall come upon you when your enemies will throw up a bank before you, and surround you, and hem you in on every side" (Luke 19:43). The more impregnable the fortress, the greater the degree of anguish, horror, and suffering that ultimately takes place to its inhabitants when judgment comes.

However, in the redemptive work of Jesus Christ, these strongholds of enemy activity in the mind and flesh can be easily removed by consent and submission of the believer to Christ. They merely await identification and agreement (i.e., confession of the truth in the sense of 1 John 1:9) to enable legal removal through God's perfect law of love and grace. By the blood of Jesus Christ, we are redeemed from the curse of the law which previously made us slaves (see Gal. 3:13) and now enabled to become free in Christ (see Gal. 3:24–4:7) by *bringing fully to light the truth of what made us captive and Who set us free!*

However, these strongholds of mind and flesh which wage war with the Spirit (Gal. 5:16–25) are not trivial. Destruction of strongholds involves judgment of their rulers according to right judgment (Ps. 149:5–9) and renunciation of the claims of those who previously had their way with us. This is the fruit of repentance. Lies must be put away! Destruction requires death of the flesh according to God's provisions, amply depicted in many scriptures:

> If we have become united with Him in the likeness of His death, certainly we shall be also in the likeness of His resurrection. (Rom. 6:5)

> He who has died is freed from sin. (Rom. 6:7)

> ...But if by the Spirit, you are putting to death the deeds of the body, you will live. (Rom. 8:13)

> ...For he who has suffered in the flesh has ceased (been released) from sin. (1 Pet. 4:1)

> For whoever wishes to save his life shall lose it; but whoever loses his life for my sake shall find it. (Matt. 16:25)

Despite clarity of our instructions and the requirement to present ourselves "as a living and holy sacrifice" to God to prove the good and perfect will of God (Rom. 12:1–2), we do not do this easily. We entertain strongholds in our mind and flesh with appetites that loudly demand satisfaction. "Needs" *demand* being met, thoughts *demand* a voice, plans *demand* highest priority, "rights" and "innocence" *demand* defense, etc. These are the selfish demands of demons that seek to convince us they are speaking for our interests. But they are not. They *usurp rule* over us, through our mind and flesh, in God's place. They replace His rightful Fathership over all things. That is why we must be crucified in Christ. Death puts possessions that need removal on the altar. When sacrificially entrusted to God to "prove" His will in a matter there is no doubt of the loss or of the pain it inflicts. A believer discovers his own frontier in the Kingdom of God when giving up *valuables upon which life has heretofore depended.* Until the very moment of death, claims of the flesh will demand their rights to continued life (not merely life, but rule and preeminence!) They will continue to argue why their presence in one's life is necessary, frequently using "religious" arguments.

The most intense pain occurs at the point of decision to nail them to the tree, *the instrument of death*, where crucifixion takes place. It is a real death scene.

Occasionally, a test is given a believer in which he or she is called upon to yield something valuable that may later be restored. At the moment of death, the will of God may still be unknown. There may follow restoration of a vision (Abraham, Joseph), resurrection after death (Isaac, Daniel, Jonah, Jesus), or other forms of confirmation or restoration that occur only after one has died in some fashion (Jacob with Esau, Judah with Benjamin, Esther with Ahasuerus, Boaz with Ruth, John, Peter, etc.). God uses this to enrich His fellowship with His children, perhaps to confirm a particular promise or vision or to resolve whether or not something has become an idol (for the believer's benefit; God already knows!) or to otherwise reveal His glory. *In such cases, God will resurrect what is put to death for His sake to magnify and glorify Himself* (see Gen. 22:1–18).

In most cases, though, the things that are being rooted out of the life of the believer are hiding places of the enemy, who prior to removal through death has consent and a legal operating base in the mind and flesh of his host. He will struggle to remain and continue his war against the soul of the believer through fear and deception, using every possible means of argument and deceit.

Hence, most voices and defenses resisting death represent *strongholds* which maintain themselves in the life of the flesh through deception, using fear of pain and death to diminish the glory of God in the believer. They belong to that which Jesus came to destroy (Heb. 2:15). Their destruction is part of the comprehensive work of Christ, who came to set the captives free.

Death for the love of Christ will prove to be the only true test of obedience in the will of God (see Rev. 12:11) and is always the door to true resurrection.

10

Defense of Strongholds

... they said to David, "You shall not come in here, but the blind and lame shall turn you away"; thinking, "David cannot enter here." Nevertheless, David captured the stronghold of Zion, that is the city of David. (2 Sam. 5:6–7)

Strongholds have basic characteristics that help us recognize what to expect in our warfare against them. First, they are basically defensive in purpose. Second, they are designed to defend territory. They react when 1) the *territory* or mission for which the stronghold was established is endangered or 2) the *stronghold itself* is directly threatened.

Enemy strongholds in men and women behave the same way, having been established in the mind and flesh of the believer. When one who would bind the strongman comes close, defensive devices come into play. Initial defenses involve attempting to remain hidden, using simple deception or distraction. When more precisely approached, a stronghold will often then argue its right to be left alone. It will explain itself with assertions that in effect justify terms of a peace treaty, posing as understandable and excusable, perhaps even "righteous" in a religious sense! A stronghold can also defend itself through discouragement or confusion, ultimately growing more hostile and using weapons which inflict pain: scorn, ridicule, accusations, and the like, potentially threatening to destroy the attacker. Fear and pain may accomplish the stronghold's work. Flight of the attacker is sufficient. A stronghold "wins" if it is left alone to maintain its grip on its victim.

These difficulties can take place between two or more persons or within a single person when the Holy Spirit begins to convict of the truth with the idea of changing one's behavior. *Methods of the stronghold can render further effort unproductive by promoting our sense of isolation, confusion, futility, and pain!*

In late stages of reduction, when warfare has failed, strongholds will sometimes negotiate, wheedle, and plead for mercy, appealing for sympathy and some settlement which authorizes continued legal residence without the unconditional surrender that the blood of Jesus Christ has accomplished.

Discerning a stronghold is only a beginning. Without agreement of its host, little can be done. *Establishing agreement that it is repugnant and against the will of God* in the mind of the host is the chief thing and may take much time, support, prayer, and forgiveness. It cannot be accomplished apart from God. Counterreactive war between two spouses learning to love God can defer progress indefinitely. Each may submit to the Lord in tearing down their own strongholds but can have little effect upon the other's by continuing to attack. We must search for God's truth and work to live it out in love. He has promised! In Christ, we will overcome Satan's lies through godly warfare (see Eph. 4:15, 25, 6:10–18; Rev. 2:7, 11, 17, 26).

Moral authority aids in reducing strongholds. Hence, a parent, employer, pastor, or other godly counselor relationship is helpful. However, this is not straightforward in a spousal situation. *It is not possible for a wife to assume spiritual authority over her husband [though she may have moral authority and position to sanctify an unbelieving husband (see 1 Cor. 7:14)]. Nor may a husband effectively possess moral authority with his wife if he has previously lost this through moral failure* (especially sexual immorality). Such failures mark preeminent strongholds which can only be restored by Christ through repentance and confession (1 John 1:9).

We noted a weapon of Satan's is wrongful use of 'religious argument' to justify wrong actions (see Matt. 4:1–10). A variation of this is to expose moral weakness of the other person. Hence, if wrongful behavior is identified, an enemy defense is to disable the other person involved by a counteraccusation that removes moral authority. Progress between spouses is therefore limited to their rate of exposure to the light of Christ and genuine renunciation of the strongholds they have thus far wrongly defended. As we will see in the study of Rahab, it is *encirclement of a stronghold by applying the Word of God to one's own life that cuts off false escape and opens us toward a godly decision.* Working in such situations without prayer and the convicting work of the Holy Spirit (see John 16:9–11) will generally prove fruitless.

We also noted from 2 Samuel 5:7 that enemy forces may establish themselves in territory claimed for God and reason that "the blind and lame" shall turn away His people. But this is futile and deceived thinking. All disciples of Jesus Christ should know that God's children will prevail in extending His light to themselves and their loved ones simply by living in Christ, His word, and His precepts (see Eph. 6:11–17).

All territories that strongholds defend in believers *rightfully belong to God.* It is only through deception and the ruination of sin that the enemy has governed under false precepts of self-interest *at the expense of trust in God.* Appetites and reasonings resist God and arrogantly proclaim lies to be in the best interests of God's children (see Gen. 3:4–5; James 3:14–16, 4:1–4), when the reverse is true. Satan assumes to rule territory which includes bodily appetites (food, drink, sex), psychological needs (comfort, understanding, encouragement), personal rights (property, time, justice, "fairness," quality and duration of life), and relations to others (responsibilities, priorities, commitments). This fleshly territory fighting for a life apart from God produces the fruit of the flesh (see Gal. 5:19–21) but *identifies the nature of the stronghold, the knowledge of which we may then use to deal with it!* When identified, it may be put to death through Christ, yielding rights to God (see Rom. 6:12–23, 12:1–3) and obeying through trust in Him.

Through obedience we thereby demolish the stronghold.

11

Disconnectedness

... bearing with one another, and forgiving each other, whoever has a complaint against any one; just as the Lord forgave you, so also should you. (Col. 3:13)

A divorced Christian meets an older woman with six kids. He soon brings her to his singles Bible study and not long after that announces their plans to be married. When an elder of the group quietly takes him aside and cautions him, he leaves the Bible study group. Soon thereafter, when his pastor adds his opposition to the marriage, he also leaves his church.

Three single divorced women who have been part of the same Bible study for well over a year express to an elder of the group their concern over unsought attention from a younger man in the group. In response to his being taken aside and requested to leave them alone, he leaves the group. Despite the successful protection of the women who have sought out protective covering, they also leave the group within a couple of weeks. When the young man is appealed to for continued fellowship, he returns for several more years. But despite appeal the women never return again.

Over a period of time a pattern emerges. What appear to be relationships turn out to be illusory; the group is only a tenuous assembly which can vaporize in a moment. I believe those who work in the gospel of Jesus Christ among the divorced will discover some behavioral characteristics markedly different from those of the never-married or never-divorced. Because many who read this come from the ranks of the divorced, I submit this discussion for the purpose of self-examination and as a general introduction to this section of spousal strongholds.

These examples were drawn over a three to four year period during which my wife and I taught Bible study for singles. My first observation was that a significant portion of singles easily took up grievances, either their own or someone else's. Incidents which would normally be unnoticed (or ignored) by most persons would cause someone to become indignant, stalk out of a room, break fellowship, even leave a church. Efforts to correct the grievance (apology and reconciliation with prayer and supporting witnesses) were difficult or unsuccessful. A second observation was that, even after periods of time in which apparently strong and committed relationships were growing, people would suddenly depart without explanation or farewell. A few seemed to be faithful and consistent, yet many others would go "in and out" a week or two at time, disappearing and reappearing with no reliable pattern. Finally, it appeared that minor circumstances could have unusually disruptive influence. Supportive relationships were easily lost because of events that seemed to intervene too easily—employment or activity schedules being common examples.

Discovery that others in ministry had noted similar behavior helped persuade me that these observations were not my imagination nor were they merely due to my own unique interactions with singles.

Puzzlement led to personal inquiry of God. Was I observing characteristics of singleness in general? Was this pattern a cause or a result of singleness or both? Then one day, I felt an urge to list the identities of those who over a long period of Bible study and prayer had exhibited the greatest levels of consistency, mutual support, and faithfulness. I got out pencil and paper and began writing down names of that came to mind. After eight to ten names, I scrutinized them and made an interesting discovery. Nearly all those on the list had never married or had lost their spouse through death. Only two had been divorced, one of those by sudden and total abandonment after over four decades of marriage.

I submitted the same question to my wife, and she came up with the same list of names. I then submitted the same question to the singles group in question, who also came up with the same list of names. Further inquiry revealed that the only questionable name on the list was that of a man whose wife had abandoned him within the first year or so of marriage. He had been unable to break a military enlistment or accomplish a change of duty to meet the demands of his wife to return to her hometown on the opposite side of the country. When he failed to comply, she abandoned him and sued for divorce. That left no one on the list who had been an active, participating partner in the disintegration of a marriage.

This exercise seemed to me to indicate (1) there is a sharp distinction in faithfulness and relationship capacities among singles, depending upon their background. In particular, those who have been involved in the war of a divorce seem to have much lower capacities for supportive relationships than those who have never married, lost their spouses to death, or even suffered sudden abandonment. It also implies (2) that even the trauma of death or abandonment by a spouse does not scar a person so that he/she becomes unable to bear faithful, life-giving relationships. Finally, the second conclusion also implies (3) that attitudes and behaviors of those who have been through divorce were probably already in place and contributed to the divorce rather than being its result.

Further review by the group considered the many dozens of others not on the list of faithful who had passed on without forming lasting relationships, appearing outwardly connected to others but proving to be inwardly separated. They were nearly all divorced.

I've attempted to summarize general characteristics of what I refer to as "disconnected" persons. They typically:

- use others for "company" rather than relationships;
- are easily distracted and unable to maintain long-term consistency;
- seek sympathy and will frequently work to provoke it;
- take offense more easily than average;

- volunteer seldomly and, when they do, are unreliable;
- have severe relationship problems in their lives;
- change jobs frequently, sometimes through totally unrelated circumstances;
- reveal, when under stress, weaknesses/problems in conflict resolution;
- have difficulty with resolution of grievances, forgiveness, and attaining reconciliation.

Strongholds of bitterness causing them to continually fall short of the glory of God rule many of them (see Heb. 12:15). They carry "accounts" of their grievances for months or years, never forgiving enemies or ex-spouses while accumulating long lists of fresh grievances which they may vent when given opportunity. Storms rage under their outer disguise of normalcy. With a few, their inability to forgive or reconcile is so strong there is question whether they have ever truly met Jesus Christ or submitted to Him in any significant way in which He can have proven His reality, power, and love for them.

Some claim convincingly that they seek reconciliation with their spouse but after months or years of effort apparently seeking counsel suddenly announce their plans to marry another, then break fellowship with all who are not supportive of their plans to re-marry. Others demand and receive strong support during times of severe need (imprisonment, illness, danger, poverty, social threat, etc.), yet immediately after the problem passes, they are gone.

To some extent these are patterns of children, stunted children who have never grown to maturity in responsibility and relationships. Perhaps they are also profiles of the wounded who have never dealt with the consequences of sin—their own and that of others. Pride, selfishness, hate, anger, greed (which is idolatry), abuse, immorality, etc. have all left their scars. For reasons only God understands, they continue to entertain and indulge enemy strongholds that have only bondage and misery as their goal.

Perhaps these patterns are in you who are divorced or whose divorce is still in the future if left uncorrected. It is for this reason that Jesus came. The Holy Spirit testifies—there is healing in Christ. Judgment begins with the body of Christ. If these patterns are recognizable in you, then search them through with God and your brothers and sisters in Christ. Bring them to a final resolution; bury them in Christ, forever. Forgive those who have wronged you and ask forgiveness of those you have wronged. Close accounts. *Do this in the full sense of the word, where both your favor and God's is fully placed upon those who have hurt you.* Do it with witnesses. Turn what was meant for evil for positive results instead and become a propitiator of sin in Christ as He has done for us and continues to do.

Then resolve to become reliable to others, consistent, faithful, and patient. Learn to keep your promises. Become a servant that others can depend upon. Let your faithfulness depend upon Christ and His strength and not upon how others treat you. Christ is your rewarder. It is the Lord Christ whom you serve (Col. 3:18–25).

Section IIB: Gender Strongholds

12

The Unfilled Appetites of Men

There is an evil which I have seen under the sun and it is prevalent among men. . . . (Eccles. 6:1)

In His design of the human race, God left the male incomplete with respect to nurture and healing. In the natural order of things, God intended his needs be completed first by his mother, then by the woman to whom he is joined in marriage. In the supernatural order of things, He provides that every man may find completeness and healing in Jesus Christ alone, with or without a wife. It is good for both men and women to comprehend the extreme degree to which men are truly incomplete, unsatisfied, and *incapable of functioning effectively in their responsibilities without nurture being provided to the man in one way or other by God.* Without it, the man is weak, unhealthy, and ineffectual.

Sin further perverts the situation so that even God's natural provision fails to bring the man satisfaction. He finds himself still unsatisfied, searching for something more. The effect of sexual sin is that a man becomes unable to find contentment and satisfaction with one woman, his wife. He seeks in vain to find it in all manner of other sinful activities, beginning with his eyes and imaginations, then leading to physical acts of sexual sin and perversions leading to death (see James 1:11–15; Prov. 4–7).

The title scripture was penned by King Solomon, a man who sought and was granted great wisdom from God. In the book of Ecclesiastes we read how he attempted all manner of finding success and fulfillment as a man. He had good cause to discover the truths stated in the sixth chapter of Ecclesiastes in which he discerns clearly the insatiable appetites that drive men, even though God has blessed them "with riches and wealth and honor" so that their "soul lacks nothing" (see Eccles. 6:2). In addition to the futility Solomon found in silver and gold, in the honor of his kingship, in wisdom, and in other endeavors (see Eccles. 2), we are given a most notable indicator of his inability to find satisfaction with one woman. He pursued gratification with hundreds of them. Scripture records Solomon had "seven hundred wives, princesses, and three hundred concubines" (1 Kings 11:3).

Solomon repeatedly uses words that depict hunger in the unsatisfied man. In the second verse of Ecclesiastes, chapter 6, he depicts it in this way: "God has not empowered him to eat from [his riches and wealth and honor], for a foreigner enjoys them. This is vanity and a sore affliction."

In Proverbs, chapter 5, Solomon uses the same metaphor to identify the immoral man's loss of manhood (his vigor, strength, and wealth) to strangers and aliens (Prov. 5:7–10); i.e., to foreigners enjoying the fruit of the labor of the man involved in sexual sin.

Solomon then goes on to say, "If a man fathers a hundred children and lives many years, however many they be, but his soul is not satisfied with good things, and he does not even have a proper burial, then I say, 'Better the miscarriage than he'" (Eccles. 6:3). He repeats the analogy in verse 6 for a man who "lives a thousand years twice and does not enjoy good things." Then Solomon summarizes the major affliction of men: *"All a man's labor is for his mouth and yet the appetite is not satisfied"* (Eccl. 6:7).

How contrary this is to the advice Solomon gives in Proverbs to a young man, promising that he can be satisfied by the wife of his youth if he will abstain from sexual sin.

Drink water from your own cistern, and fresh water from your own well. Should your springs be dispersed abroad, streams of water in the streets? Let them be yours alone and not for strangers with you. Let your fountain be blessed, and rejoice in the wife of your youth. As a loving hind and a graceful doe, let her breasts satisfy you at all times; be exhilarated always with her love. For why should you, my son, be exhilarated with an adulteress, and embrace the bosom of a foreigner? (Prov. 5:15–20)

There is a dark outcome to Solomon's pursuit of wisdom and satisfaction. It seems that in his vain pursuit of satisfaction through many women he lost discernment regarding the safety of his nation, the people with whose welfare he had been entrusted. He opened his nation to the legal entry of enemy spirits to draw them away from their true source of security and fulfillment, the God of Israel. *The very same verses that count the number of women King Solomon had as wives and concubines end with the words, "And his wives turned his heart away. For it came about when Solomon was old, his wives turned his heart away after other gods; and his heart was not wholly devoted to the LORD his God, as the heart of David his father had been" (1 Kings 11:3–4).*

This is the pattern of many men today. Seeking fulfillment of their appetites through ungodly means, they open their families up to destruction through the legal access of the enemy to devour the wives and children they are responsible for protecting. There is indeed such an intimate connection between sexual sin and the entry of evil spirits into a nation and family that it is difficult to separate them. Possibly it was primarily the sins of Solomon, driven by his unsatisfied appetites and quest for many women, that set the stage for the "sins of Jeroboam" that followed him; i.e., this is the particular idolatry and immorality which is solely attributed as the cause of destruction of the northern kingdom of Israel. This sin of Solomon's may even be traced to his father David, who, among his sins, appeared to have a major generational sin which he passed onto his son; that is, David's undisciplined love of many women. *A strong biblical case can be made that sexual immorality resulting from the inability of men to satisfy their appetites and be satisfied with one woman may be one of the major "doors" that opens the human race to the destructive onslaughts of Satan.* Hence, repeated pictures of death are drawn in Proverbs for those who indulge in it.

An unsatisfied man is drawn deeper by his lusts into sinful habits. Eating and drinking excesses, sensuality, pornography, adultery, sodomy, child molestation, incest—things beyond his control that fill him with disgust and fear, fear that his wife will find out his most shameful secrets, as she eventually will.

What is the impact upon a wife when her husband's stronghold of "unsatisfied appetite" is eventually revealed? *She discovers she is inadequate to satisfy her husband!* She is wounded in her place of greatest need—her value, her need to know that she is preeminent in her husband's eyes and life, that she alone fulfills his needs. She is thereby removed from her unique place of identity and security. His love and her adequacy make the vital foundation upon which she flourishes. With it she has freedom and power to love others. Loss of it brings anxiety and grief, injury and loss of vitality. How can she be a true fountain of nurture to a man declaring her to be inadequate? She will not likely perceive the problem as her husband's sickness or inadequacy. Rather, she will see it as her own inadequacy as a woman. It bruises and diminishes her. The accuser comes in.

Can a woman with such a husband still live freely for him? Unless she is quite secure in her relationship with God and equipped in Christ to overcome the evil in her husband's life, she cannot! A damaged breast cannot nurture. A husband who cannot be satisfied takes a wife beyond her natural capacity. She becomes conditional and restricted in her responses to her husband's real needs. As her insecurity increases, a vicious cycle ensues. She is diminished in her nurture and he is further weakened. The husband blames the wife for her inability to satisfy him and the wife blames her husband for his incomprehensible evil appetites. The man who cannot be satisfied with one woman and allows his wife to be usurped from her position of preeminence consequently destroys himself, fulfilling the scriptural warning against a man hating his own body (see Eph. 5:29).

This is the normal cycle of destruction in such a marriage. Apart from Christ, both spouses have correct basic perceptions but incorrect fixation of blame. Both are locked in their own self-centeredness and incompleteness. There is no ultimate solution for this outside of God. Evil strongholds are firmly in place in both the man and the woman. Only Jesus Christ can destroy these strongholds and enable completion in Him with their mates.

13

Insecurity

The wise woman builds her house, but the foolish tears it down with her own hands. (Prov. 14:1)

The information of the preceding chapter is explicit with respect to the nature of the fallen male and his insatiable bodily appetites. However, in a larger sense, it also portrays the behavior of any human appetite in either men or women related to a basic need that becomes insatiable through the corruptive power of Satan.

Women also have a fundamental basic need established by God's design upon which they are dependent. They need security. A secure woman is a free woman, pouring out life in an awesome display of creative power for the welfare of others (Prov. 31:10–31). An insecure woman is stifled, pursued by fear, spending much of her energy in her own devices attempting to gain the security she needs. She is sapped of creative power and unable to respond to need. Insecurity becomes a raging appetite that dominates her life, robbing her of her beauty and power to bless others.

God has provided that the female find completion and full security in Jesus Christ—always available under any circumstances to those who trust in Him. In the design of the family, God placed the function of security (the "shield") in men, who are to be the model of Jesus Christ with the woman and tasked to be that security. Due to sin, many men violate their responsibilities and fail to provide women, wives, and daughters the security they need. To the contrary, they wound them and destroy female capacity to trust in them (or God) for their security. Through destruction of trust, the door is opened in women to begin building their own security devices, strongholds of Satan in which women build their lives around the precept of being keepers of their own security.

Insecurity is a most powerful stronghold, occupying illegitimately as it does the place of Christ that God intends man to occupy as Christ's model and agent. The basic need for security is real, powerful, and legitimate. However, the fostering of attitudes and behavior that the woman must be the keeper of her own security, unable to trust God or the relationships He has provided, is founded upon a lie that works to keep the woman in bondage.

Satan's deception and pattern upon which he builds all his strongholds can be seen in his own perversion and lie to Eve that brought about the fall of man. In lying about God's trustworthiness there is a pervading thought that Satan originated in the world—that we can be like God while being independent of God. Or similarly, that we are complete within ourselves and do not have an inherent need for dependence upon others. By fostering the lie that women must provide their own security, Satan seeks legal residence to promote himself against God, war against other souls (especially men), and oppose the free giving of life inherent in God's design. Hence Satan's lie is to destroy women as givers of life and fountains of nourishment (see Prov. 5:18–19) after the nature of El Shadday, the "very able, (more than) enough, very sufficient breast" (Gen. 17:1), the attribute of His own name which He gave to women.

Scripture is evocative regarding the beauty of a righteous woman. It is founded on the imperishable quality of a "gentle and quiet spirit," precious in the sight of God (1 Pet. 3:4). Why is it described as having "imperishable quality"? Because it is based on inner confidence, trust in unseen things (see Heb. 11:1–2), the resolution of eternal issues once and for all. Life is free from fears of uncertainty. It is the same confidence that enables a woman to carry "strength and dignity as her clothing" and to "smile at the future" (see Prov. 31:25). It is founded on the only kind of trust that can produce godly submission in a woman according to the model of Sarah described by Peter, the power to "do what is right without being frightened by any fear" (1 Pet. 3:6).

Women not scarred by sin have an inherent sense of confidence and freedom. They do not naturally embrace conflict or concerns about their future. They have a naive, perhaps even unfounded, trust in their husbands and in others. However, this all changes when they are damaged by sin. What was previously only incompleteness (resolved through trust in God and husband) now becomes perverted to a prison of isolation and mistrust.

The centrality of a woman's need for security and the nature of enemy strongholds which become established in them as sinful alternatives to faith in Christ correlates with the strongholds of destructive lusts for nurture that become established in men. They are two of the central themes throughout the remaining chapters of this book.

14

The Sins of Jeroboam

He did not turn away from all the sins of Jeroboam the son of Nebat, with which he made Israel sin. . . . (2 Kings 13:11)

An unusual and evocative repeating pattern is emphasized in the history of the northern kingdom of Israel after the death of King Solomon. One may enter the Bible at any subsequent point in the history of its kings and find the above verse or a close paraphrasing of it entered after each king. It is a judgment against their lives and rulership. Every king of Israel commencing with Jeroboam, the founder of the northern kingdom, through Hoshea, the last king (taken captive by the Assyrians when Israel fell and was scattered over the earth) is without exception condemned by God for not departing "from the sins of Jeroboam." This takes place over approximately 236 years and with 18 kings in succession!

What were the sins of Jeroboam?

The Bible records that Solomon's son Rehoboam, after inheriting the throne, foolishly threatened to place an even heavier yoke on the ten tribes of the northern kingdom than had his father. This caused the northern kingdom to revolt and separate itself from Judah. They selected Jeroboam, the son of Nebat, "a valiant warrior," to be their king, thus fulfilling a prophecy that had been made over Jeroboam by the prophet Ahijah the Shilonite during an earlier period when Jeroboam had worked under King Solomon (see 1 Kings 11–12).

Shortly after he was made king, Jeroboam decided he had a problem with allowing the center of worship of his people to continue to be Jerusalem, which remained under the rulership of Judah and the southern kingdom. For he said in his heart,

> Now the kingdom will return to the house of David. If this people go up to offer sacrifices in the house of the LORD at Jerusalem, then the heart of this people will return to their lord, even to Rehoboam king of Judah; and they will kill me and return to Rehoboam king of Judah. (1 Kings 12:26–27)

So he consulted advisors and made two golden calves and said to the people, "'It is too much for you to go up to Jerusalem; behold your gods, O Israel, that brought you up from the land of Egypt,' and he set one in Bethel and the other he put in Dan" (1 Kings 12:28–29). There is a remarkable similarity here to the sin of Aaron when Moses failed to return quickly from the mountain; Aaron had led the people of Israel into sin with the fabrication and worship of a golden calf (see Exod. 32). *Fear of the people drove both Aaron and Jeroboam to disobey God and to draw the people to worship idols.*

As a result of this and the festival days he established, "which he had devised in his own heart," Jeroboam set in motion the apostasy of his entire kingdom. A foundation of worship of the true God of Israel, the Creator and Redeemer, built over previous hundreds of years, was cast aside. The gods that they began worshipping included not only the two golden calves but also Ashtaroth and Baal, the same gods of the land which God had earlier declared to be abominations and which produced iniquity warranting God's extermination of the nations who had so worshipped. Note that for Aaron's prior failure to control Israel during Moses' absence and for leading them to worship and orgy before a golden calf, God had pronounced the destruction of the entire nation of Israel. *This had been turned aside only by the intercession of Moses* (see Exod. 32).

Scripture takes unusual pains to frame the identity of the repeat entry of this sin into Israel. After two chapters of discussion of Jeroboam, his ascension to the throne, and his sinful official endorsement of idolatry into the worship of the nation, the thirteenth chapter of 1 Kings ends with, "And this event became sin to the house of Jeroboam, even to blot it out and destroy it from off the face of the earth" (1 Kings 13:34).

Thus God announced again the same judgment of extermination on Israel. First a man of God pronounced before King Jeroboam that a king of Judah, Josiah by name, would sacrifice the priests of Israel on its altars. Then Abijah, the one who had first prophesied of Jeroboam's kingship, again prophecied, "I am bringing calamity on the house of Jeroboam, and will cut off from Jeroboam every male person, both bound and free in Israel, and I will make a clean sweep of the house of Jeroboam, as one sweeps away dung until it is all gone" (1 Kings 14:10).

Why is this subject being raised in a book devoted to the destruction of enemy strongholds in marriages? What is there in the worship of false gods and the genealogy of a corrupted nation that relates to the spirits that destroy husband-wife relationships?

Please listen carefully.

The sins of Jeroboam were a generational curse (see Exod. 34:7; Num. 14:18; Deut. 5:9) which successfully *destroyed the marriage covenant between God and Israel. The gods involved were gods of sexual immorality and child destruction* (see also Hos. 1–2). They worked to destroy right relationships, to remove the blessings of God from His chosen people, and to destroy their seed. Satan's purpose is to destroy the seed of God (see Gen. 3:15). These are the same spirits at work today destroying marriages and the fruit of marriage, our children. It is also important to recognize that *the central motivation by which the sin of Jeroboam gained access to the people for whom he was responsible was insecurity;* i.e., his fear of loss of material position and his life. This same motivation continues to work in marriages today, especially through brides, as it worked in Jeroboam, who represented Israel, the wife of God. In the case of Israel, it resulted in giving the enemy access into the kingdom and building a stronghold powerful enough to ultimately destroy her generations later.

These are the same strongholds with which we deal with issues of life and death for our children.

The utter seriousness with which God views the resulting perversion of Israel's worship of false gods and their sexual immorality is made excruciatingly clear in how God dealt with the subsequent intermarriage of the daughters of King Ahab of Israel into the line of Judah, thus threatening Judah and it's promise of the Messiah (see Gen. 49:10–11; 1 Chron. 5:2). This took place about six generations later in the history of Israel's kings. In 2 Kings, chapter 8, it is recorded that Jehoram, the son of Jehoshaphat, king of Judah, became king. "And he walked in the way of the kings of Israel, *just as the house of Ahab had done, for the daughter of Ahab became his wife and he did evil in the sight of the LORD*" (2 Kings 8:18). Hence we see that infection of the bloodline of Judah had taken place through intermarriage with the bloodline and idolatry of Israel. What could this produce as a result other that the extermination of both Judah and Israel? God's need for drastic correction is obvious in order to protect His promises, for the following verse says, "*However, the LORD was not willing to destroy Judah, for the sake of David His servant, since He had promised him to give a lamp to him through his sons always*" (2 Kings 8:19). God does not forget! Keeping in mind His Messianic promises and the required purity of the bloodline, God was committed to intervene.

Scripture records that God raised up another man, Jehu, and had him anointed by command of the prophet Elisha to be king of Israel with instructions to utterly destroy the house of Ahab. However, in carrying out his instructions, Jehu killed not only King Jehoram of Israel but also King Ahaziah of Judah. Who was King Ahaziah? He was the son of Judah's King Jehoram and a son-in-law of Ahab to whom we referred above. He had become a close associate with Israel's King Jehoram and happened to be actually present with him when Jehu came to carry out his instructions. Woe to those who become yoked with evil! Beware of marriage to idolatry!

Thus God *destroyed the king of Israel and the king of Judah in the same day*, along with destroying Ahab's entire house. In so doing He thereby destroyed as well the legal door of access by which the sins of Jeroboam could enter the nation of Judah through the bloodline of its kings.

This profound picture reveals how generational sin is conveyed through bloodlines of children and marriage; also, how doors of access by the enemy are gained into families and nations through sinful alliances, especially marriage.[1] The door of access into the bloodline of Judah had to be closed through the judgment of God and death of those judged in order to provide for comprehensive healing and protection of Judah. These laws are immutable!

These precepts apply vividly to marriage today in the widespread adultery and harlotry associated with marriage, divorce, and remarriage. This is especially seen in the associated dramatic growth of wife and child abuse accompanying the destruction.

It is unfortunate but true that women who have been abused by men bring into marriage severe insecurity. Beyond their normal incompleteness and need for a shield, enemy strongholds have already been established before the marriage, lies by which women, like Jehoram, seek to gain their own security by devices "which seem best to them." By experience of abuse from their fathers and/ or sexual immorality with their boyfriends or husband before marriage they have learned that men are untrustworthy. The enemy stronghold constantly whispers that they have little value and must provide for their own security. They pursue the idolatry of material possessions in their lust for security; they seek rulership as a means of self-control and of usurping God as the head of the husband and leader of the family, thereby constantly tearing down their economic base, their husband, and their true security. *The husband is constantly denied opportunity to seek God's answers and to face the pressure that his position requires.* In usurping God's position as the husband's head, the wife opens the family to the most destructive forms of deception and idolatry, working against both her and their children. It is repeated over and over again in each subsequent generation until, as with Israel, complete destruction of the seed of the marriage takes place.

In the meantime, the husband, fearful of death, performs the same death dance, chasing after false idols that cannot save him but have a blood lust to devour his children

There is a common irony in the sin of Aaron, the sin of Jeroboam, and the sins caused by strongholds of insecurity working in women. All involve the enemy's success in deceiving a person to turn away from the true Deliverer, the true Shield, the only true God of blessing and security and toward a false god, a deceiving spirit which cannot deliver or bless. *Thus Jeroboam actually declared by his thoughts and actions that the God who prophecied and anointed him king over Israel was not able to sustain him in that position unless he should pursue a strategy of worshipping other spirits!*

How strange and incredible! This is the same form of deception which holds many believing women in bondage today, women who urgently seek the blessing of God on their marriage but are captivated by their strongholds from enjoying true security and joy.

Who can deliver from this body of death? Praise God for His grace through our Lord Jesus Christ!

Only God's judgment and resurrection power can correct the situation. Christ is the only solution—His death on Calvary (see Luke 14:27, 33), His shed blood, His mercy and power. We must flee to Jesus. The judgment and death of Jesus for our sins provides a place for us to judge and repudiate our sins, placing them on His body and under His blood. He has become our curse that we may go free (see Gal 3:13).

Yes, husbands are untrustworthy. But God is trustworthy. *Trusting God and letting* the husband make mistakes will not jeopardize a woman's security. It will only enhance and ensure it. A woman's faith in God to work through the mistakes and foolishness of her husband is not misplaced at all. It is based on God's character, not her husband's. It is reckoned to her as righteousness (see Gen. 15:6). God will never let the righteous be shaken or suffer hunger (see Ps. 55:22; Pr. 10:3; Isa. 49:10). We have the assurance of Jesus in Matthew 6:33: "But seek first His kingdom and His righteousness; and all these things shall be added to you." Does the reader believe this? If so, you will see the glory of God.

This working out of trust in God is in a woman's weakest place—both by God's design of her dependence upon security and by the subsequent corruption of her nature. It is precisely in the area where she is most in need of Jesus Christ (see 2 Cor. 12:9); it is the most difficult area for her to develop and exercise her faith in God. But it will be the most fruit bearing and powerful in ministering to her husband, to her family, and to the world. May the enabling grace of God fall upon all women who purpose to place their trust in God and to obey Him in this critical area, destroying strongholds and bringing every thought captive to Jesus Christ, to the glory of God. "Wives, be subject to your own husbands, as to the Lord...See to it that you respect your husband" (Eph. 5:22, 33). "Love your husband" (Titus 2:4).

Though Ahab was destroyed and Judah was protected, the sins of Jeroboam had thoroughly infected Israel. Though prolonged for many more generations, Israel's fate remained unchanged from that of Ahab, kept until the iniquity of the nation became full. Israel was utterly destroyed as all the pagan nations which preceded it, the names of its children removed from the face of the earth. Let us pray that this will not happen to our own families and nation.

Dear Lord Jesus, please give us grace to be a pure and holy, trusting Bride to You and to our earthly husbands, able to keep our eyes on You, though calamity all around may strive to deceive us. Help us to identify and remove idolatry, all false sources of security. Help us to identify the windows through which insecurity has been established in our lives as unrighteous strongholds of mistrust against You, to see and repudiate ungodly behaviors in which we usurp Your authority working through those placed over us. We place all of this sin under Your blood to have it washed away from us forever. Give us a quiet and peaceful spirit—the mark of a godly bride, in which we smile at the future, not frightened by any fear. Thank You, Lord, that we can trust You for our security. Give us Your strength in our weakness. Please let us see more of Your beauty as we conform to walk in Your paths of righteousness. Amen.

15

The Spirit of Harlotry

But you trusted in your beauty and played the harlot because of your fame and you poured out your harlotries on every passer-by who might be willing. (Ezek. 16:15)

A male's uncontrollable appetite for sex and a female's insatiable demand for security have a common meeting point—harlotry or prostitution. Sex for payment is the ultimate culmination of lust in these two areas for both the man and the woman and has many progressive steps, especially in cases where sexual immorality has preceded marriage.

Rooted in deep deceptions, harlotry has its basic elements in how it first leads both the man and the woman into *initial* sexual immorality, frequently disguising itself with elaborate schemes to capture its slaves and hold them in bondage. Sexual sin is committed under many lies, all responding to the lust of the flesh for gratification in both men and women (see Ezek. 23:8–16).

Later in this book chapters 37 and 38 describe how God has placed His own desire to reproduce His seed into His design of the human race. They also describe how vastly different the reproduction urge manifests itself in male and female. The underlying drive for sexual gratification within the male originates with different forces and in a totally different context than it does for the female. The man is seeking personal gratification of seed planting in a context of his need for nurture. In the initial union there is also a context of sealing headship or sovereignty over the woman. Ejaculation is an end-in-itself and very fleshly in its gratification to the man. The woman is seeking gratification related to her desire for relational intimacy and desire to nurture and satisfy the man. Her context is her need for security in union with him.[1] It is much deeper, more soulish (affecting her mind and emotions), more process-oriented and less fleshly than the man's experience. She is centered on her function of enjoying and enhancing the chief relationship through which she finds identity and security.

The perversion of sex is also vastly different in the male and female, especially in the lusts and deceptions which lead to harlotry.

Through various deceptions, the enemy initially hides the fact that enticement toward sexual immorality is actually prompting a trade between two people seeking two different things. It disguises this by seeking to persuade that the two are in some form of "love" or that there is other rationale between their desires and needs that can be met through sexual relations outside of marriage. The lies that lead each of them to believe that sex outside of marriage will fulfill their needs (even the female need to nurture and promote relationship) lead them into terrible bondage and destruction, with repeating cycles of deeper degradation and perversion. Payment of money or goods is the logical end point for a man willing to coerce and oblige a woman to satisfy his lusts in return for his provision. For a woman driven by an ungodly appetite for security, the only alternative to overt power over a man and his finances is to yield her body in order to gain it. Both the man and the woman are tremendously degraded and defiled by their enslavement to these conditions.

Although both men and women can possess harlotry (see Ezek. 23:17–18), harlotry is described as an enemy spirit (see Hos. 4:12, 5:4) belonging particularly to the female. Women "play the harlot" (Gen. 38:24; Ezek. 16:15, 16, 26, 28, etc., 23:3, 5, etc.; Hos. 2:5, 4:12, 14, 15) and are repeatedly cited as the owners/possessors of harlotry (Ezek. 16:20, 22, 25, 26, 29, etc., 23:7, 8, 11, 14, etc.) while men can be joined to it (Prov. 29:3; 1 Cor. 6:15–16). Harlotry is closely compared with adultery (Ezek. 16:38, 23:37, 43; Hos. 4:13–14) and is associated with idolatry, the harlot misusing her husband's provisions as sacrifices to her idols. It is identified as *able to draw a woman into the sacrifice of her own sons and daughters* (Ezek. 16:20–21, 36, 23:37, 45).[2] There is also an extreme form of harlotry cited for the nation of Israel (and perhaps for modern nations also) in which the woman will pay for the attention of her lovers rather than receiving payment from them (Ezek. 16:33–34).

The man's walk into this enslavement is characterized by foolishness and lack of wisdom. With each step he loses manhood; i.e., his vigor and strength to support life. His substantive capacity is thus poured out on the ground together with his sperm as "streams of water in the street," thereby destroying his ability to fulfill his God-given functions of providing security for a woman and raising up godly seed. Sexual immorality leads the man to death "...as an ox goes to the slaughter...costing him his life" (See Prov. 5–7, 29:3).

Scripture cites that harlotry also involves foolishness in the woman. "She does not ponder the path of life; Her ways are unstable, she does not know it" (Prov. 5:6; see also Hos. 4:11–14). In addition, several other specifics are cited. *Ingratitude is reflected as a closely related basic sin.* By this a woman is "made exceedingly beautiful and advanced to royalty" by God or her husband, yet because she trusts in her fame or beauty, pours herself out in harlotry (see Ezek. 16:1–22). In addition, the words of Hosea and Ezekiel evoke powerful images of certain appetites of harlotry which are never satisfied, seeking either to increase material satisfaction or recapture the visions of youth: "They will eat and not have enough; they will play the harlot, but not increase" (Hos. 4:10). Ezekiel indicates that a woman may seek through harlotry to recapture the essence of her original sexual experience(s) as a young woman, visions that will persist in her later days, drawing her back in attempts to relive and satisfy them (see Ezek. 23:8, 19–21).

In marriages where sexual relationships have been allowed to be defiled by the enemy, these forces constantly work to destroy the intimacy between husband and wife. Premarital sex by the wife with other men prior to her husband has destroyed her natural capacity to be bonded to and live her life for her husband. In her lovemaking she will revisit visions of the man or men of her youth who preceded him. Her use of sex as a vain instrument to gain the love and security of previous men will carry into marriage as a device to be used on her husband, quite contrary to the manner in which God designed it in that neither spouse is to deny his or her body to the other (1 Cor. 7:2–5). Sex becomes a form of prostitution to extend the wife's security and control. Yet, because it is harlotry, her spirit causes her to recognize her defilement (see Ezek. 23:17) and to resent the sale of her body to her husband. She will come to hate her husband and herself for it. The husband recognizes this, but in his own impotence as a man and slavery to sexual appetites, he has no power or wisdom with which to escape coercing his wife into lovemaking. In so doing he allows the enemy to increase hatred and bitterness and all the other aspects of their strongholds rather than minister freedom and healing to her. Their relationship is torn apart.

In situations where the husband has compromised his own wife's virginity prior to marriage, he has even more grievously defiled her. She will continue to resent this for years, knowing deep in her heart he was not capable of defending her integrity prior to marriage and is therefore untrustworthy thereafter as her keeper. As explained in *Restoration of Men*, the conspiracy between them to sin perverts their relationship, sets the stage for the husband's giving up of headship of the family to the wife through role reversal, and usurps God's ideal for the husband's accountability to God for the family. Women who come into headship of the marriage also frequently use sex as one of their control devices. Any such use of sex by the woman to manipulate or control her husband is a perversion of the sexual relationship and is a form of harlotry used to gain the things she seeks. Through it, Satan gains added authority to work against the marriage and reproduction of godly seed.

Where the wife was not previously a virgin and premarital sex has taken place, she also enters marriage without knowing that her husband's love for her was sufficient for him to deny himself for her sake. She senses she is "worth" something less than the price he was unwilling to pay for her and that he has character insufficient to defend her. This denies her one of the aspects of her value that God intended her to have. Instead of receiving the love of a woman who has certain knowledge of her value and his character, the husband is now placed into the "bondage of expectations," having to constantly prove his love and character to his wife after marriage. As another aspect of stronghold control to enhance her self-image, it is to no avail. Gratitude and thanksgiving are never forthcoming from the wife, since these things become "necessary" according to her soulish demands. She has accepted the lie of "paying her way" and requiring the husband to also "pay his way" by proving his love. The husband's offerings become constant payment for past guilt and insecurity, sealed into a constant cycle of proving love to affirm his wife. Giving by the wife tends to either become conditional upon the husband's doing this as yet another form of harlotry or take other forms of denial or trade. They all remove sexual union from its intended place, the *free* pouring out of body, soul, and spirit by a man and woman committed to each other, affirming their mutual life covenant to each other's well-being, as well as the raising of children resulting from their union.

Only the power of God can overcome the spirits so established in a marriage. They will not yield to intellect. Only the blood of Jesus can heal and restore the things otherwise permanently lost through sexual immorality. Unless the provision of Jesus Christ for the removal of sin is appropriated by the marriage partners, both the sin and its consequences will continue to manifest themselves in the lives of the marriage and the children. Sex will continue to have various degrees of harlotry manifesting themselves in the mind of the husband or wife or both and will also produce the same lack of satisfaction which harlotry produces.

The stronghold of harlotry can be recognized today as one of the foremost enemy strongholds throughout the land, defiling men and women everywhere and spreading its seed to the destruction of families and ruination of millions of children. Public polls of teenagers in the United States in 1990 reported that over 50% of boys and 30% of girls believe that sex is warranted as return payment by girls who are taken out on dates by boys! Thus has the spirit of harlotry spread its lies to our young ones! The *unsatisfied lusts which harlotry in turn fosters* are now being magnified in the second and third generations of its victims in the most extreme forms of sexual perversion: homosexuality, rape, sodomy, and child molestation. Law enforcement agencies, courts of justice, welfare programs, foster care homes, and relatives of broken families are struggling vainly to maintain pace with the exploding problems of sexual perversion and violence now running rampant and still multiplying rapidly. Harlotry is the major enemy power behind the millions of unborn babies every year sacrificed through abortion to the blood lust of Baal, the ancient God of Canaan, thus illustrating the direct link between harlotry and idolatry.

Many women spend some years in marriage where they demonstrate an outward guise of normalcy, then suddenly revert to the habits and demands of the spirit of harlotry which occupied them decades earlier. Now they devour the goods of even faithful husbands while sleeping with new lovers under the delusion that strange men will satisfy their lusts.

The husbands for their part (usually always having tasted of the earlier harlotry) continue to rage in frustration and impotence at their wives, demanding satisfaction that cannot be met. Thus they also go outside the wife into pornography and adultery in a vain attempt to find it. The flight of their wives reaps what they have sown. Such men are greatly deceived, trapped into illusions that draw them into the destruction of their families, creating demeaned women who live wounded and defeated lives and yet another generation of children to be served up to Baal. Both spouses fail to accomplish the things that would bring them satisfaction and fulfillment. Broken lives and families built upon personal lust litter the land, as countless children serve as innocent victims.

Who will save their own children rather than sacrifice them to the spirit of harlotry? Husbands and wives must repent of their sins, the appetites of their lust and insecurity, their lewdness, the abominations of their sexual immorality. They must turn to God. "Everyone who calls upon the name of the Lord will be saved!" (see Joel 2:32; Acts 2:21; Rom. 10:13.) There is no other hope! Jesus Christ alone, the Lamb of God Who separates us from our sin, can save!

Men must take the lead. They are responsible for the leadership of their families and the deliverance of their wives and children.

Behind every harlot is an ungodly man. God has provided for men to take their places of responsibility in their marriages; He can give them the strength and wisdom to prevail against the enemy. In the Lord Jesus Christ, we have power to reclaim what the locusts have eaten, to find freedom from the power of sin, and to liberate our wives and children to lives of joy and fulfillment in the power of God through Jesus' unmatchable name.

What is the pathway of destruction of harlotry? Its root is lack of knowledge and Lordship of Jesus Christ, lack of faith in the character, nature, and provision of God. The man who lacks trust that God can nurture Him through right relationships (if necessary, without a wife) subverts protective authority in the woman's life and uses coercion to establish his rule over her. He seduces her outside of marriage. The woman who lacks trust and confidence that God can protect her through right relationships (and, if necessary, without having a husband) fails to embrace God's protective authorities in her life and seeks to establish her security through her own devices. She is deceived into believing that yielding her body to the man will secure for her the things she desires. She awakes instead to the discovery that she has been sold into even deeper bondage, emotionally bonded to the first man through sex and captivated by visions of lies thereafter as to how she can find fulfillment through the continued use of sex as a tool.

Healing requires a reversal of failure to trust God through the Lord Jesus Christ.

Only the blood of Jesus can cleanse. Only the blood of Jesus can destroy harlotry. God's Word says we have redemption through the blood of Jesus Christ (see Eph. 1:1–12), the power to break the curse of sin through Christ who became a curse in our place (see Gal. 3:13; 1 Pet. 3:18) so that we might be dead to sin but made alive in the Spirit through God's free grace.

Lord, let us be used as instruments of righteousness rather than instruments of sin (see Rom. 6:13–14).

To all those who would renounce the spirit of harlotry, its stronghold, power, and consequences in their life, and claim the redemptive work of Jesus Christ in restoring them to freedom, purity, and His Lordship, the following prayer is offered:

Dear Lord Jesus, I repent of my wicked ways of lusting after perverted fleshly satisfaction, rule, control, nurture, relationships or security. I repent of the place I have given the spirit of harlotry, the use of sex as a tool in my life to obtain the things I have falsely claimed I needed without regard to You. I repent of partaking in it and renounce it as sin, abominable in Your sight and destructive to Your interests of bringing peace, joy, and fulfillment into my life. I want to tear down this stronghold forever by Your Word and with Your blood. I need a clean heart within me and the joy of my salvation. By faith, I claim the power of Your Word to do this. I place it under Your Holy blood, shed for my sin, and I claim its power to deliver me from the curse of sin.

(**Men**: As Lord of all things, I know that You are able to meet my righteous needs as a man for nurture and healing apart from the obedience and godliness of my wife, if necessary. Help me to promote the well-being and security of my wife regardless of her capacity to meet me, and do not charge any of her shortcomings against her account. I place my trust in You.)

(**Women**: As Lord of all things, I know that You are able to meet my righteous needs as a woman for security in Your own power and apart from the obedience and godliness of my husband, if necessary. Help me to promote the well-being and health of my husband regardless of his capacity to meet me, and do not charge any of his shortcomings against his account. I place my trust in You.)

Give me wisdom and a giving heart to honor You in this marriage, with all of my gifts being made in Your Name only and with no conditions for return or recognition from my spouse. I place my sex life under Your Lordship and control as an instrument for Your righteousness. Please protect our children from the spirit of harlotry and give them Your divine deliverance for salvation and the power to live for You. Thank You for being both the Author and Answerer of this request made in Your will and with confidence that it will surely be answered through Jesus Christ. Amen.

Jezebel

And it came about, as though it had been a trivial thing for him to walk in the sins of Jeroboam the son of Nebat, that he married Jezebel. . . . (1 Kings 16: 31)

Jezebel was the daughter of Ethbaal, king of the Sidonians. She drew Ahab into serving and worshipping Baal. In addition to erecting an altar for Baal, Ahab made "an Asherah," the female sex deity common to the surrounding pagan nations. "Thus Ahab did more to provoke the LORD God of Israel than all the kings of Israel who were before him" (1 Kings 16:32–33). The spirit of Jezebel is one of the most powerful controlling spirits of women, maintaining a stronghold relatively easy to identify but difficult to break. It is being described in increasing detail by Christian writers as discernment of enemy principalities and powers matures in the body of Christ. It displays certain personality traits as well as physical characteristics in the persons it dominates [1] and affects those who war spiritually against it with certain identifiable influences.

From Scripture we know that Ahab had many characteristics of a little boy who had never grown up. He was in a man's body but without manhood. When Syrian King Ben-Hadad besieged Samaria and demanded Ahab's riches, wives, and children, Ahab agreed, having no stomach to defend either his wealth or his own flesh and blood. He was an ineffectual shield, an impotent man. If Ben-Hadad had not then overstepped what Ahab had already granted, thereby involving Israel's elders, Israel could have fallen without a whimper (see 1 Kings 20).

But at his elders' urging, King Ahab began to resist the further demands of Ben-Hadad. Ben-Hadad was a boaster in his false gods. One thing quickly led to another and Ben-Hadad was provoked into war. God intervened on Israel's behalf and gave Ahab a great victory, not related to Ahab's merits but possibly to Ben-Hadad's blasphemy of Israel's God. This became more explicit when, after escaping with his life, Ben-Hadad was provoked in the name of his "gods of the plain" to return to Jerusalem and try it again. God again provided Ahab a great slaughter of the Syrians and capture of Ben-Hadad. But Ahab foolishly let him go, bringing a curse upon his family and nation.

The poisonous effects of Ahab's emasculation (loss of manhood) through ancestry and marriage are evidenced in the fact that God's miraculous delivery on these two occasions did nothing to awaken Ahab's consciousness toward God. He remained trapped in his impotence and idolatry.

Ahab had been eyewitness as Elijah called down fire by the God of Israel against the prophets of Baal. He didn't respond to God, reflected in the fact that it was Elijah, not King Ahab, who put the prophets of Baal to death. Jezebel then went murderously berserk upon hearing from her husband the news of what had happened. She was evidently a completely lawless person, operating without any identifiable constraints whatsoever—certainly none from her husband.

Later, when Ahab admired the vineyard of Naboth and had his offer to purchase it rejected by Naboth (on righteous grounds because it was the inheritance from Naboth's fathers), Ahab became petulant and peevish. He refused to talk or eat, behaving just like a spoiled boy.

The bullying, scornful spirit of Jezebel was immediately evidenced by her response to her husband: "Do you now reign over Israel? Arise, eat bread, and let your heart be joyful; I will give you the vineyard of Naboth" (1 Kings 21:7). Her brutal and lawless approach to getting her way was illustrated by her summarily staging an execution dinner. Naboth was seated at the head of the people and "two worthless men" that Jezebel had appointed falsely testified that Naboth had cursed God and the king. Naboth was then taken outside and stoned to death.

Ahab was so dependent upon Jezebel and apparently unable to discern anything other than his own selfish appetites that he is not recorded as being either a party to nor an inquirer regarding Naboth's murder scheme. Jezebel took care of everything. It is recorded that Ahab afterward went "to take possession" of the vineyard. Picture a little boy taking possession of something his mother has provided, with no moral consciousness of how she obtained it for him. That God nevertheless holds a husband accountable for the actions of his wife is recorded in God's words to Ahab through Elijah the prophet, "Have *you murdered* and *also* taken possession?" (1 Kings 21:19, emphasis added).

The power of Jezebel to keep in her subservience one whom God holds accountable is one of this stronghold's chief characteristics. She is able to powerfully discourage and diminish men who are not in Christ. She has devastating power to control and maintain dominion over a husband, keeping him emasculated and incapable of growing in wisdom and responsibility. The power of the Jezebel stronghold holds the husband prisoner, as a butterfly pinned to a board, while the wife usurps (1) his headship of the family and (2) God's place as the husband's head. She will also usurp, where applicable, her husband's work. If he is ill, crippled, or otherwise in need of real healing, he will not receive it through her. She does not want a healthy husband who can compete with her control.

In *The Three Battlegrounds*, Francis Frangipane points out many of these aspects, including the level of principality in which the spirit of Jezebel operates.[2] The spirit of Jezebel is the antithesis of and wars against the spirit of Elijah, which Jesus said in Matthew 17:11 would come ("Elijah is coming and will restore all things") and which Malachi prophesied would mark the end of the age prior to the coming of the Lord: "Behold, I am going to send you Elijah the prophet before the coming of the great and terrible day of the Lord. And he will restore the hearts of the fathers to their children, and the hearts of the children to their fathers" (Mal. 4:5–6). Jezebel fiercely resists work by the spirit of Elijah to bring about reconciliation and restoration of all things in preparation for the return of Jesus Christ.

The unique power of *teshookaw* in women to reach out and move the spirits of their husbands makes women highly susceptible to entertaining and giving residence to Jezebel in their own lives. It is to the effect of better controlling and manipulating their husbands. Because of the particular susceptibility of women to deception into false ideas that might provide them with security, abused and injured women are especially susceptible to the Jezebel spirit. As Frangipane states:

> Jezebel is more attracted to the female psyche in its sophisticated ability to manipulate without physical force. Look for Jezebel to target women who are embittered against men, either through neglect or misuse of authority. This spirit operates through women who, because of insecurity, jealousy, or vanity, desire to control and dominate others.[3]

It is also especially important to note that Jezebel's religion was based upon sexual perversion and witchcraft, the foundations of the idolatry she brought with her from her pagan nation. The use of sexual attraction to control the male and sexual immorality to emasculate and render him powerless is a chief strategy to bring men to ruin, in accordance with the word of God (Prov. 4–7). Satan uses this with license to kill, as is highly evident in the world today.

In Jezebel's more advanced forms in abused women, its manipulation and coercive devices (even by women seeking counseling) are frequently so powerful, deceptive, and pervasive as to be essentially indistinguishable from witchcraft.

With regard to the power of Jezebel to control men through sexual stimulation, it is noted that in God's ultimate judgment and execution of Jezebel, *He used eunuchs to throw her off the city walls and kill her.* In ancient times, eunuchs were uniquely those men who gave up their power to reproduce their own seed to live lives of service to royalty. They could be trusted to serve without being susceptible to the pervasive temptations and influences of sexual immorality in the king's palace. Either voluntarily or forcibly, they were castrated as means of enabling them to remain free from these influences. The men used as instruments of Jezebel's judgment were *free from her powers of sexual manipulative control.*

Although women may be deceived into believing they are gaining security by their control over their husbands, they pay a terrible price for their bondage. The Jezebel spirit occupies many women who have allegedly come to Christ but in whom the Word of God has never circumscribed and destroyed their strongholds as God intends. Rather than becoming free women, they remain slaves to fear and ungodly passions they cannot control. There are a number of symptoms evident:

1. Perhaps most immediately evident symptom is their exposure to constant torment and stress of bodily illnesses and supposed spiritual warfare. By removing themselves from under any human agent of spiritual authority (husband, father, mother, pastor, brother(s), etc.), they have no shield operating in their lives. Such human authorities are intended by God to intercede and take a woman's infirmities in their place. By failing to submit to any such authority these women have, in effect, given the enemy full legal authority to attack them directly.

2. They have a critical spirit toward those in spiritual authority. They are unable to submit to pastors and elders in churches and are frequent church-hoppers, unfaithful to long-term commitments within the body of Christ that require peaceful relationships with authority.

3. They seek to aggrandize themselves, coveting places of ministry and frequently claiming themselves to be "prophets" (Rev. 2:20).

4. They use manipulative appeals for sympathy in an effort to extend control over those around them, frequently using either their bodily ailments, their self-debilitating efforts of spiritual warfare, or other types of appeals for understanding, including tears. (Note: Frequently there are heart-rending causes of their conditions that warrant utmost sympathy and efforts to intercede and work with God for their healing. It is the pattern nature of how such women will use these things to manipulate sympathy that is being noted here.)

5. There is a spirit of distraction which opposes efforts to deal creatively with exposing and bringing the interfering spirit to account. Lines of thought in the discussion seem to constantly change. One example is to focus accusations and guilt upon others—a feature present in all of human nature, but apparently a particular device in the defense of this stronghold to deflect attention from itself.

In addition, Joyce Strader, a pastor's wife who has reported her encounters with the spirit of Jezebel, states that Jezebel also frequently uses flattery (words that entice), "pseudo-superspirituality" (i.e., religious-sounding complaints against leadership), intrigue and gossip, and desire to gather supporters—common devices of the enemy to divide and create factions within the body of Christ.[4]

An experience reported by Strader in which a woman was able to identify and renounce the spirit of Jezebel within her while being supported by intercessors also occurred in the life of this author. My initial confrontation with the spirit of Jezebel was in a woman undergoing counseling who revealed a characteristic spirit (or spirits) that could not be identified. We worked for several weeks praying for deliverance from this spirit according to its symptoms of behavior. Then through another (female) counselor, the spirit of Jezebel was identified in her through the use of Strader's article, which cited in almost complete entirety the list of symptoms that we had identified and against which we had been praying for deliverance. By her renunciation of this spirit by the power of the blood of Jesus Christ, this woman was delivered from Jezebel and real healing began.

I've also seen confrontations with Jezebel in which more hostile activity took place. All have feigned various degrees of godliness and, in my opinion, been seemingly intermingled with real discernment and gifts of God. All held their husbands prisoners. In one case a husband who was severely crippled by arthritis had been unable to receive healing over years of earnest prayer and support group activity. Yet, he began to walk again within weeks after he had been removed from under "her" roof by her apparently unwitting decision to have him committed to a rest home.

I have also seen Jezebel bully a husband to the ludicrous extreme of rudely forcing him to anoint a gift with oil and pray after he had already declined and asked her to do it. Her demand was founded upon it not being "right" that she pray because he was the "head" of the family! Her submissive-sounding words were directly contradictory to the actual bullying behavior of her spirit in which she illustrated she was not subject to her husband at all.

It is important, as Frangipane points out, to recognize that those who work in the spirit of Elijah will come under attack by Jezebel. When this happens, one is exposed to powerful influences seeking to promote fear and discouragement, as in the case of John the Baptist, who ministered in the spirit of Elijah (Matt. 17:10–12). This is especially true in the restoration of men and marriages, where men are coming under the restorative power of God and working to rebuild godly relationships with their wives and children. It is not uncommon that the most powerful stronghold and one of the last for God to reach is found in the wife, from whom all manner of disparagement and venomous scorn are heaped upon a husband who has truly begun to seek God and find true manhood in Jesus Christ.

Homosexuality:
More Male Dysfunction

> I, the Lord your God, am a jealous God, visiting the iniquity of the fathers on the children, and on the third and the fourth generations of those who hate Me. (Deut. 5:9)

Most men fail utterly to grasp the centrality of the above scripture, repeated four times in the Old Testament (see also Exod. 20:5, 34:7; Num. 14:18). Closely linked is God's redemption from this curse prophesied in the last verse of the Old Testament, in which He says that through the spirit of Elijah He will "restore the hearts of the fathers to their children, and the hearts of the children to their fathers, lest I come and smite the land with a curse" (Mal. 4:6).

It cannot be too strongly stated that it is the fathers, not mothers, who are ultimately responsible for the guarding, reproduction, and raising up of their seed. They are the *husbands* of their wives and *husbandmen* for their seed. "Do not be deceived, God is not mocked; for whatever a man sows, this he will also reap" (Gal. 6:7). Every father should know that his iniquities pass with his seed into the lives of his children. Only Christ, The Seed of God, can alter the outcome of a man's fruit.

Homosexuality is a variation on the common theme of the day that sexual immorality destroys ability to raise up godly seed. It produces the same sort of dysfunction. It destroys capacity for the crucial male-female relationship needed for reproducing children in God's likeness, the first step of which is to produce earthly children. Earthly children always assume some likeness of their earthly father, not only in physicality but also in attitudes and behavior. They are in turn a seedbed for God's perfect reproduction of His Seed, Jesus Christ, in lost sinners. This "second birth" is in exact likeness to The Heavenly Father (see Heb. 1:2–3). This central theme of Scripture is summarized by the following foundational precepts:

1. God's purpose in man is the creation of life in His own likeness (see Gen. 1:26a);
2. The first commandment which God has given men is to reproduce (see Gen. 1:27–28);
3. The first identifier of the Messiah is as *Seed*, key to reproduction. (see Gen. 3:15);
4. The chief motivator for successful marriage is the desire of parents to seek godly offspring (see Mal. 2:14–16);
5. God declares that His children will be "conformed to the image of His Son" (John 1:12–14; Rom. 8:29).[1]

Nothing has changed. God will accomplish His word. Not even the fall of man will set aside God's purpose or provision for reproduction of His own children. Though Satan opposes Him and has been given license to wage war through many strongholds, he is doomed by The Seed, who died to accomplish His work and was resurrected (see John 12:24–27, 10:17–18). There will be a myriad in the exact likeness of Christ with whom He will share His kingdom.

Because homosexuality is a stronghold which manifests identical obstruction and destruction to the above reproductive purposes of God, it is therefore included among spirits and attitudes which war against marriage *and its central purpose of reproducing godly seed.*

Homosexuals have common kinship in the general dysfunction of most men by being unable to: (1) relate well with their fathers,

(2) keep faithful to a wife, (3) maintain a marriage, and (4) responsibly raise up children to maturity. This should sober all of us. Even outwardly successful marriages face the same temptations and potential ravages. In all the above key areas there is no difference between many heterosexual men and homosexual men. All have been victimized by sin to produce death to their seed. It is a curse. Homosexuality is one of many forms of destruction to what men were designed and created to do with God: create good seed.

Because it is derivative of the sins of the father, we therefore should anticipate all related curses to point to the same means of healing; i.e., reconciliation through Jesus Christ with both the Heavenly Father and earthly fathers (see 2 Cor. 5:17–21).

The common factor in male homosexuality in nearly all studies of the past century is (a) an absent or ineffectual father or (b) traumatic experience(s) with the father. This link is not essentially different from the common broken link to fathers found in other sociopathic behaviors, creating adverse impact to individuals and society at enormous public expense.[2] This finding supports many reparative therapies which lovingly emphasize healing of the scars of youth that came through father and/or peer rejection and is in agreement with the biblical identity of fathers as those primarily responsible for the outcomes of their offspring.

Effectual work to bring healing and good fruit into the lives of homosexuals requires that they be brought to God through the love of Christ, through His disciples. A reparative model which illustrates this is provided by the following example.

Dr. Elizabeth Moberly, a psychologist who specialized for many years in gender identity research, has proposed that homosexual behavior is based upon repressed love-need of the young child which may be reactivated in later years. According to her model, every child receives its gender identity through the love of the same-sex parent during its childhood growth, especially during its first three years of life.[3] Failure to receive this love-need leaves the child incomplete in gender identity until the need is met, causing him eventually to seek a male source of love. Dr. Moberly presents persuasively the idea that the need for the same-sex source of love is essential for therapy and natural in terms of the completion of gender identity. She advocates that it should not be thwarted but provided in an appropriate therapeutic manner leading to the man's security in a loving relationship which helps him complete his gender identity. *Lacking gender identity, he will never achieve interest or capacity to love a woman and find the greater level of personal fulfillment in a stable heterosexual relationship.*

Being greatly persuaded of the biblical strength of Dr. Moberly's model, the author attempted to apply it to the situation of a close friend with a homosexual son. The following chapter provides some limited personal testimony tending to corroborate the ideas of Dr. Moberly's model, at least for male homosexuals.

The evangelical community commendably opposes approval of homosexuality as a lifestyle. However, opposition is based almost totally upon biblical admonitions against it. Little other information required for public debate of the issues of homosexuality has been included in the argument. In an increasingly secular world antagonistic to biblical standards, simple appeals to those standards will no longer be heard nor will they persuade the public toward correction. It is more useful to support debate with compassionate understanding of the underlying issues of homosexuality, its long-term life consequences, and methods of bringing about healing and modification of the destructive behavior. In particular, personal and public health and education issues require such informed debate.

Appendix A is therefore devoted to providing some such background on the subject in the belief that it is crucial for the evangelical community to become better informed in the continuing research regarding homosexuality's causes, consequences, and susceptibility to therapy.

Homosexuality:
A Father's Testimony

For you who fear My name the sun of righteousness will rise
with healing in its wings; and you will go forth and skip about
like calves from the stall. (Mal. 4:2)

Dr. Moberly's model of gender identity introduced in the previous chapter, seemed to me close to a biblical explanation of homosexuality, *at least with the male.* Her model accurately reflects
and amplifies the scriptural portraits of (1) an intact dual-parent
family as the preferred means of successful child rearing, (2) the
father's responsibility for iniquities passed down to the children,
also discussed previously, (3) the father's ultimate responsibility
for the family, including reconciliation with the children (Mal. 4:5–
6), (4) love as God's basis for all growth and healing, and (5) God's
prescription (undertaken through His love, initiative, and personal
expense) through Jesus Christ, by which men find reconciliation,
personal identity, and completion in the love of God, the Father.

I made an early application test of the Moberly model which
has further persuaded me of these views. I went to a friend who
had a homosexual son, twenty-eight years of age at the time and
sharply estranged from his father. I presented the Moberly model
to my frient, then asked if he had ever had a traumatic separation
from his son during his son's first three years of life.

His response was, "No! I had a great relationship with my son. We used always to wrestle and play. Every evening we would hug and rough and tumble together. I only had one occasion where I was separated from him when he was about a year or two old, when my ship deployed for 9 months."

He then paused a bit, started to continue, then stopped in midsentence, "Wait! I remember now that right after I got back I fell into the dry dock and crushed both my legs. I was hospitalized for nearly a year!" After another moment, he continued, " Oh-h-h! Wow! And when I got out of the hospital, I was then in a wheelchair for nearly another year!"

By this time, his hand had gone to his forehead. Then he said slowly, "Then my wife and I had our second son. I see now that I never really reestablished my relationship with my first son!"

Based upon his corroborating testimony of Moberly's model, we discussed various approaches as to how he might draw closer to his eldest son, in particular, how he might take responsibility and initiative as father for the unmet love-need of his son. We prayed for God to provide for restoration and completion, but for months thereafter my friend never seemed to undertake any specific effective actions to draw closer to his estranged son. I was disappointed, thinking that somehow he had failed to grasp the significance of his opportunity to correct a matter clearly related to his responsibility as father.

However, some time later I received this report, "Guess what! For some reason, my son has started coming over to visit with us a lot more often—and he's staying longer, too! At Christmas he stayed with us for three days. And all the time he was with us, he kept coming up to me and hugging me. He would just wrap his arms around me and hug me and run his hands through my hair (what there is of it!). And you know what? I made sure I never touched my hair after he messed it up!" The father was smiling from ear to ear!

I receive such reports in amazement of my own shortsightedness and lack of faith. Why could I have not have anticipated that the Father, Himself, would be involved in this father-son restoration? He was answering our prayers! One senses Dr. Moberly's model to be close indeed to the truth and that restoration of fathers must be close to the very center of God's own heart. The Holy Spirit seems to testify of two Fathers now enjoying this blessing of seeing a son restored in the knowledge that he is loved.

Over the next year or two further growth took place. Both mother and father purposefully planned and spent increasing time with their son, both at their home and at his, in a large city an hour or two away, and with their son's homosexual friends. They attempted to support him without his misunderstanding that they support his lifestyle. Now at age thirty-one, he has told his parents that his homosexual friends frequently remark as to how obvious and great is the love of his parents for him, in contrast to something they never had. These parents' love of their son has become a testimony to the whole homosexual community.

In addition, it appears that their son has grown emotionally and changed internally. He has grown in his ability to discern behavioral patterns and maturity among his friends. Yet more recently he has decided he no longer desires a roommate and has commenced living alone.

The father's testimony is still one of comfort and joy in the changes he sees in his son. "You know, he still comes up to me often and hugs me and messes up my hair! And I still leave it that way!"

It is possible that Dr. Moberly's model is not as symmetrical with respect to girls as she postulates. She points out both genders having close relationship to their mothers during the first year of life and that female gender identity with a same-sex love source is much more naturally secured than for the male. Perhaps for this reason there are far fewer female homosexuals than male. However, a fair proportion of lesbians appear to be drawn to that lifestyle based on abuse and bitterness related to the failure of men (fathers, stepfathers, boyfriends, or others) rather than traumatic experiences with their mothers. Perhaps it will be eventually determined that with girls also everything comes to rest on the functional performance of fathers.

Disciples of Jesus Christ should be able to identify with the incomplete person; they themselves are completed only by faith in Christ. The homosexual cries out for compassion as one who needs to know real love. The male homosexual, at least, is a vivid case of one who is incomplete—and *crying out for completion.*

Anyone who has experienced excessive appetites (i.e., alcohol, drugs, cigarettes, sex, possessions, money, power, food, recognition, or other evil habits and desires) knows personally what it is to be lost in discontent and dissatisfaction. These appetites are never satisfied. How much more would a person *crave love and seek its false substitutes?* If appetites of the flesh can be perverted, how much more can love be perverted?! How does a homosexual differ from men who have abused, cheated or abandoned their families, or squandered their lives on gambling or alcohol? How does one differ from women who turn their lusts to illicit "romance" or waste years seeking primary fulfillment in a marketplace? The homosexual is human incompleteness seeking sinful solution, common to all self-centered depravity. Where would any of us be without the love of God? Would we not all be ashamed if God were to share with the world our attempts to satisfy ourselves outside of Him?

What the authors of the Bible tell us from beginning to end is that all of mankind's problems are rooted in failure to know the love of the Father and thereby to trust Him—and of His expensive and painful steps to resolve that problem for us. *Homosexuality is a particular stronghold that sums up the very essence of lack of knowledge of the Father and its critical need to be rightly expressed through a human earthly father.* By failure as earthly fathers we cooperate with Satan's plan of hatred against human offspring and his opposition to the reproduction of God's Seed, Jesus Christ, through the human race.

Section III: Tearing Down Strongholds

Destruction of Strongholds: A Study of Rahab

. . . how can anyone enter the strong man's house and carry off his property, unless he first binds the strong man? (Matt. 12:29)

As the above scripture suggests, successful warfare requires proper strategy and tactics. Successful warfare in the Kingdom of God obviously requires them, too. In Joshua, chapters 2 and 6, we receive instruction. The account of the destruction of Jericho contains a picture of God's plan for spiritual warfare for nations and for God's people to destroy enemy strongholds.

Less recognized, perhaps, is the fact that this story also portrays both "friend" and "enemy." In addition to the destruction of the enemy, it reveals the strategy for liberation and spiritual transformation of the people of God from enemy strongholds. This is personified by Rahab, the harlot. She models our own liberation in Jesus Christ as He destroys our enemy strongholds.

We know that Rahab's transformation was powerful and complete because after the destruction of Jericho she was taken as the wife of Salmon, a direct descendent of Judah. She became the mother of Boaz, God's example of a man's man. Boaz is distinguished as one of the most godly men of the Bible, the one who modeled the work of our Lord Jesus Christ as a kinsman-redeemer and who brought the gentile woman, Ruth, into a place of exalted fulfillment as a wife and mother. Boaz's excellence helps focus our attention upon what so transformed his mother.[1]

How did a woman become transformed from prostitute to mother of one of the most godly men in the Bible? Let us look first at God's overall strategy for destroying Jericho, a powerful city "tightly shut" and filled with "valiant warriors" (Josh. 6:1–2). There were a number of chronological events which together brought success.

First, God raised up strong men, tested and refined through forty years of hardship in the wilderness, to whom His words "be strong and courageous" (Josh 1:6, 7, 9, 18) were not ineffectual as they had been to Moses' generation. Israel was now ready to obey God.

Second, God gave Joshua wisdom to "view the land, especially Jericho" (Josh 2:1). In a manner reminiscent of the actions of Moses, but now much more focused on the single objective at hand, Joshua sent two spies into the city to "search out" (i.e., to gain personal knowledge of) the nature of the enemy's stronghold.

Third, God responded to their initial obedience to cross the Jordan by performing signs and wonders to build their faith further. The spies experienced providential protection and evidence that the word of God had preceded them; i.e., the woman who protected them knew that, "the Lord your God, He is God in heaven above and on earth beneath" (Josh. 2:11). They came back with enhanced confidence in their mission with an encouraging report. "Surely the LORD has given all the land into our hands" (Josh. 2:24). In addition, the Lord then dried up the Jordan River, further building the faith of the Israelites while melting the hearts of the inhabitants throughout the land (see Josh. 5:1).

Fourth, God announced the result of the war against Jericho beforehand. He declared, "See, I have given Jericho into your hand, with its king and the valiant warriors" (Josh. 6:2).

Fifth, God announced His tactical encirclement plan for its destruction, requiring further obedience. The children of Israel were to carry out a daily encirclement process, walking around the city once for each of six days. On the seventh day they were to do so again successively, "seven times, and the priests shall blow the (seven) trumpets. And it shall be that when they make a long blast with the ram's horn, and when you hear the sound of the trumpet, all the people shall shout with a great shout; and the wall of the city will fall down flat, and the people will go up every man straight ahead" (Josh. 6:4–5).

This prescription for destroying Jericho is not merely an isolated example. We note it to be God's basic pattern of warfare and judgment against strongholds of rulers, of principalities, of the earth, of sin, and of final judgment. All involve encirclement, the removal of options, melting of hearts, announcement through trumpets, final destruction, and fire (See Jer. 30:1–11, 33:1–9; Matt. 24:1–31; 1 Cor. 3:12–15; Heb. 10:25–31).[2]

The sixth aspect of God's plan depends upon further obedience of His people. A key part of the judgment of Jericho required further obedience in faith on the part of God's children to actually carry out God's instructions. They faced death in carrying out tasks contrary to the wisdom of the world. God seems to delight in raising up people of every generation who will do this. The children of Israel successfully carried out God's instructions to the letter, foolish though it seemed.

Seventh, God fulfilled His word by accomplishing the complete destruction of the stronghold of Jericho by His own power.

The only exception to the complete destruction of Jericho and its inhabitants was with Rahab, with whom the same process took place. The difference is that, in the destruction of what had (until recently) been her stronghold, she was set totally free!

Rahab was a woman brought to a most extreme form of degradation. She sold her body to men similarly depraved to momentarily satisfy their lusts. She bore the accumulated effects of sin in her life. She knew that men were not trustworthy. So she followed her own plans for security: money. It became a stronghold that held her in bondage. She sold herself for cash and what it could buy. Prostitution put bread on the table, a roof over her head, and perhaps also temporary riches. But outside of her immediate family, she was probably despised, having no reputation, self-esteem, or future. She had no husband and possibly no children. As she grew older and her parents died, she would see only increasing loneliness, fear, and doom. Lacking the Word of God, there was no way of escape for Rahab.

Then, amazingly, the Word of God was given to her. In a most wonderful display of how God can reveal His true identity and nature to any He chooses, He mercifully revealed Himself to Rahab, who had never heard a sermon nor a word of Scripture, had never set foot in a synagogue or church, and had never met a man or woman of God. She merely heard testimony of how the true God, the God of Israel, had "dried up the water of the Red Sea" when the Israelites came out of Egypt and what they "did to the two kings of the Amorites who were beyond the Jordan, to Sihon and Og, whom (were) utterly destroyed." She knew this to be the work of the only true God (See Josh. 2:10–11).

Upon this, she staked her life. When given an opportunity to exercise her knowledge of God, she risked death to save the two spies Joshua had sent into the city. She did this with no prior conditions. It was unconditional. She hid them and protected them with a false story when the king of Jericho sent word to her to turn them over. As she later explained her actions to the spies, she made repeated references to God as "Lord" and identified Him as true God, saying, "for the Lord your God, He is God in heaven above and on earth beneath" (Josh. 2:11). Following this, she asked the two men to "swear by the Lord" to deal kindly with her father's household and to "deliver (their) lives from death" (Josh. 2:12–13).

God's humor surpasses ours. What could be more preposterous? What could better illustrate the power of God to overturn man's wisdom than the "foolishness" of a prostitute placing her future into the hands of *soldiers*? Enemy foreign soldiers at that! And on top of that—spies!

But consider this. How capable would Rahab have been to exercise her knowledge of God had her other ways of escape not been cut off? Would she have risked her life had there been any other hope? Would she have been willing to risk loss of her life and relationships to protect a couple of foreign spies bent upon their destruction? We sense the death of alternatives. Rahab was out of options. "If I perish, I perish!" (Esther 4:16) seems to echo across Scripture as men and women consider other potential sources of hope then place their trust in God. As Peter said to Jesus when questioned as to whether he would turn away, "Lord to whom (else) shall we go? You have words of eternal life" (John 6:68).

No! God circumscribes each of us with the Word of Truth and cuts off other ways of escape. He reveals the futility of our lies and false hopes. Removal of false escape is part of His plan for deliverance. The "strong man" of the stronghold is bound, revealed to be a liar. Before making a "leap in the dark" with God, our lies must be demolished. Rahab had been completely encircled, not merely within the city walls but in her own life. The walls of Jericho no longer offered protection, hence they no longer had power over her.

Now the Word of God offered her true escape—the Word of a living, trustworthy God. She knew what He was doing with Israel. She decided to cast her lot with them. Rahab took the opportunity to choose life with God (Deut. 30:19).

We see that essentially the same seven elements of destruction of Rahab's strongholds were involved as in the seven elements identified in the destruction of Jericho.

First, God raised up *strong men*, spies, agents—both of deliverance and judgment.

Second, God provided Rahab with opportunity to search out the matter and gave her *wisdom to know what to do.*

Third, God built up her faith as *she saw the divine providence of God* in her favor (through precisely the same events which enhanced the faith of the spies).

Fourth, having activated her faith, *God announced the results to her beforehand,* conditionally, based upon additional required steps of *obedience* (see Josh. 2:14–20).

Fifth, she received instruction for *further obedience.* They were the tactics of personal identification with God leading to life in the midst of destruction. Rahab was told to formalize the encirclement of her household with a scarlet thread, from which no one was to "go out."[3]

Sixth, *she was obedient* to the additional requirements God had set before her.

Seventh, with the blast of trumpets and great shout of the people outside of the walls, *the power of God destroyed her strongholds.* While Jericho was destroyed, she was delivered. She became a free woman.

The simultaneous destruction of the enemy Jericho and deliverance of Rahab from her stronghold is the pattern of deliverance we seek for our own lives. It involves trusting God unto death.

From the insecurity of harlotry to security in the love of God for her, Rahab became a new creature. Done away were anxieties and human solutions. Done away was life behind walls. Rahab was given instead by the God who loved her, a husband who also loved her. She became the mother of Boaz, the very model of a godly man working on behalf of a woman. What a wonder! God's arm is not short that He cannot save!

Rahab is the example of how working knowledge of the true and living God can demolish strongholds of insecurity and depravity to bring forth righteous relationships. True fulfillment in marriage and, as with Rahab, the marvelous fruit of godly seed are founded upon this.

Demolishing a Stronghold

But prove yourselves doers of the word, and not merely hearers who delude themselves. (James 1:22)

Pain brings us to seek relief. Hopefully, we find right relief! An example in my life illustrates the nature of warfare with strongholds. For years I would come home from work seeming to have no capacity whatsoever for listening to my wife's discussion of the events of her day. From the moment of my arrival home I would become irritated and angry at her as she commenced to eagerly share with me. It seemed to me that her discussion usually included (even focused upon?) identification of problems at home with which I had to deal. I would therefore usually retreat to the bedroom to change clothes, read the newspaper, and otherwise "transition" from my own hectic day of work to the situations which existed at home. Only after an hour or so by myself could I seem to deal rationally with my wife. *However, for years the situation did not strike me as a personal problem in my attitudes or behavior.* It seemed rather to be a problem of not having an understanding wife, a "cross" that I had to bear. Does this sound familiar?

However, one day God allowed circumstances to focus my attention more fully upon the problem. I came home having had an extremely blessed day, indeed one of the most God-filled days of my life. The providential blessings and answers to prayer that had fallen upon me during the workday had filled me with praise, and I had literally sung and praised the Lord aloud all the way home from work. The moment I came in the door, however, it was all shattered by something my wife said to me. In an instant I was angry and bitter. All sense of the presence of God vanished. The contrast in my attitudes and impotency in controlling my emotions was so dramatic and powerful, it finally captured my serious attention; *it seemed to demand immediate action on my part to determine and resolve the problem in me.* (The fact that I was slated the following day to counsel a marital difficulty also helped highlight how utterly ludicrous my failure was and seemed to "shout at me" an urgency for dealing with it.) But now I was convinced it was *my* problem!

I retreated to the basement with the Lord and began to deal. Because the problem was rooted in my own sin (buried in lies for years) and the solutions involved required fixing my own behavior, the answers did not come easily.

After hours of what seemed to be the most agonizing and demanding prayer, it appeared God revealed to me that the basic nature of the conflict occurring everyday when I came home was that my wife was intruding into something I was defending; the whole repeating scenario was one in which she presumed entry into an area where she was prohibited. My angry responses were defending something I thought was "mine." As I inquired further about this, it seemed God revealed to me that I had built a protection system complete with reasonings, emotions, and defense mechanisms, around my "time" after coming home from work. In the name of my own needs, I had built a stronghold around my right to unwind, relax, and transition from my hectic workday to the affairs of my home. Until this was done, I refused my wife any entry into "MY time!" justified by MY needs, MY emotions, MY problems, MY peace of mind. Any forced entry on her part, prior to MY deciding I was ready prompted angry defense of MY rights.

When I finally reached clear conclusion regarding the nature of this conflict, I asked the Lord what I should do with it. He immediately responded, "Place it on the altar. Give that time to your wife. From now on, when you come home, your time is to be immediately devoted to listening to what is important to her." He further gave me exacting guidance on what to do the following day. It didn't sound easy but I began that evening to make detailed plans. Even with such specific direction from God, I initially dreaded the prospect, but by the time I arrived home the next day, I had become eager about it. My wife knew nothing about what had happened or what I was going to do. In obedience to God I just came home, went immediately to where she was (in the kitchen), sat down, and listened. A miracle followed.

The tearing down of this particular stronghold in my life (anger, defending the territory of rights to MY time) was honored by God that day through a remarkable opportunity to serve my wife in an area in which she was hurting. That very day, an unexpected incident over her horse had resulted in a serious broken relationship between her and some close friends. Through my personal attentiveness God fully exposed the matter within five minutes of my arrival home, then provided immediate wisdom on how to restore the relationships. Within only a few more minutes and a single phone call, God accomplished a complete healing of her relationship problem (more amazing because it involved a man, his wife and their daughter). Her grief was transformed into tremendous joy! It seemed so easy! But even her joy must have been small compared to mine. I sat amazed! Joy overflowed through me! I saw God at work in our midst. He had provided specific opportunity to demonstrate His faithfulness and power in upholding His word to me in a very beautiful way. The death I had died the previous night was totally transformed.

In this example we see a stronghold which had been operating freely in me for years in an area in which I had been previously blind, reacting in anger to defend its territory (deceiving me that it was for *my* sake!) and justifying its existence through reasonings that appealed to my fleshly sense of rights. In its dominion, this stronghold thereby gained power and authority in me to bring destructive accusations against my wife, hurting her and working against our marriage, generally through accusations of her failure to understand and sympathize with me and her inability to change her behavior. But these were all lies. *Once I was convicted by God to relinquish rights to the territory I had been defending, the stronghold was destroyed.* It was effectively reduced by prayer and the Word of God. God closed off all my escape routes, eventually allowing the lies I had believed to produce enough pain to prod me into action. Any other alternative to finding God and His solution became unacceptable. Obedience to His Word became my escape!

It is also an example typical of marriage, where most of our strongholds tend to be most easily identified by the nature of the warfare they bring against a helpless and unwitting partner.

There are many similar examples of greater and lesser strongholds which are torn down continuously during the life of a believer living under the discipleship of Christ. Left alone, they will generally grow in their appetites and demands until they cause such a degree of pain that they may serve to bring the believer to God. Unfortunately, the pain levels which are required to gain our attention are often so severe that the threats to life and happiness are well advanced before we become willing to seek God's solutions to their removal.

Yet, He is ready to help in time of need and is certainly "a rewarder of those who seek Him" (Heb. 11:6).

Occupying the Land: The Spirit of Caleb

But My servant Caleb, because he has had a different spirit and has followed Me fully, I will bring into the land which he entered, and his descendants shall take possession of it. (Num. 14:24)

There are two distinct types of people who occupy territory. One is an owner who holds rightful title and authority to the territory he occupies. The other is a usurper, one who claims territory which rightfully belongs to another. The difference in behavior between the two is immense. The first reflects identity and stewardship; real responsibility. The other is an imposter. He reflects deception, bravado, and pretention, glorifying himself rather than promoting his stewardship. One requires a man; the other attracts boys desiring to be perceived as men but unable to accept men's responsibilities.

Godly women are able to discern the difference. But many women are neither godly nor mature and cannot tell the difference. They may select men as a covering who are really usurpers by nature, pretenders, boys not really committed to the responsibility of manhood, nor capable of rising to the occasion when trials come. Or some women may think they can "train" the man into responsibility. Disaster follows.

Even legitimate occupation can be destructive if given to an irresponsible man. Authority and responsibility must go hand in hand;

authority cannot be properly administered until the one assigned has *entered responsibility*. Otherwise, in addition to the challenges he faces anyway, he only tempts other usurpers to challenge him. Irresponsible men and thieves, seeking easy territory to usurp from other irresponsible men, will attempt to steal his stewardship. He must be able to defend it.

It is not a job for boys or pretenders.

Men have been involved in usurpation since they were kids, constantly contesting each other in ways that require enforced game rules to maintain order. It is impossible to get boys to even form a line without game rules, especially if it is even implied that another will gain a superior position! Their fallen nature leads them into lying, cheating, and stealing in a myriad of ways and degrees to obtain things not properly theirs because they lust after the prestige or power that attaining a superior position may provide. They carry these tendencies into their relationships with women, first as they seek sovereignty over girls and then as they enact husband-wife relationships. The result is that they generally seek to gain and maintain a place of headship over a woman and family (with its perceived prestige, power, and satisfaction) without actually entering and occupying God's assigned place of attendant responsibilities. Few men really perceive the death associated with husbanding when committing before God and man to maintain a wife. [1]

When men occupy God's true place of responsibility, confrontation with death is unavoidable. This cannot be accomplished by the ordinary nature of flesh, which clings to life. God therefore identifies in His word the availability of a "different spirit" to enable men to occupy their assigned territory. *It is identified with following God fully and "enabling our descendents to take possession of it."* We will call this the "spirit of Caleb," since it is specifically identified by Scripture as a spirit in Caleb, while recognizing that this spirit is also profoundly portrayed by other godly men and women in Scripture who similarly confronted life threatening tasks.

Let us consider some of the many Bible illustrations of places to which God has assigned men, women, and nations that struggled to

find obedience while confronting fear and death. Foundational illustrations are found in Abraham and in the nation of Israel, both
having been taken from secure environs and brought into the desert.
Both were told to go to Canaan, a land they were to occupy, and
given the promise that God would make them a great nation. Considerable training was required to prepare Abraham and later, Israel,
in this critical issue of occupying their assigned land to "enable their
descendents to take possession." It involved difficult training.

Abraham took his nephew Lot with him after having been told
to leave his relatives behind (Gen. 12:1–5). God propitiously used
this disobedience to further develop Abraham's character, separating the two of them and having Abraham give Lot the best land
when strife developed between their herdsmen (Gen. 13). He later
used this to further draw Abraham into the responsibility of defending his nephew with his life when Lot and his family were
carried off by the kings of the east (see Gen. 14). Defending bur-
densome relatives as a task of territorial stewardship was a noteworthy aspect of Abraham's training! He pursued and defeated the
four kings and their armies with a trained force of only 318 men,
recovering all of his relatives and goods.

Other stages of Abraham's life were marked with fear of death
and cowardly lies hiding Sarah's true identity as his wife. After
twice refusing to risk his own life for his wife, Abraham came to
face personal death in its most extreme form, offering up his own
son for sacrifice according to God's instructions. By this obedience
he was given God's unconditional, sworn promise that he and all
of the nations of the world would be blessed in like fashion (see
Gen. 22:16–19).

Israel went through a similar fashioning process in which God
produced from a nation of slaves a people capable of obedience,
fighting for and occupying the land, no longer incapacitated by a
fear of death. We see in Israel both the process and its results for
individuals and nations.

We must note in the biblical record that a long, painstaking
process is not necessarily required for individuals to be freed from

a fear of death! We see in Numbers, chapters 13 and 14, that God can raise up people able to decide immediately they will occupy territory God has assigned, despite risky obstacles.

With Joshua and Caleb, God demonstrated that vital working faith and obedience are possible even from within a nation of slave mentality. Training in government or in warfare was not prerequisite for either of them to obey the call to occupy Canaan. Joshua and Caleb saw the same circumstances as did the other spies. Yet they argued forcefully to the people for entering Canaan, despite the opposing report, "The people in the land are strong, and the cities are fortified and very large; and moreover, we saw the descendants of Anak (i.e., giants) there" (Num. 13:28). The other men, however, caused the whole congregation to cry and weep with their bad report.

> We are not able to go up against the people, for they are too strong for us...The land through which we have gone, in spying it out, is a land that devours its inhabitants; and all the people whom we saw in it are men of great size...there also we saw the Nephilim (i.e., giants) and we became like grasshoppers in our sight, and so we were in their sight. (Num. 13:31–33)

The story goes on to describe how, because of their fear and mistrust of God, these doubters were removed from God's promise and other men were raised up in their place to occupy the land.

What was it that was different about Joshua and Caleb? It might be argued that Joshua had a special advantage, having worked at close quarters as the servant of Moses (see Exod. 24:13, 33:11), "more humble than any man who was on the face of the earth" (Num. 12:3). As such a servant, Joshua had later been selected by God to take Moses' place when he died. No doubt at some point Joshua had gained from God the eyes and spirit of his master. As with all effectual servants, Joshua was eager to fulfill his master's goals; therefore perhaps it is not surprising that even shortly after leaving Egypt, Joshua would have supported Moses. But Caleb was in a different position. It could not be presumed of him that he would willingly enter into the risks of occupying a land of giants. He is therefore specifically recognized for having had a "different spirit" from the others. It is this enabling "different spirit" we therefore desire to possess, to identify its behavior and God's promises that come with obedience to it.

Why is this necessary?

The fact is that most men occupy in their marriage only the boy's position described at the beginning of this chapter. They've taken territory for which they've never really been tested and which, through fornication, was unlawfully usurped. The average husband has never truly submitted to his wife's father, but rather "took" her in sexual immorality prior to marriage. He was never thoroughly scrutinized nor found acceptable as a husband in terms of how he really regarded and treated the girl prior to marriage. He has not only failed to honor her protection, he has violated her himself. He has considered sexual immorality with another man's daughter to be normal, rather than the monstrous sin it really is, and continued on without repentance. He is therefore carrying great weakness and a curse of God in their marriage. He obtained his wife without a true proof of love. His actions would not be approved by her father. Not until years later may such a man's territory be contested. But the time will come eventually. The enemy is licensed to do this. Men's sins will eventually overtake them.

In other ways as well, these men have never faced death for their wives and hence regard the occupation of their territory (i.e., their position of husband) much as a boy looks at his having gained the top of the mountain in a "King of the Mountain" contest.   It is an *assumed position for which the real issues of life and death, which bond the soul of a man to his wife, have never been successfully confronted.* When things get difficult, many husbands are ready to quit, leaving their wives and children to the next man. As for facing giants, they are fearful and lazy, shrinking violets with no stomach for fighting or responsibilities. So they leave, usually with much loud whimpering about how they have been mistreated by their wives! Their pain is real, but their responses to it totally miss the mark.

This deficiency of manhood is especially apparent when the wife has finally had enough with her little boy who refused to grow up and she divorces. After a few painful weeks or months of agony, the boy generally gives up his family in despair and recrimination. He can't comprehend that occupying the place God has designed for him (as his wife's provider and protector) is a personal decision that must be resolved regardless of his wife's attitude. He never correctly comprehended it in the first place.

Land must be responsibly occupied first, before it will bear fruit. Prior to the break in marriage relationship, the man we are discussing above never knew that he was living under false assumptions, that enemies could some day come to legally contest his territory, that a price was required for possession, that if he failed, other men would compete to take his place. Now the prospect of fulfilling his responsibilities without a supporting wife, nurture, affirmation, and assurance of a successful outcome overwhelms him. He wants to negotiate, to trade for his needs in exchange for what he gives to his wife.[2] But this is wrong. God requires him to occupy his land without condition, based on a call to responsibility and obedience! He must face the giants. If he doesn't do it, God does not intend to neglect his wife and children's protection while he abdicates. He will be removed just like the disobedient men of Israel!

It is precisely this unconditional occupation of responsibilities, with its attendant uncertainties and terrifying "giants" which men must face. The portrait is accurate. Men must face and overcome fear of death if they are to be successful. Men must be willing *to die in claiming their assigned territory in order to know it as their own.*

When the day of reckoning comes and floods beat against his marriage and offspring, the boy who has squandered his manhood in sexual immorality will have little to draw upon. He will be frustrated by all the normal signs of "impotency." He will have no wisdom to know what to do. He will have no vigor or strength (see Prov. 5). He will be dismayed and incapacitated by his own pain and fear of what is happening to him. He will find, in short, that he has no capacity as a man to do right by his own wife or in the raising of his own seed. These are the broadest and most profound meanings of "impotency." It is what confronts our society on the broadest scale today. Boys quit marriage because they never truly possessed it and are impotent to do so.

What does a boy who is resolved to become a man do when he is willing to pay the price? He has the Word of God and a personal decision. Will he or will he not occupy the place God has assigned him in marriage? Does God have the power and provision to enable him to possess it? Yes, He does!

What do we see in Caleb's decision? We see a man saying, "We should by all means go up and take possession of it, for we shall surely overcome it" (Num. 13:30). Where did he obtain this confidence to oppose giants? From God, Who had stated it explicitly to them. Repeatedly over years of captivity and again only forty days earlier, God had promised he was "going to give" the land "to the sons of Israel" (Num. 13:1–2). Caleb believed God; so he committed.

We have other examples in the Bible of similar propositions which God has placed before men, "giants" which threatened to slay them. Consider David and Goliath. From where did David obtain confidence? To those who were dismayed, David said, "The Lord who delivered me from the paw of the lion and from the paw of the bear, He will deliver me from the hand of this Philistine" (1 Sam. 17:37). He occupied a place in battle *representing an army, a king and an entire nation.* Comprehend—truly lay hold of and appropriate for yourself— *that God gave this task and test regarding responsibility to occupy kingship to David many years prior* to his actually assuming the throne for which he had been anointed and promised. It was David's test of kingship.

Or consider Judah's decision to take his brother Benjamin's place as a slave of Pharaoh. God had convicted Judah's heart that his father would die if Benjamin were not restored to him. The only hope for this was if Pharaoh would allow him to redeem his brother with his own life. He was as good as dead when he stepped forward to speak to Joseph. He had no conditions. The deed was done. He was committed (see Gen. 42–44). It was out of this that God honored him by placing the Messianic line in the house of Judah, the house of manhood restored! (see Gen. 49:9–12).

Consider John's decision to appear at the cross during the crucifixion of Jesus Christ, to be publicly identified with the One "who loved him." It amounted to a self-imposed death sentence to be publicly identified as a disciple of Christ and related to Him during His execution. John had decided alone sometime after fleeing with the others (see Mark 14:50) that he would accept the consequences of identifying with Christ. He went to the cross of Jesus as a man already dead. What were the results? The scripture records that John was accorded the place as Jesus' replacement in the care of Mary, the mother of Jesus, ahead of all Christ's brothers (John 19:25–27). Tradition also records that John was the only disciple who did not later die a martyr's death. He had already died!

Consider Gideon (see Judg. 6–7); consider Peter preaching the gospel publicly to those who had only recently crucified Christ (see Acts 2); consider Stephen facing his accusers (see Acts 6–7). Consider all those who died occupying the place God had given to them in faith (see Heb. 11). Did God enable them to follow God fully? Did He keep His word to "enable their descendents to take possession"? For whom are we living—ourselves or our seed? Jesus said, "Unless a grain of wheat falls into the earth and dies, it remains by itself alone; but if it dies, it bears much fruit" (John 12:24).

Consider Esther Here was a woman challenged to occupy her assigned place. Her uncle, Mordecai, recognized the situation and her fear of likely death if she went before the king without summons. He made a second appeal to her to take action to rescue her people. He said,

> Do not imagine that you in the king's palace can escape any more than all the Jews. For if you remain silent at this time, relief and deliverance will arise for the Jews from another place

and you and your father's house will perish. And who knows whether you have not attained royalty for such a time as this? (Esther 4:13–14)

Do you see her territory defined? Do you see the promise that if she denied occupying it, God would raise another source of relief and deliverance?

Here is a model for men! She grasped the issue firmly. She confronted what was required of her and began preparations to go before the king without summons, though it was against the law and the king had shown no interest in her for over thirty days. She resolved the issue of her own death. Hear her spirit as she says, "Go, assemble all the Jews who are found in Susa, and fast for me; do not eat or drink for three days, night or day. I and my maidens also will fast in the same way. And thus I will go in to the king, which is not according to the law; and if I perish, I perish." (Esther 4:16)

Here is the word of God! Here is the spirit we are seeking! The spirit of Caleb is also the spirit of Esther! "I will do it! I am committed! And if I perish, I perish!"

Where are the men willing to occupy their places? Far be it that women may rise to the occasion and modern men prove unable! Lord, give us men who will occupy their places like Esther and Caleb did. Give us more men like Esther!

Once God raises men who are willing to face death on behalf of their wives, killing the giants and tearing down strongholds will be easy! Come to us quickly, Lord Jesus, to help us!

Crossing the Jordan

For which one of you, when he wants to build a tower, does not first sit down and calculate the cost, to see if he has enough to complete it? (Luke 14:28)

Husbands and wives, do you desire to occupy your God-assigned territory in your marriage? In the context of the last two chapters, we should pause and contemplate the serious nature of a decision to occupy one's proper place in the marriage relationship. God's promises are infallible, but they are based foremost upon seeking Him and His righteousness, rather than merely trying to grasp worldly things or fix one's spouse (Matt. 6:33). Quite often the one to whom the appeal to rightfully occupy is given is one who is hurting emotionally, is spiritually immature or otherwise unable to discern between flesh and spirit in understanding their true motives. We have been given sure promises by God, but they are not mere cookie cutters for regaining a spouse whom we (and others) may have damaged beyond our capacity to reach and heal. God's promises lead along a difficult road purposed to build godly character in us in Christ and to bring glory to God. This chapter is therefore devoted to helping one discern his or her true motives and toward enabling sound decisions upon which the cost has been counted.

It should be helpful to note at the outset that ten of the twelve spies which Moses sent into Canaan (Num. 13–14) failed to make the grade of right decision making, even though they had been exposed to the same promises and confirming evidences of signs and wonders as Joshua and Caleb were. As we have said, perhaps Joshua had unfair advantage, being as close as he was to Moses and perhaps only Caleb has the fullest measure of the spirit we are seeking.[1] One or two out of twelve are not good odds. If the fabric of man is no different in the body of Christ than in the newly liberated nation of Israel, can you expect better odds? You might even argue that if you have no stomach for this and fail to rise to the word of God, you are in the large majority! This will not help you. "Enter by the narrow gate; for the gate is wide, and the way is broad that leads to destruction, and many are those who enter by it. For the gate is small, and the way is narrow that leads to life, and few are those who find it" (Matt. 7:14). There are indeed forces of fear and unbelief working from your own still unseen strongholds attempting their deadly work to turn you aside from your God-given tasks. But God will uphold you if you commit to serve Him and seek His righteousness. Faithful duty in Christ toward spouse and family is your chief task.

Consider the underlying motivations of some of God's chief examples of those who occupied their assigned territory to His glory. Boaz was a righteous man who always had God and a desire to please him on his lips. He upheld righteousness on behalf of a lovely woman at great personal cost, in the end giving her up in order that the "greater good" could be accomplished for her in accordance with the laws of kinsman-redeemer. After Boaz denied himself gratification with her in both the short term and long term, could God have denied Boaz?[2] In Boaz's case, he was rewarded on earth with marriage to the woman he had died for and given an exalted place with her in the annals of Christ's genealogy (Ruth 1–4).

David also had the righteousness of God foremost on his mind when he undertook to accept the challenge of the uncircumcised Goliath. David was indignant that Goliath could get away with challenging the God of Israel and knew the God that had upheld him during his battles with bears and lions would do so also with this giant. He was upheld by God in this battle and over many subsequent years of patience in fleeing Saul before finally coming into his kingship (see 1 Sam. 17).

After many years of trials, Abraham finally passed his own supreme test of trusting God with a life more important than his own, his son Isaac's. He got up early in the morning to carry out his instructions to sacrifice his only son at a place God had designated. He knew somehow that God would keep His earlier promises that had been placed in Isaac. Perhaps he had a grasp of substitutionary sacrifice or resurrection of the dead; he made statements to this effect during the journey. But he kept to his work until God intervened and he obtained God's unconditional promise of blessing on his lineage and upon all believing mankind (see Gen. 22).

Esther, for of her people and the one who had raised her as his daughter, committed her life at great risk to interceding with King Ahasuerus ("If I perish, I perish.") The result was deliverance for an entire nation in exile (see Esther).

Joseph remained sexually pure against the enticements of Potiphar's wife as a matter of righteousness, refusing to betray his master or do wrong in God's sight. The results of his faithfulness were his glorification as prime minister of Egypt and deliverance of his father's family.

For the love of his father, Judah submitted to Pharaoh and requested slavery for himself in exchange for his half-brother Benjamin's freedom to return home. It secured deliverance for all and the lineage of the Messiah in the line of Judah.

Is a picture beginning to form? These are people who gave up everything human life can call dear for the sake of God and others. They are all portraits of the deliverance of God through Jesus Christ, but they are all also the lives of real flesh and blood men and women who trusted God in fulfilling the two great commandments. As Jesus said:

> You shall love the Lord your God with all your heart, and with all your soul, and with all your mind. This is the great and foremost commandment. And a second is like it, You shall love your neighbor as yourself. On these two commandments depend the whole Law and the Prophets. (Matt. 22:37–40)

Jesus, for the love of His Father, fulfilled all of the above portraits in His own life, delivering for the sake of His Father, rescuing brothers and sisters and nations, winning a bride, proving Himself for a Kingship, and fulfilling the resurrection of the Son from death. But He wasn't the first to face death. God enabled predecessors and successors to do the same, overcoming fear of death in resolving to accomplish what God had ordained them to do. Please grasp for yourself that as disciples of Christ, we are called upon to face the same death.

Despite years of teaching, training, and exhortation in Scripture, many never seem to overcome fear of death. Many never come to place these two commandments at the forefront of their lives. God knows why. Without discernment regarding Christ's other provisions for them, nor judgment as to their ultimate salvation, I will only give opinion that neither will they ever taste the glory of God in this life for having traveled through the valley of the shadow of death for the sake of God's righteousness.

The sad fact is that almost no modern man marries with a real comprehension of what his marriage vows mean, and fewer have confronted the painful, humiliating discovery of their depth of love unto death for their wife before marriage. They really don't know if they love their wives and neither do their wives. God does not intend it to be this way. To resolve this in a modern society, they must both discover it (if they are to discover it at all) after the marriage vows. Better late than never! Of those who've made the discovery later, albeit through fire and water, Christ has produced marriages founded on solid rock. We'll speak more of these later.

For those resolved to move ahead, consider how God took Israel across the Jordan. Then develop your own corresponding prayers, studies, and decisions accordingly.

- First, you must belong to God and desire to obey Him. Your will must be submitted to His. You must be strong and courageous (see Josh. 1).

- Second, you must be trained in warfare and able to face its responsibilities (see Deut. 2–3).
- Third, you must go in company. Courage and obedience are enhanced when you have others of like mind supporting you and when your actions are accountable to them (see Josh. 1–3).
- Fourth, honor the Lord in what you do, trusting that He is with you (see Josh. 1–4).
- Fifth, expect confirming signs and wonders at the point you are committed in faith and have taken the first steps to do what seems impossible for you to do (see Josh. 3:15–17).
- Establish a remembrance, with witnesses, of what you do in faith and of God's work in enabling you to do it (see Josh. 4).
- Don't be surprised when your hidden sins erupt to cause distress and loss. Repent, purify yourself, and go forward (see Josh. 8–9).

God gives us sacred promises that are absolutely reliable. He will not fail us! But we do not know the immediate outcome. God always answers exceedingly abundantly beyond what we ask or think, according to the power that works within us (Eph. 3:20). But, "how do you know you will save your wife...or your husband?" (1 Cor. 7:16). Christ died for the world, yet not all are saved; only the faithful, whom the Father calls, will respond to Him. Are you willing to go forward in obedience to your responsibilities, to be made into the One who is faithful, without preconditions and without knowing for sure that your particular desires will be granted in the way you hope?

I have seen men faithfully pursue wives who divorced them, discovering a love they hadn't previously known was there and enduring great fire to perfect and prevail in winning back their wives. The ex-husband of the girl who was instrumental in leading me to Christ in 1976 pursued her faithfully for several years until she consented to remarry him. He did all this as an unbe-liever in Christ![3]

This man is not alone. Others have made similar discovery of love and paid the price of commitment, fasting, prayer, humiliation, and accountability to maintain faithfulness to their unfaithful wives. As a result of God's intervention, they have seen miraculous regen-eration of their marriages, hardly recognizable except for the names of the spouses involved.

Others, though, quit. Even after extended periods of disciple-ship in which their attitudes and faithfulness in Christ have seemed to grow (their ex-wives beginning to pay close attention to the changes apparently taking place and beginning to ask for help in ways which could have led to reconciliation), some men give up and flee. Even a counselor can be deceived by the appear-ances of change.[4]

Wives, is it your purpose to get your husband to change? Be-ware! I've heard no end of women who have attempted to argue convincingly that their motive has been to please God in submit-ting to their husbands, but whose continued complaints reveal torrents of bitterness toward God for *not honoring their faithfulness by changing their husband's behavior.* When changes in their own attitudes and behaviors are explored, all of these women will un-failingly reply, "I tried that and it didn't work." Thus they reveal that their only purpose for years has been to get their husbands to change, not to serve and become pleasing to the Lord.

Contentment must come from serving the Lord. Let everything you do be for His sake, not for men (see Eph. 6:5–7). If He has given you a place to occupy and told you to occupy until He comes, then be content that He is a rewarder of those who diligently seek Him, and make your peace with Him in setting and holding your course. He will not fail to do right by you and the one for whom you intercede. You will see the glory of God.

The Poor in Spirit:
A Study of Sarah, Part I

Blessed are the poor in spirit, for theirs is the kingdom of heaven. (Matt. 5:3)

A close look at the relationship between Abraham and Sarah raises disturbing questions as to just how effectual Abraham was as a husband. It is disturbing because it appears to identify remarkable similarities between how that giant of faith, Abraham, treated his wife and the same shortcomings of husbands today. Even paragons of faith may treat their wives pretty poorly. The scriptural picture of this indicates severe difficulties of self-image and worth which Sarah must have had as a result, laboring for years under the weaknesses and blind spots of her husband. We will look at this as closely as possible through a woman's (Sarah's) eyes.

Consider how Sarah (then Sarai) must have felt about herself when she suggested to her husband that Abraham (then Abram) have a child by another woman, her maid Hagar (see Gen. 16:1–3). At this point, age seventy-six, Sarai had given up hope in having a child of her own. *She thus saw the end of her hopes of fulfillment and value as a woman.*

She saw the only hope of fulfillment of her husband's aspirations in bearing seed to be through another woman, and she was also grasping at straws for her own self-fulfillment when she said, *"perhaps I shall obtain* children through her" (Gen. 16:2, emphasis added). Ask yourself honestly how you would feel about yourself if you were in her position, having always aspired to bearing your husband's offspring, but now believing this to be impossible. Now hope had finally died with Sarai. It was a terrible day. She offered a generous gift to Abram, but it must have hurt terribly. It was a final pronouncement of her own failure of success in life, the death of one of the chief dreams of womanhood, to reproduce offspring from her husband.

Consider, too, that Abram apparently didn't pause to defend Sarai or his faith in God, but had immediate sexual relations with Hagar. If you were Sarai, what would you have preferred your husband's response to be? How would you feel with Abram's actual response? Would you feel your life was worthwhile? Would you feel valued? Do you think this is characteristic of strongholds of futility and unworthiness established in many women?

This was furthermore only the beginning of even more difficult trials for Sarai. Soon she had another woman living under her roof carrying her husband's baby. Instead of finding relief, Sarai found only a sharp increase in her agony as she became despised by Hagar for their "difference" in womanhood—the ability to bear children. Then, when she appealed to her husband for defense, the best he could muster was to turn Hagar over to her to do "whatever was good" in her sight (Gen. 16:4–6). What poor defense of one's wife! Abram's actions left much to be desired in protecting Sarai from emotional abuse.

But these actions fit quite well with what we see to be a consistent pattern of similar poor treatment of Sarah by Abraham over many years.

One of Abram's earlier failures of faith involved his departure, on account of famine, from the land which God had promised him. He went to Egypt, where he became fearful of being killed because of Sarai's beauty. For self-protection he turned his wife over to Pharaoh, identifying her only as his sister. Sarai went submissively, but oh, how grieved she must have been. Her husband did not consider her worth protecting, but only handed her over to another man. God intervened and sent great plagues upon Pharaoh, informing him of the truth. Abram was strongly rebuked and sent away with his wife and "all that belonged to him," (apparently even getting rich on the deal!—Gen. 12:10–20).

Later, Abram risked his life to rescue his nephew Lot. Lot was a considerable difficulty for Abram, extra baggage and a liability, having been brought from the homeland after Abram had been told by God to leave his relatives there (Gen. 12:1). When strife developed between the "herdsmen of Abram's livestock and the herdsmen of Lot's," Abram generously offered Lot his choice of land to separate the two. Lot responded by taking the best for himself. Then sometime later, having settled in Sodom, Lot was taken captive by invaders.

In contrast to his nondefense of Sarai, Abram bravely went to battle for Lot's rescue, mobilizing all his men and allies and defeating a superior enemy. It must have seemed striking to Sarai that Abram would react so sharply to the defense of his nephew, who had earlier taken advantage of her husband, but to leave her completely undefended (see Gen. 13, 14).

This pattern did not change. Some twenty-four years later, even after some of the miraculous blessings we are about to discuss, Abraham still could not get it right! He was fearful of risking death on his wife's behalf. *Husbands please listen!* Abraham again "went south" into the land of another king and again offered his wife up as his sister to protect his own life. The spirit is willing, but the flesh is weak! Abimelech, King of Gerar, took Sarah and narrowly escaped with his life. Thank God for His intervention a second time to protect not only Sarai but also her husband.[1] Thank God also for revealing to us in unmistakable clarity *Abraham's stronghold of fear of death!*

The evidence is powerful that Abraham was confronted with the fundamental issue of the flesh of all husbands, i.e., fear of death, and that his treatment of his wife in nearly every instance discussed by Scripture was that which would ruin a woman's sense of her true worth. Abram's basket case treatment of his wife surely placed a tremendous burden on her heart. She had every reason to be poor in spirit, poverty stricken regarding her own worth, knowing her husband valued her little when it came to his life or hers. Whatever had been her younger vision of a knight in shining armor willing to risk his life for her had surely by now been smashed to smithereens!

We will consider now how God mercifully ministered to Sarah's problem. We first note that God did not neglect Abraham's problem either. *But he did not solve it through Sarah! Wives, please listen!* God solved Abraham's problem in an extremely excruciating and personal manner in which Abraham was directly confronted by God. Husbands cannot be confronted and corrected in such a manner by their wives. It is a work of God to fix husbands!

Abraham's fear of death was ultimately resolved through God's command for him to sacrifice Isaac. There can be little doubt in any parents' heart that after he received this command, Abraham worked through all the alternatives and personal resolutions of attempting to satisfy God's requirement by allowing him to take his son's place. Any loving parent would so offer himself/herself up if it would spare their own offspring. But, God did not immediately retract His command. Through the ensuing events of Genesis 22, Abraham not only had his fear of death resolved experientially but was also afforded a grand exposure to the greater picture God had in mind for substitutionary sacrifice, exceedingly abundantly beyond anything Abraham had asked for or thought.

24

New Life:
A Study of Sarah, Part II

After I have become old, shall I have pleasure, my Lord being old also? (Gen. 18:12)

When Sarah asked the above question, she was being cynical. She clearly implied that there could be only one possible answer to her question—a resounding "No!" But this incident took place just a moment prior to a personal miracle. To a woman poor in spirit, crushed down by despair in ever finding value in her husband's eyes or fulfillment in life, God came for a personal visit to resurrect life! There are many women today for whom such a miracle is needed through personal intervention by God.

Sarah was an old woman, ninety years of age, when one day three men came to visit her husband Abraham and were served a meal outside their tent. It is specifically recorded that she was past childbearing age (Gen. 18:11). Her statement also reveals that she was a dead woman from a number of standpoints. Not only was her body dead in its ability to reproduce children, but her hope and expectations in God's earlier promises that she would have children by Abraham (see Gen. 12:7, 15:4, 17:19) were also dead. Her faith in God had waned. If God could not be trusted on specific promises, how could He be trusted at all? When she overheard from inside the tent one of the men outside suddenly say, "Where is Sarah your wife? . . . I will surely return to you at this time next year; and behold, Sarah your wife shall have a son" (Gen. 18:9 –10). She responded with sarcastic laughter, despite having been given explicit promise earlier that she would bear a son by Abraham (Gen. 17:19).

Yet, an amazing amount of other information is also contained in her brief response. First is evidence of her knowledge of where her fulfillment lay. Even in old age and death she expresses herself in classic terms of husband and children! Out from under accumulated years of dashed hopes she was able to depict the truth in her pithy remark. "Hah!" she says in effect, "Now that I'm too old to experience the things in which a woman finds fulfillment, a complete know-nothing stranger is telling my husband I'm going to have a son next year! What a joke!"

Also present in her brief expletive are the aspects of her deadness in body and soul, as well as lack of fulfillment. "Shall I have pleasure," she says? She is old and so is Abraham. How can she come alive again? Can her body become young again for childbearing? It is almost the same proposition Nicodemus gave to Jesus 1900 years later, being told that he must be born again (John 3:3–5), asking how it was possible for a man to go back to the womb. Sarah identifies her dream of fulfillment, of having her husband's offspring, as well as bearing the promise of God's blessing for nations for generations to come, *even while she is ridiculing the idea!* What expressive sarcasm!

We see too in her statement that she realizes her fulfillment is tied to her husband's life, "...my lord being old also." Beyond that, we see further in her choice of words her submission to him, "...obeying him and calling him lord" (1 Pet. 3:6). Life and death, relationship, grief, and vision are clearly gathered together in this one classic, pithy proposition. Her situation is now full-term, bursting with implications regarding her personal relationship with God, her husband, and her personal needs. *It is a moment which God has prepared.*

Precisely at this moment, in the midst of her summary of her situation, the Lord meets Sarah personally and addresses all of her issues, conscious, subconscious, and spiritual.

The scripture records that her laughter and statement were "to herself." Yet, the man outside the tent immediately responded to Abraham, "Why did Sarah laugh, saying, 'Shall I indeed bear a child when I am so old?'" Then He *repeats* his promise that "this time next year, Sarah shall have a son" (Gen. 18:14).

Whoa! This is not an ordinary man, is it?

The scripture records that Sarah denied that she laughed, saying, "I did not laugh," for she "was afraid." Why would she be afraid? Because something fearful was happening; this man with the ridiculous promise had accurately heard her thoughts! He had overheard and testified to both her laughing *and* speaking to herself.

Then the man speaks yet again, "No, but you did laugh" (Gen. 18:15). Now she has certain proof from this man she fears! In one instant He overcomes her lie, her fear, and her denial. This man is not bluffing. He speaks with authority. He *knows* the truth and *He knows her*.

Here is the personal meeting place, an intimate intervention of God in the life of His beloved Sarah. The man outside the tent making this ridiculous promise has just validated His promise by validating His identity. He knows Sarah in her innermost! He is the Lord God of Israel!

Why would God reveal Himself to Sarah in just such a special way? Why would He intervene in the very midst of her cynical statement summarizing her futility and death? Could it be because He already knew these were the fundamental issues of her life and desired to intervene with them in a precise personal manner—which reveals His nature? A nature in which He provides Sarah with intimate, profound, and authoritative personal attention? Why, unless...He *loves* her?

For what other reason does God intervene in any life? The Designer with His creation; the Shepherd with His flock? We are valuable. He knows our needs and is eager to meet us in them personally and intimately. In a great sense it is precisely our poverty which delivers us to Him so we can discover His true nature.

This sudden, deep realization of God's personal love for Sarah is totally life transforming! She discovers she is precious to God!

Amazing! She is beloved! Wow! Suddenly, her faith in and love of God are awakened! God's word springs to life in her. His seed takes root in her heart. Her personal assurance of His truthful promises and power come alive! She becomes alive to God. She becomes alive to her husband. Her body comes to life! She becomes pregnant!

This is true resurrection, one of many examples in the Bible. A dead woman is brought to life. The woman who lived behind the door of the tent, who did not go out to meet strangers and perhaps had no other function than unfulfilling menial service for her husband is now a totally different person. On the outside things may have looked the same. *But never again were they the same on the inside!* She is now free, vital, filled with new life! God has fulfilled her in Himself and Abraham.

This is precisely the reproduction of God's seed: life founded on believing confidence in His promises. This also demonstrates the precise overlay of reproducing God's seed and human seed.

And perhaps most amazing of all, God did all this *in precise response to her cynical proposition!*

How can we capture the fragrance of the aroma of the knowledge of God and what it produces (see John 12:3; 2 Cor. 2:14–16)? We see Sarah's resurrection commenced with her knowing:

a) God, the Truth, validated in His intimate knowledge of Sarah's thoughts and needs;
b) the fact that God's personal promise to meet her need and desire was therefore true, also; and
c) life coming into her in all its manifest variety of spirit and body by activation of her faith.

So, it was a package deal! She got new life and a son, Isaac, to boot! True life in God enabled Sarah to become pregnant and have a son! She was first *enabled by God to know and receive Him* in order to reproduce life in herself!

Are not we all in need of God's enabling love to find life and fulfillment? Ask for it. Recognize the truths which were contained in Sarah's heart. In Sarah's honest proposition, made in the supposed secrecy of her thoughts, we have the foundation of a woman's fulfillment; i.e., of "finding pleasure" in right relation to a husband (even a basket case). Her poverty in spirit was God's problem and He resolved it. Her husband's problems were also God's, and she let God resolve them while she continued to relate to him with a peaceful and quiet spirit, "precious in the sight of God" (1 Pet. 3:1–6). God is faithful.

So we sense a right relationship with her husband is a powerful part of a wife's ministry and responsibility, regardless of the demeaning actions of her husband. This may have been a precondition which Sarah satisfied.

Paul said, "Who is adequate for these things" (2 Cor. 2:16). Searching the deep things of God still leaves this a mystery. God's enabling affirmation to women and the fulfillment of His will in their lives are crucial and should be earnestly sought (Matt. 7:7). We cannot predict how God will circumscribe us with His word in a manner which will set us free from strongholds. A woman must make her way in right relationship with her husband and retain vision that she is truly a vessel of God to be poured out in living for her husband and their offspring. In due time, we claim that the true Jehovah God of Israel will show up! This is the means by which Sarah found her greatest fulfillment in life and has passed it on to many women.

So, the man must die for his wife. But she lives for him, just as we, the bride of Christ, live for our Bridegroom, who died for us.

Dear Jesus, may the fullest measure of Your grace be upon all women who read this in providing them with the personal miracle they need, falling nothing short of Sarah's, that each might know her inestimable value to You, her preciousness beyond any price except the One You paid Yourself. May this preciousness also be evident to their husbands, whom You have given to know Your love through their wives, to the glory of the Father. Amen.

25

The Only Safe Place

I am convinced that He is able to guard what I have entrusted to Him until that day. (2 Tim. 1:12)

Possibly the most difficult task for those with marriages in deep trouble is to break their previous habits of attempting to control and/or change their spouses. Sometimes this is made a bit easier if their spouses leave them. Nevertheless, unless old habits are broken, every bit of progress toward reconciliation will only be thwarted by more "broken glass" in the relationship by each person reverting to the same behavior which brought their opposite numbers to despair in the first place. It is amazing to observe the lying power of the "old man" to draw husbands and wives into acting as though a relationship will improve if they can just get their spouses to "come back," "get a job," "stop manipulating," or otherwise *do what they want them to!*

Wide varieties of anxiety come to someone whose spouse has left. The pain experienced includes not only the anguish of personal rejection, but other forms of loss, as well, ranging from loss of the "control" of one's nurture or security through the control of the spouse to sincere concern over the welfare of the one who has left. It may take some time for true motivations and emotions to clarify. It is possible for a spouse who has driven the other to desertion to be overcome with guilt over their actions and extreme concern over what will happen to the spouse as a result. The same concern can be further mixed with flaming rage over injustice in how the spouse has treated him or her, especially when the person has been left for an adulterous affair, frequently the case. In nearly all cases the manner usually *first pursued by the one seeking counsel* is to find a way of re-establishing control (!) over the spouse. The assumption is falsely made that all the sources of anxiety (viewed self-centeredly, of course) will go away if only the one who has left will return. But such a simple solution usually achieves nothing at all in the way of permanent corrective change. In this light, a sincere "final" departure of the spouse is frequently God's opportunity to commence permanent correction.

Nevertheless, there is a real problem. *Sincere* concern over the prospects of the spouse, if present, must be dealt with to aid the work that must go on in the one undergoing counseling.

Counselees must be persuaded to seek righteousness first while the spouse is put in a safe place and kept there until God has worked His pleasure (Matt. 6:33).

As stated, it is usually at the point of worst crisis, where the other spouse has finally left, where hope has been destroyed, where one will begin to get serious in searching for God and His solutions for one's life. This takes place when the person is in the worst pain, most threatened or despairing, and convinced that he or she is being dealt with most unjustly by the opposite number. Even if and when it finally dawns on one of them that God's primary agenda (Read: ONLY agenda) is with him or her, not the spouse, great difficulties remain. It is also possible that under all of this, there is little real concern over the spouse's future happiness.

But when sincere concern is evidenced over the future welfare, health, prosperity, and happiness of the spouse who has left (as opposed to merely regaining *control* or reasserting personal rights and needs), there is good opportunity to appeal to this sincerity in a manner which will produce change and reveal the glory of God because *it trusts God and enables* God to work and keep the promises of His Word! It enables removal of distractive focus on the faults of the spouse and aids in God's loving correction of the one remaining, while freeing God to work with the other spouse without interference!

It involves putting the other spouse in a place of safe keeping with God and attending to ourselves! Of course! Why didn't we think of that?!

Strong deceptive forces work against letting go of the spouse to specifically trust God for the spouse's welfare.

There is an almost overwhelming tendency of the "old man" to continue to attempt to control the spouse from the strongholds of many years. The old nature clings to it. Thinking primarily of themselves, two spouses have few effective motivational goals for each other. The husband has no real motivational concept of building his wife as a free woman and the wife either despairs of ever enabling her husband's success or never had it as a personal motivation in the first place. *During crisis, the two will only modify their techniques for controlling each other.* In fact, the response of a man during a separation in which his wife has taken control is quite frequently to change his control methods to those normal for a woman and the reverse is true for a woman whose husband has left. He begins to use more subtle techniques like those his wife used toward him, while his wife shifts to overt, forceful methods previously used by her husband. Instead of ruling in a perverted manner, he now attempts to manipulate. She begins to confront and antagonize in a masculine style. Instead of learning to behave like a man in Christ, he behaves like a woman not in Christ. It is the classic example of role reversal for the emasculated man and only causes his wife to despise him more. Instead of behaving as a godly woman, she discards the remaining vestiges of her nurture and picks up the sword! They will usually end up hating each other.

The wife who readily perceives that her marriage is in trouble and desires personal change is usually without real comprehension that she may be occupying God's place of headship with her husband and that under her tutelage he will never be free to experience the Lord's tutelage. Attempting godliness, she is likely to only increase her activities to "help" her husband find God and to make decisions which are "correct" in her sight. Strife and pain will only continue to increase as she becomes stronger in her frustrations and assertions. "The wise woman builds her house. But the foolish one tears it down with her own hands" (Prov. 14:1).

So, even for disciples of the Lord Jesus Christ, the battle is usually still cluttered with old habits of attempting to control or change the spouse. It is really a problem of trusting God while being responsive to one's own discipleship.

There are a thousand reasons or more for not turning a spouse over to God and really letting go—all of them lies. "Maybe he/she won't come back to me;" "I need to know what he/she is doing so I can provide protection/correction;" "If I don't tell him/her what to do, they'll make a mistake;" "We'll lose the house!" "They'll think they're winning;" "I want the kids;" "They'll continue to treat me unfairly;" etc. In all these reasons there is apparent justification for taking things into one's own hands. There is self-righteousness, fear, jealousy, and other deeds of the flesh in which Satan uses fear and unforgiveness in fostering further bondage (2 Cor. 2:7–11; Heb. 12:15).

Can it be overstated? There are huge blind spots in this area! Unless very drastic changes in circumstances or pain levels take place, most spouses will continue in unawareness of the problem. As long as the other spouse is present and dialogue continues, the old habits persist. Even apparently sincere attempts to entrust the spouse to God seem usually to be futile; personal control and self-promotion are frequently just too powerful, lacking sufficient pain levels or mature discipleship to the Lord Jesus Christ.

Therefore, one of the few reasons a counselor might potentially rejoice over drastic difficulties which introduce high pain levels into a marriage is that such overwhelming circumstances often are the critical ingredient to bringing someone to seek lasting solutions with God. Bankruptcy can enable someone to throw away their worthless stock; spiritual bankruptcy can also cause one to abandon false values, idols, and habits and to seek really new approaches for dealing with problems.

This is all an unusually long introduction to present a really simple truth for one who really loves one's spouse and wants the best for him or her in the face of dreadful difficulties, things that are available only from God.

The truth is this: *True security is available only from God. True blessing, health, understanding, and wisdom are available only from God. True ownership belongs only to God.*

The best place of safety for one's spouse is totally with God. It is the only safe place. He is the one who created and redeemed our spouses. He is the only one with power to uphold them and the purpose to do so. He is the only one infallible in knowledge and righteousness. It is right that he should be given opportunity to exercise His ownership and relationship rights. The things our spouses need are available from God. They are available only from God. Apart from God they are not available. *Apart from God, there is no safe place.* In God is complete safety—with God and Him only.

Apart from God there is no safety. We shouldn't want our spouses in any other place!

Therefore, it should be our desire to resoundingly, wholeheartedly, and fully place our spouses with God for safe keeping—and to leave them there! Do not be persuaded to take them back, attempt to control, threaten, or persuade them. Give them to God!

To enable such a decision and prayer to work, one must remove control goals from all communications. If this cannot be done, then reduce communications themselves until levels are reached where it is possible; i.e., to communicate without attempting to control the other spouse. When these levels are reduced (or deteriorate) to a point where communications only support acceptance of the other spouse exactly as he or she is, then success may be close at hand.

In my experience, such an unshakable position regarding the opposite spouse is achievable only under the following conditions:

a) a working trust in the character and promises of God;
b) a sincere, loving concern for the welfare of the spouse;
c) a realization that controls over the spouse violate God's sovereignty and ability to bless the spouse with the best He has

purposed for the spouse; therefore a heartfelt desire for the spouse to be in *no other place* except the place of blessing;

d) recognition *that it is the authority of any spouse to sanctify (set apart for God's true purpose) the other spouse with God, acting in faith (1 Cor. 7:14).*

Though we talk about sanctification frequently and loosely, we seldom apply it fully, except perhaps for our children. It is quite often only those men and women whose marriages are going down the drain after years of unsuccessful attempts to change each other who get a chance to fully apply this important aspect of successful marriages. Counselors should diligently pursue it.

An example of the life changing power of this form of spouse sanctification is contained in the application/testimony section of this book.

26

Affirmation

Behold, this has touched your lips: and your iniquity is taken away, and your sin is forgiven. (Isa. 6:7)

God is an affirming God. We see in His Scripture that God is always encouraging and building up His people, even while warning them or pronouncing judgment. He "knows our frame that we are but dust" (see Ps. 103:14) and lives by His own Word which says, "The spirit of a man can endure sickness, but a broken spirit who can bear?" (Prov. 18:14). There is something wonderful and empowering in discovering we are valuable and loved and that this extends to there being no account in Christ kept of our iniquities. God addresses this need for love and forgiveness at the outset of the gospel of Jesus Christ and anticipates no response from us until He has helped us to resolve this need.

The verse at the heading of this chapter was spoken to Isaiah after he had seen the Lord and knew that he was undone because of his sins. It was only after Isaiah had been touched and cleansed, experiencing, no doubt, all the amazing grace which accompanies divine cleansing, that God asked Isaiah to respond. "Whom shall I send, and who will go for Us?" In his new condition, Isaiah was able to respond, "Here I am. Send me!" (Isa. 6:8).

So why is it so difficult for us to do things in the fashion that God does? Why do we so often insist on people first changing or obeying as a condition for affirming our love to them? Why shouldn't they first be seeing their extreme value to us instead of the other way around? We should understand that it is love and affirmation that provide the power to respond and grow. This is a central theme of attacking and destroying strongholds in the lives of others we love. Therefore, we will spend considerable time in this and following chapters exploring various aspects of the power of affirmation, of positively attesting to the value of others.

First let us look more thoroughly at this consistent pattern in God's own behavior toward us. He affirms His obedient servants. "Be strong and courageous...I (am) with you" (Josh. 1:5–7, 9). He affirms in messages of angels. "Do not be afraid" (Matt. 1:20; Luke 1:30) and "You are highly esteemed" (Dan. 9:23, 10:11). He affirms also in giving sharp correction and warning. The whole book of Malachi, which is full of reproof, also illustrates affirmation of God's love and the power of that love to overcome evil among God's people.

As a short example, consider the opening verses of Malachi. The words commence with "I have loved you" and ending with "and you will say, 'The LORD be magnified beyond the border of Israel'"(Mal. 1:2–5). They reaffirm God's love and positive purpose for Israel, despite many years of their having profaned Him. They *precede* a stinging rebuke of the priests, men, and leaders of the nation. As further example, the prophetic revelation of the coming of the Messiah (the refiner's fire) in chapter 3 also opens with the preceding affirming description of Christ as "the messenger of the covenant, in whom you delight" (Mal. 3:1). In the closing verses, even in the midst of impending doom and blazing judgment, the salvation of those that love God is reaffirmed.

This pattern of affirming prior to reproving is seen, too, in the sequence of God's curses at the fall of man. Prior to judging Adam and Eve, God first cursed Satan and gave the promise of "The Seed" who would redeem mankind from the dreadful consequences of sin (Gen. 3:15–19). In effect, God pronounced not only that Satan was cursed but also that God would bear Himself the judgment in His vicarious sin sacrifice, proving His committed love for mankind and His active work on our behalf. Only after this promise did He proceed to the curse upon mankind resulting from sin.

Because men and women are God's design and marriage is God-ordained, we would expect to find biblical provisions for affirmation between husband and wife in marriage. We do indeed find them, but because men and women are designed differently, they also give and receive affirmation differently. The differences are not immediately evident and require study.

In Proverbs 31 a man named King Lemuel took pains to write down praise of his wife as a record and example of the virtues of his wife, of her essential character to his success and the success of his family. There is no doubt that she also received these praises directly from her husband for "Out of the abundance of the heart, the mouth speaks" (see Matt. 12:34). The writer of Proverbs 31 clearly had an abundant heart toward his wife; writing under the influence of the Holy Spirit, he also explicitly commanded all men to praise their wives. Assuming, perhaps, that men (by design) cannot sufficiently discern instruction from example itself and therefore need it spelled out, King Lemuel's instructions are *actually repeated three times in the closing verses!* Following his cue, we will also review the praise instructions for men explicitly.

In the closing verses of Proverbs 31 we read of the woman that "Her children rise up and bless her; her husband also, and he praises her, saying; 'Many daughters have done nobly, but you excel them all'" (vv. 28–29). If this is not sufficiently clear, we read further that "a woman who fears the LORD, she shall be praised" (v. 30). Note the implication that even if the husband does not praise his wife, the Lord shall assure it, regardless! Finally, the closing words are "Give her the product of her hands, and let her works praise her in the gates" (v. 31). Since an earlier verse of this same passage establishes that her husband is known in the gates (see v. 23), this again assigns to her husband responsibility for the praise of the wife and her reputation in public and makes it clear that her praise is one of the "products of her hands."

The Proverbs 31 man does not devote a single word to the external appearance or beauty of his wife. He actually points out the futility of such by saying, "Charm is deceitful and beauty is vain" (v.

30). Many husbands make the mistake of imagining their wives can find security and esteem by words that praise external beauty when the opposite is true. Words that extol temporal values only encourage the wife (or daughter) to erroneously pursue them.

The world considers it open season to compliment a woman on her appearance and, if possible, to win and possess her through flattery. *If a wife or daughter do not already know their place of high value and esteem in the eyes of husband or father*, then the first usurping man who offers value through praise will tempt the woman or girl to move toward him since he offers a place of apparent greater value according to their need for praise. This is the case today in many fragile marriages and weak father-daughter relationships; the first man with a good line has a potentially easy conquest of what God has placed under another man's protective trust.

Men with difficulties in their marriages should realize that, regardless of what the world may say, God designed females to *receive a portrait of their value from their husband (or, earlier in life, their father)*. Their actual value is inestimable! But their view of it is shaped by his words and attitudes. Women live and measure their positions in relationships through words (whereas men may have harsh words one minute and have totally forgotten them the next.) A woman's security, her capacity to trust God through trials and her personal fulfillment (i.e., the "product of her hands") are all determined by words!

Unfortunately, carnal men carry gratitude in short supply. Praise is a matter of spirit and not merely intellect. Men who do not easily see the incredible miracle of life support God has given them in their wives will have a hard time merely praising them through will power. God must be in a man's heart and mind if he is not to remain blind to God's gift of life support!

King Lemuel was not blind! Proverbs 31 has nearly thirty character qualities which are ascribed to an excellent woman. There is little doubt that a godly man will be able to see a majority of these in the woman he married. When his eyes are truly opened to the love of God for him, he should also see the awesome attributes God has brought close to support him. They reflect the nature of God in his wife in areas in which he is in poverty.

A special attribute of the Proverbs 31 woman is her sense of security. She "smiles at the future" (Prov. 31:25). This reflects well upon the husband and on the wife's trust in God. But it is in short supply in this day and age since a woman's natural capacity for trust in her husband is severely damaged by sexual immorality. Most men have only themselves to blame for this loss in their wives and in a whole nation of women.

This introduces the question of a husband's need for affirmation by his wife. Is this also a legitimate need of his? Yes! The preceding paragraph and scripture provide a broad hint. Does Scripture present a clearer picture? Yes, it does, but it is not affirmation based upon words. *It does not provide for a man to receive affirmation from his wife from her praise.* In fact, *exactly the opposite* is true.

A godly wife affirms her husband by a "gentle and quiet spirit" free from fear, reflecting her *contentment and confidence in God and her husband to do right by her.* By this reflection, her confidence "to do what is right without being frightened by any fear" is the silent statement of a godly woman (1 Pet. 3:1–6). Lacking the anxious bondage that drives an insecure wife to express lack of confidence in her husband and/or to attempt controlling him, she also affirms by quiet confidence that her position cannot be shaken. She "smiles at the future." She is secure while God and her husband "work it out." Whether or not a godly woman's husband is a foolish man is irrelevant. She submits to her husband even in the face of potentially awful foolishness, as Sarah did when fearful Abraham lied about her and gave her to Pharaoh (see Gen. 12:11–20) and then twenth-four years later to Abimilech (see Gen. 20). In both cases, God intervened to protect her as we saw in preceeding chapters.

Hence, a man is affirmed when he knows his wife to be free of anxiety and that, regardless of wisdom or foolishness, the respect of his wife is secure. Ultimate responsibility for resolving a problem that threatens her happiness falls squarely upon his own shoulders, and she trusts him to find the right answer. She will not abandon him if he makes a mistake. Her confidence is a working faith that releases God to do everything necessary with the husband to bring him to success. Praise God for women who can do these amazing things!

However, though this is how God has provided for his affirmation, the husband must find his way to do what is right regardless of his wife's affirmation, fears and anxieties, sins, or whatever. He is to follow the example of Christ, Who gave Himself up for His Church...

> ...that He might sanctify her, having cleansed her by the washing of water with the word, that He might present to Himself the church in all her glory, having no spot or wrinkle or any such thing; but that she should be holy and blameless. So husbands ought also to love their own wives as their own bodies. He who loves his own wife loves himself; for no one ever hated his own flesh, but nourishes and cherishes it, just as Christ also does the church, because we are members of His body. (Eph. 5:26–30)

Few cheering sections support men faced with a crisis. Finding obedience to God on behalf of a wife can be a lonely search, in the company of God alone.

God died for us for us without condition, and the Bridegroom proceeded without any affirmation by His bride. Fulfillment was promised Him, but not of the same nature as the bride's. His fulfillment, the "bridegroom's joy" (see Zeph. 3:17; Is. 62:5; John 3:29, 15:11; Heb. 12:2,) is not related to the hearing of words of praise. He finds it in the building of a free woman, free to be all God has created her to be—*free of any visual defect*. Whereas her fulfillment is through her ears, *his fulfillment is to be through his eyes*. His fulfillment is to be the same as that of Jesus with His Church.

God describes this for the Bridegroom of the ages in Isaiah 53: "As a result of the anguish of His soul, He shall see it (the result) and be satisfied" (v. 11). This is His promise for each man who lays hold to the position God has given him and who is resolved in Christ to accomplish the work regardless of the cost.

He shall see the results and be satisfied.

27

Affirmation:
The Proverbs 31 Man

A woman who fears the LORD, she shall be praised. (Prov. 31:30)

Men wonder why women would ever go to other women to seek fulfillment in lesbian relationships. The reason is these women have never found a true place of value and growth to maturity in a male relationship.

Fathers wonder why their daughters would rebel against them, abandon their protection, and foolishly seek to be their own agents in bringing a man to marriage, knowing that sexual immorality and self-destruction are the most likely results. The reason is the same; daughters think they find higher value given them by their boyfriends than by their fathers.

Women were designed to seek a place of value. They also depend upon words to nurture their relationships and upon praise as their primary means of receiving gratification. By nature, unless damaged by men and until they come to know the Savior as their true Source, they instinctively seek this from men. Finding a place of true value is the key to unlocking a woman's incredible capacity to love and pour out her life on behalf of a husband and family.

Ultimately, women need to know that they are valued enough to die for. When they find a man with such a love they will gladly suffer shipwreck with him, knowing that to him they are precious pearls, diamonds, rubies; jewels fit for a king! God's design of the female is to reflect the gospel of Jesus Christ in the relationship of the Bride of Christ to the Bridegroom. It is gender-specific in the human marriage relationship.

Girls find their initial value through the words and actions of their fathers, then from their husbands. They are to be praised! Praise is not an option for men. God commands husbands to praise their wives in creative and poetic words. He says specifically that praise is a woman's reward.

Many men read Proverbs 31, perhaps even to their wives, in extolling the many qualities of an excellent woman, a woman who "fears the LORD." But then they leave it at that. They should rather go on to emulate the man who wrote Proverbs 31. Though written about a woman, the *commands contained in it are for men*. Proverbs is much more instructive for men than for women!

Consider King Lemuel, the man who praised his wife. With a spirit of gratitude, he describes her attributes. Husbands, have you ever done such a thing? What is more significant: the attributes of the wife or the attitude of the husband moved to describe them so poetically?

There are over two dozen specific character attributes which King Lemuel cites of his wife. In addition, he emphasizes that praise for a wife is part of her just reward from both God and man. In fact, counting the example of King Lemuel himself, there are four explicit commands or examples within Proverbs 31 that the wife is to be praised (and praised publicly) by her husband (see vv. 28, 30 and 31 in combination with v. 23).

True praise is to be directed at a woman's character qualities, not external beauty. Beauty does not convey value, whereas character does. The warning is explicit: "Charm is deceitful and beauty is vain" (Prov. 31:30).

Many men have difficulty grasping this issue, proving unable to praise their wives in words describing anything other than their hair, clothes, or physical beauty. They thereby demonstrate their own shallow and temporal value system, plus their lack of gratitude and humility in giving credit to their wives. Their eyes are blind to the love of God in their wives. Oh, the depths into which men have fallen! Despite behavior that should rightfully drive them away, God has given husbands amazing and faithful creatures to care for them! They are called wives!

The same neglect usually applies to fathers raising daughters. Failing to properly recognize the vision young girls carry for a 'knight in shining armor' (who will value her and love her unto risking death on her behalf), fathers tend to let their daughters invent their own solutions to finding the man of their dreams. Fathers, have you ever praised your daughters in areas of their character? What do you think your daughters dream about when they think of romance? Unlike most boys or men, it is not sex! It is about soul intimacy, words of endearment which lift up, enhance, and appreciate their inner qualities and their nurturing such a man. Lacking fathers who appreciate their qualities, daughters tend to drift about seeking knowledge about men from their mothers and girlfriends, who know little or nothing about men. They fantasize and believe many things that are untrue. They should instead be finding reality through their fathers. A father knows a lot about men, but unless he is seen by his daughter as the forerunner of her husband and an agent for a secure marriage, who values her highly and is committed to help find a godly husband, he will be rejected as unsympathetic about the important issues in her life.

Insecure daughters especially reject the refining process every young man is to receive from a girl's father. Though she desires one willing to die for her, an insecure girl prefers to control the situation and will not trust her father; she won't tolerate a potential true love bearing actual difficulty on her behalf. It is every woman's mercy instinct to try and relieve her lover from the pain of accountability which every man requires for character building.[1] She remains bound to the deception that "she can do it better herself" (see Isa 53:6), but "its end is the way of death" (Prov. 14:12).

So, when a girl hears the first words of endearment which exceed the value she enjoys from her father, she is vulnerable to fleeing her father's true protection. "Higher value" is often merely a boy admiring her physical beauty and claiming that sex with her will make him happy. She may believe she can win him by satisfying his needs. What evil! Girls who believe this lie will sooner or later have their dreams and marriages shattered.

Even a thousand warnings will make no impression on girls who are not secure! Daughters must be greatly loved; they must know it and be accustomed to living freely under the protection God has provided. That is the security of family, for which the father is responsible, continuosly, actively, ALWAYS!

God secures us in Christ the same way. Ahead of everything else is the realization that God is alive and loves us. We are precious to Him and His power is directed at protecting and blessing us. It is in this context alone that the power of God's love expressed in the offering of Jesus Christ to pay for our sin has become a reality. The knowledge of the Son of God's death for me is the reality that secures me. This is the truth that sets me free! Love unto death cannot be denied. It wins my trust and eagerness to be in right relationship with the One who did it. It is God's word that has changed me.

It's the same thing needed by women from men. Men are asked by God to love wives the same way Christ loved the Church (Eph. 5:25–33). That means expressing our love to them in the same fashion that portrays our willingness to die for them. They thereby receive the same understanding of their value. Men are God's agents for expressing value in practical ways, even as King Lemuel did for his wife. Ultimately, we of the Bride all seek the same reward from our Bridegroom: "Well done, thou good and faithful servant."

Many men are out of shape, inexperienced, and untrained. Some eventually desire to change their ways (the biblical word is to *repent!*). If a man is really serious, *he will begin to exercise and train.* He will go to school and to the gym! This need is evident in men who have never recognized their responsibility to create a place of security for the jewels entrusted to their care, their wives and daughters. All men would benefit greatly by attendance at the King Lemuel "School of Female True Value Training"!

This exercise will produce good fruit through men who work at it. Guys, write a Proverbs 31 poem, song, or letter to your wives (or daughters) according to a prayerful listing of some of the qualities that God has placed in them. God will reveal these to you if you will diligently seek God to open your eyes. If all the verses of Proverbs 31:10–31 are used, about thirty or so traits can be identified. Then launch off on your own to write those additional wonderful attributes that apply to your own wife or daughter. Be another King Lemuel! Let God speak through you!

Men, this personal project is recommended to take you in a new direction. Turn on some *teshookaw* for the sake of your wives! Be concerned regarding your inadequate efforts to affirm the value of your wives and daughters. Ask God to take away your blind spots! Purpose fulfillment for the women and girls under your protection! God has done it for you and desires you to enjoy doing the same work as our Heavenly Bridegroom!

Dear Father in Heaven, abiding with me through Christ, please give me the spirit of gratitude and praise of King Lemuel for his wife! Equip me to see and express the wonderful qualities that make my wife and daughters so priceless and valuable and to do this with Your eyes and love. Though I may yet be weak in discernment and unskilled in praise for skills and character, You are not! Please give me words that will let them know with certainty that they are valuable and are a blessing to me. Let me bless them with my gratitude! Enable them to see I am committed as a man to protect them with my life. And dear Lord, in the name of Jesus, I pray that they will find fulfillment in their ability to live their lives for You, pouring out the riches of your grace in mercy upon others. Thank you. Amen.

Section IV: Applications and Testimonies

28

Testimony:
An Affirming Woman

An excellent wife, who can find? For her worth is far above jewels. (Prov. 31:10)

There have been occasions in my life where I became involved in extensive search with God for major life direction. Unwittingly, I was ultimately drawn each time to inquire of my wife in a manner in which I expected to resolve the issue by discovering her desires. In each case I was totally surprised by her response. *Surprised* is not an adequate word.

The last instance took place during my last of a thirty-one-year Navy career. As my departure grew imminent, we sought God's direction for our future. I thought the foundational call of my life to be establishing men in Jesus Christ. I anticipated counseling, writing, and teaching men in a manner in which God could heal them and enable them to minister to their wives and families. But I was in a quandary about where to live.

At the time, my wife, Gretchen, and I were living in Alexandria, Virginia—our fourteenth year in a home we had owned for seventeen years. We had a choice. We could continue to live there where our roots were deep and extensive in many areas of our church, community ministry, and Boy Scouting. The alternative was to move back to an older home in the Pacific Northwest where we had lived nearly 20 years earlier, before knowing Christ. We knew only one remaining family in the town of Port Orchard, Washington, where we had moved away in 1970 when our son, Kenny, was three months old. Now he was graduating from high school. We seemed to have no clear direction to resolve where we would live after I left the Navy. We loved the Pacific Northwest where my parents still lived, but our roots were deep in Virginia.

For nearly a year, we sought direction in a myriad of ways: praying continually, submitting issues of ministry to our local church, analyzing the pros and cons of alternatives, and relating certain indicators of our potential direction to circumstances which God might develop. Anyone who has been through such major efforts at finding life direction will know how agonizing such a quest can be until the time arrives for God's answer. It seemed like no tentative indicators, direction, or reasonings could be sustained for more than a day or two before being completely demolished by new indicators, direction or reasonings. It seemed awful at the time, but out of it came something so wonderful and rare I am writing this chapter just to share it.

There came a day when I finally resolved in my heart that the only way to find definitive direction was to search the inner heart of my wife and resolve the issue on that basis alone. I would make the decision to please her.

At an appropriate time I got her seated without distraction at the kitchen table. While perhaps sipping a cup of coffee, we discussed the situation for the umpteenth time, and I brought the discussion around to the following query: "Honey, if there were no other considerations regarding things [i.e., Kenny's forthcoming college selection, our daughter Suzy's choice as to where she would live, my parents, Gretchen's many friends, her activities and horses, our church's decisions, ministries, etc.], what would your preference be regarding where we should live? If we had a completely clean slate, where would you prefer to live?"

I was very careful, I thought, to put the question in a manner in which I could discover even the slightest inclination of her heart.

She thought quietly for perhaps twenty seconds. I was eager and attentive, for I was certain she understood the question and would answer it. Then she answered. "I'll be completely happy to go wherever you decide."

I hid my dismay, thinking, *Surely, she did not understand the question, after all! I must present it again more carefully.* I was still sure she had an inclination just under the surface of her first response. So I rephrased the question.

After another even longer pause, she rephrased her answer, "I will be happy just to be with you, no matter where we live. Whatever you decide is fine with me."

Efforts to elicit even the slightest further thoughts were unavailing. She just continued to state in very creative and beautiful ways that she would be happy as long as we were together.

How many men have tasted what my wife gave me that day?

It is difficult to express fully how ennobling and rare an experience like this is for a man.

I experienced two extremely powerful things simultaneously. First, I was in awe that God could create someone with that kind of security and trust, with no conditions whatsoever. How could Gretchen have such inner confidence and capacity as to place her whole future and happiness in such a frail vessel as me, without even expressing an opinion? How could she be so assured that things simply made no difference as long as she was with me? I could not contain it. It was the most enhancing event of my life to experience the reality of my own wife sitting there before me exercising such extreme personal trust and contentment in me.

I suppose her trust may have actually been in God, but the resulting voice of her resolve was that her happiness was in me, not in where we lived, and that she was committed to this with her whole life.

Second, came the impact of realizing the *value* of such a trust. I was in the presence of an amazing treasure entrusted to me! It was not merely that I needed to determine a place to live or to guard my wife's future! Like a tender baby or a priceless work of art I now had her trust to preserve. It was her trust and contentment in me which suddenly became most precious. I could not afford a

mistake! Her confidence amplified my need to find the right an-
swers! God had placed the buck squarely on me! I was responsible!
I could not deal falsely with Gretchen by dealing half-heartedly with
God! I had to find God's will for us, no matter the cost.

Hence, my wife's determination that her happiness resided only
in me and not in my decision had the actual effect of *further inten-
sifying my purpose* of discovering God's will in order that I could
make a right decision!

I realized later that Gretchen had also taken this position in
some earlier years, but with less stunning impact. But never had I
inquired with so much specific care and firm intention of fully
responding to even the slightest indication of her heart. Of course,
God knew what was going on all along. He honored my love for
my wife and desire to do His will by giving me a greater grace
through her. God met me through her words and further refined
me as a man. Yes! My wife had given me the freedom to either get
it right or get it wrong. It was up to me and the Lord.

These things are not merely affairs of the intellect. Human
intellect cannot produce the type of freedom and response that
Gretchen gave me that day. Nor can it be faked. It is a reflection
of the spirit. She spoke out of the abundance of her heart. Her
heart is full toward me. She does me good and not evil all the
days of her life. She is a free woman able to live with me in a
manner which ministers power to me too—power to seek out
God and bear the consequences on her behalf with joy! Her freedom enabled her to deliver me up to the Lord that day. It made
me responsible. Yes, it also greatly increased the pressure on me!
On the other hand, my senses of personal value and self worth
have never been higher! How many women could do that? They
must have greatly empowered husbands!

Well, we eventually did obtain our answer from the Lord. We
were told to uproot and move. But in many respects, discovering
God's direction and working through all the affairs of moving were
anticlimactic after that day, when compared to this single experience. How can the affairs of this world compare with discovering

the supernatural things of God, so rare in flesh and blood, even in one's own spouse? How lovely to find a gift so intimately close, to be affirmed that God loves me and can uphold those who trust in Him. How remarkable that such power can be placed into God's beloved creatures, His people, my wife.

I pray in Jesus' name that other men and women might also share such things. I have attempted to supplement God's Word on the power of a woman's quiet and peaceful spirit in Sarah, Esther, and King Lemuel's wife with these additional words testifying of my wife's beauty. It is a substantive reflection of the power of God's Word brought to reality in my own life—something for others of His children to admire and seek for themselves as a gift of God. *It is not illusory!* God's word is vital, substantive and life giving and can be claimed in Christ in your own life!

29

Testimony:
A Modern Marriage

> And they overcame (the accuser of our brethren) because of the
> blood of the Lamb and because of the word of their testimony,
> and they did not love their life even to death. (Rev. 12:11)

In many respects Gary and Holly had a typical modern marriage—a marriage that wouldn't last long unless a miracle took
place. Gary was in his midthirties and second marriage, having
brought with him two kids from a previous marriage. He had
gone into construction work after over a decade of work as a
rock band guitarist. He had a background of drugs, alcoholism,
and sexual promiscuity.

Holly's background was similar; she also brought two children
of her own to this, her second marriage. Difficulties between the
children and their parents/stepparents were great, Gary being continually at war with Holly's oldest child, who was ultimately sent
to a private institution for care, and Gary's children, though younger,
growing more and more unruly and disrespectful of Holly. Anger,
impotence, and attempts to rule his family by force were typical of
Gary's behavior. Whenever the stress levels in the home reached
certain extremes, Holly would just disappear, running away for
days at a time with a friend, returning to a life of partying and
drinking and threatening to end the marriage.

All of the behavioral patterns of discontent, insecurity, harlotry, impotence, and lack of fulfillment outlined in this book were present for both spouses. Gary was emotionally and financially impotent to deal with the issues of being an effective husband and father. Holly attempted vainly to control and direct her husband according to what she thought best. Failing and returning to despair, she would again flee the marriage.

Both claimed and gave evidence of having a personal relationship with the Savior Jesus Christ. However, though faithful in church and surrounded by other believing friends, little early evidence of Christ's work in the marriage itself was visible other than that the marriage had somehow lasted seven years. But God was preparing a major work in their lives.

One day Holly took off again, convinced that she had had all that she could take and telling her husband to start the divorce proceedings. (She said she wouldn't legally initiate divorce because "that would be a violation of Scripture"!) She disappeared with the family van and Gary, based on the identity of the friend Holly left with, assumed she had gone to Florida.

His despair and pain over the failure of the marriage plus the advise of a friend led him to counseling which applied the scriptural information and principles set forth in *Restoration of Men* and this book. A short synopsis of what took place follows.

Gary was immediately presented with his responsibility and failure as a man to effectively serve his function as head of family. He was convicted by the Holy Spirit that it was indeed his own background of sexual immorality that had dissipated his manhood in accordance with Proverbs, chapter 5, and left him impotent to lead, protect, and fulfill his wife—that her frustration and unhappiness *were a direct result of his own impotence as a man.* The evidence was overwhelming. The conviction of sin and the death sin had produced was powerful. Its effect upon Gary was a shriveling experience.

Gary purposed as a goal in life to provide for a happy, fulfilled wife. He accepted total responsibility for the marriage failure, repented, asked for forgiveness from God, and began to deal with the new revelation of his responsibility and the belief that he could experience restoration of his manhood in Jesus Christ. He committed to occupy the territory God had provided as his area of responsibility for his wife, resolving that no price was too great to pay for her. Within a short period he became committed that he was going to be a complete husband for his wife in Christ and that, "if he perished, he perished." God magnified for him the true beauty of his wife and revealed to him her pain. He developed *a strong desire to deliver her from her pain and for her to be a free woman.* He began to pray and fast for her continually, many days at a time, losing twenty pounds of weight over the next month or so. Within a few early days he had surmounted a good deal of his incapacitating pain and began to make effective prayer intercession for Holly.

Despite God's dramatic revelation of His Word in Gary plus Gary's vision and personal commitment for his wife, Gary still had considerable difficulty for the first month in praying for Holly due to double-mindedness in his prayers. In committing her to God and thereby claiming her total security and protection [hemming her in by thorns from harlotry (Hos. 1, 2:1–7)] he was often buffeted by either (1) desire to control the situation and know for himself where she was and what she was doing, or (2) sexual lust for other women and impatience or despair over ever restoring his marriage. He also exhibited strong habits wanting to manipulate the situation. But he was obliged by the circumstances God had provided (total separation and no knowledge of his wife's whereabouts) to do the only thing he could: *trust God for her security*, pray, and perfect his attitudes in Christ. God used this time to do a major work in Gary. The effort to resolve where he stood with Christ on these matters took about four or five weeks—less time than most men require.

Gary's attitudes toward the counselor were excellent. He became very open, transparent, and teachable, quick to confess his temptations and sins and to apply counsel to his actions. The Holy Spirit gave him open ears and a desire to work at his task with great vigor despite deep and tormenting pain. Through continuing prayers and counsel, the Holy Spirit built (1) a deep confidence regarding God's love for him and (2) *amazement regarding the love God had for Holly*. (He correctly perceived that the dreadful fire and painstaking attention God had given to him for Holly's sake was a measure of God's great love for her and the method to make him fit for expressing God's love to her.)

Given a clear choice part way through counseling to quit the fire or continue in it for the sake of his wife, Gary made a free-will decision to stay in the fire until God's work was completed.

A few weeks after she had left, Gary discovered through the institution in which her oldest son had been placed that Holly had not gone to Florida but to Alaska. He was, however, unable to establish communications with her. As he continued to pray for her safety, protection, blessing, relationships, finances, etc., his heart became more and more abundant toward her, and he began to write poetry for her. He composed a lovely poem to Holly, entitled "To My Friend," which is included in the Appendix of this book. He continued to pray and fast for her, now having lost about thirty pounds over a period of about two months!

At this time Gary obtained Holly's address from her son's school and began to send her money and flowers plus a copy of the poem. For a while he had no idea whether or not she was receiving them. But, at this time his spirit began witnessing to him of her complete safety and protection. He received assurance in his heart of the things for which he had been praying, and his double-mindedness disappeared. He still had no visible or verbal evidence as to Holly's circumstances.

As he prayed, the Holy Spirit frequently gave him specific wisdom on how to pray. Many aspects of how she was to be hemmed in against temptation and destructive influences were given to Gary in his prayers, including how to pray for such things as her employment, transportation, residence, and associates.

One of the purposes for which Gary prayed during this period was to take onto his own body Holly's infirmities, exactly as Christ has ordained for husbands (Eph. 5:25–33). This was exemplified for us as the Bridegroom of the Church died for our sins and removed our infirmities in His own body. Gary recalled, in particular, a large cyst on Holly's hand and prayed that God would enable him to bear it as her substitute.

In the meantime, Holly received the poem and knew immediately something had happened to her husband. At first she was incredulous and thought someone else had written the poem. Shortly after, she placed her first phone call to Gary.

What took place during the call is difficult to describe. Holly heard a man speak who had fullness of heart for her (Matt. 12:34b; Luke 6:45b). Out of his mouth came words which ministered to her. He took full responsibility for the problems of the marriage; he spoke confidently regarding their future together; he expressed his love for her and of God's love for both of them. He did not attempt to manipulate her with words or ask her to come home but expressed the strength and confidence that God was giving to him as he occupied faithfully the position God had given. It spoke to her spirit. She was so eager to hear more, she began to call him regularly and was quite unabashed in confessing that she thought his words were "different, changed, beautiful."

Over the next few conversations, Gary discovered that Holly had driven their van off a road, destroying it, and had been reduced to using a bicycle for transportation. From an initial life of "freedom" and dissipation upon her arrival in Alaska, she had been rapidly reduced to bare subsistence, being hemmed in through other circumstances as well regarding her activities and lifestyle.

She had also found a place to live with a dysfunctional relative with uncontrollable spending habits. In this woman's compulsions to spend (in which she dissipated over three hundred thousand dollars of inheritance in less than two years), Holly was able to see her own anxieties and compulsions to spend for material things—a habit which had brought hardship to her marriage with Gary. In addition, Holly met a cleaning woman who advised her that many years earlier she had also left her husband under similar circumstances, thinking to return to him "after he had learned his lesson." But when she returned after six months, she had found her husband had given up and found another woman. Holly believed she'd heard a clear admonition from God that she needed to return home.

In one conversation, Gary inquired as to the condition of the cyst on Holly's hand. She described to Gary how one morning she had discovered it to have suddenly disappeared! Gary was able to correctly tell her the exact date of its disappearance—the date of his prayer to take it upon himself, in Christ.[1]

During this period Gary also focused his prayers upon building up/edifying Holly as a free woman. He did not coerce her in any way to come home. He kept sending her money and resolved with the Lord that God alone would be judge regarding when it was time for Holly to return. Her inquiries were always met with, "Any time you want to come home is fine with me. Come home whenever when you feel completely ready," or similar words.

During this period Gary also resolved that sexual freedom would be ministered to his wife after she came home. This included a resolution for celibacy until she expressed her desire for sexual union.

The conclusion of the story is only the start of another. Holly came home after about a four-month absence. She was a different woman, transformed by God in a mysterious fashion that can be reported but not explained. *She was now convinced of God's love for her.* She had a different man for a husband, not one whom she had produced through manipulation and coercion but one *whom God had produced.* She settled back in for life on the frontier with her children and stepchildren, but now things were different. She had hope and security in her relationship with her husband. She knew he loved her and was willing to die for her; he had demonstrated this in many ways. She became a beautiful, free woman, no longer withholding herself from her husband. Prior habits of blackmailing or manipulating her husband in order to get him to give her money or meet her demands disappeared. Other women with marital problems immediately sensed a change in her and began to seek her out for help.

The problems with the children have continued to be difficult and may well remain for the rest of their lives. They all have many difficult problems but are laboring to solve them. Gary's business and creativity has been blessed; his finances have begun to heal, and he ultimately built a permanent home big enough for his expanded family. It is the first real home Holly has ever had, fit for a queen. Despite the problems with their kids, they can truthfully be said to be a transformed family.

What were the critical factors here that make this such a success story? It is a mystery, but I have an opinion as to how and why God intervened in glory.

1. Both spouses knew Jesus Christ and had some purpose in their lives to please Him.
2. Gary was deeply convicted by the Word of God regarding his failures as a man and came to take responsibility for the underlying true scriptural causes of his failures.
3. He yielded to God on all the important matters, including taking his place as husband unto death, if necessary, and making many free will offerings to God, regardless of what his wife did or what happened with the marriage.
4. Gary applied his convictions to his prayers, fasting, and actions, putting his heart, mind, and soul into obeying God. God amply encouraged and strengthened Gary in his weaknesses.
5. Gary was particularly responsive in putting away his control devices over his wife, recognizing her as a creature of God for whom he had been entrusted to protect and love. He was also particularly faithful in dealing with fleshly appetites which had raged in him for years, experiencing real death in his responses to God.
6. God intervened with a gift; He revealed and amplified Holly's true beauty as a woman to Gary. In addition, the more Gary invested in her, the more precious and beautiful she became.

7. Gary bonded to Holly with fire. *He paid a tremendous price in having spent his life on her behalf in a number of areas in which his flesh, mind, and attitudes were put to death.* She is now worth all that. Both he and Holly know this and know it to be a work of God.

8. The knowledge of her value in her husband's sight and in God's sight has made Holly secure and therefore a free woman. She is no longer afraid to deal with the difficulties still facing them in their children and the perplexing ups and downs of a difficult family life.

Here is some of their personal testimony.
In Gary's words:

The Lord never said this life would be a bowl of cherries, but that we would suffer to become more like Him. I now see clearly why God allowed me to be put through such heart-wrenching anguish—to purify me (as part of His body, the Church) and to allow me to take an active part in the building of my faith by seeing the miracle of God's transformation of my life and my wife's life while she was twenty-seven hundred miles away.

I believe with my whole heart that God will move heaven and earth for a man who will really lay it down and intercede for his wife (see Jer. 32:27). After praying and fasting for six weeks, there was an Alaskan earthquake fifty miles from where Holly lived. I hadn't prayed for an earthquake. But the Lord is sovereign over the earth. I shall ask Him when I meet Him how this related to my prayers. But that evening Holly placed her first phone call to me, and God blessed me with great calmness and godly authority to speak peace and spiritual life back into Holly and our marriage. From that day on, our relationship has been greater than we ever imagined, and I hope I will stand as a living encouragement for all men. Men must learn to weep before the Lord in humbleness and petition—probably the key factor in dying to yourself and presenting your wife as spotless, holy, and blameless before the Lord (see Eph. 5:26).

Here are the priceless words of the bride:

When I look back and see how the Lord has taken us through muck and mire and has placed us on His sure foundation, I can only call it a miracle. The trials and difficulties that Gary and I had were larger than life to us. Anyone outside of the grace of God would have given up on this marriage years ago. But Gary and I both had that hope that Christ has given us and knew that somehow we would make it. The Bible tells us that He, Christ, will not give us anymore than we can handle, and when I ran away to Alaska I felt I could not do anything more for the marriage.

But the Lord took that situation and through prayer, willingness, and a desire to serve him, taught Gary how to intercede for me and to show me a kind of love I had never known. Even though I was twenty-seven hundred miles away from my husband, there was a sense of security and love from him that I had never experienced before. A lot of what happened I could never explain because it was only between the Lord and Gary. But I do know that it has changed the way I feel about love, life, marriage, and the Lord Jesus Christ.

Praise the holy name of Jesus Christ!

Testimony: A Father's Role in Marriage Restoration

I am a shield to you. (Gen. 15:1)

John's daughter had fled her marriage and come home several hundred miles to live with her parents. Her reported background of marriage difficulties (alleged abuse plus neglect and emotional difficulties occasioned by the fact that her husband was living very close to his parents) produced anger and division among her parents. Her husband's parents allegedly controlled him and nearly all aspects of his marriage, his employment, and his family affairs.

John and his wife, Irene, were believers in Christ but were divided regarding how to deal with their daughter's problem. They both believed in the importance of rebuilding their daughter's marriage, but the son-in-law's actions had greatly alienated them. Irene, in particular, felt that the son-in-law's alleged behavior was despicable and could not bring herself to support reconciliation. She had been further provoked by a number of abusive phone calls he had made to their household after their daughter had come home.

Counsel with John and Irene revealed that the circumstances of their daughter's marriage were rather typical: there had been little oversight of John over his daughter's relationships, and the son-in-law had never come under John's serious scrutiny nor testing as a condition for his dating or marrying John's daughter. He had never been through any process which could have clarified his attitudes or resolved her value to him prior to their marriage. The circumstances of their daughter having come home to live under her father's roof seemed to suggest that it was time that John established the protective shield over his daughter which he had failed to provide previously. For her security and for the peace and serenity of his household, it was evident John needed to cut off free access of his son-in-law to his daughter. Henceforth, it would become necessary for him to go through John as a precondition for further contact or relationship with his wife. John was to fulfill his task as a refiner and purifier of the bridegroom, not having any certainty as to the outcome but because it was his functional responsibility to be an effectual shield for his daughter and the agent of her successful marriage to a man who truly loved her.

The involuntary aspects of this strategy were significant. Irene's strong sympathies for her daughter made it unlikely she could be strongly supportive of a means of perfecting the son-in-law toward a meaningful reconciliation. Also, the daughter would be required to submit to her father's policy; living at home under his roof required living under his rules. Yet she was already a married woman and used to living independently of her father. Further, it is a general principle that if discipline and refinement of a bridegroom begin to bear fruit (i.e., a bride begins to sense that she is really loved), she will attempt to circumvent her father's discipline in order to relieve the pain of her bridegroom and restoratively build that relationship.[1]

Soon the son-in-law called again. John got on the phone and explained gently but firmly that they needed to talk face-to-face before the son-in-law would be allowed to meet or speak to his daughter. John suggested he come for a visit, stay at a local motel, and meet with John, who would help with the expenses. The son-in-law refused, gave excuses, and insisted upon his "rights." The father firmly persisted in this position over several such conversations. But it was not evident that any change in the son-in-laws' attitudes were taking place. Also, with time, it seemed evident that John's daughter was to some extent circumventing her dad's constraints on communications.

After several months, though, the daughter made plans for an extended overseas trip. Without notice or discussion, the son-in-law suddenly quit his job in his hometown, left his parents, and moved a long distance to another large city to seek a new job. He found a job and then contacted his wife through John to seek reconciliation. She continued with her planned trip, but it was clear that the basic requirements of reconciliation had occurred. After she returned home, she rejoined her husband in their new home. The marriage was successfully reconciled. Possibly unrelated, several years later, he is today studying and preparing for potential ordination in ministry.

What were the key elements of this demonstration of God's love?

1. The wife of a failed marriage, either deliberately or inadvertently, sought protection under God's chief agent for her safety and happiness—her father.
2. Her father resolved that he would establish a godly means of protecting his daughter from the undisciplined, abusive behavior of her husband, fulfilling his function as a father and providing opportunity for the younger man to perfect his inner heart's true attitudes toward his wife.
3. Despite imperfections of the human participants involved, God used the obedience of the girl's father to perfect the heart of her husband. The husband discovered that he really loved his wife sufficient to take significant risks on her behalf. He resolved to make the sacrifices necessary to establish a sound basis for their marriage, regardless of personal cost. Without any apparent support, he left his father, mother, and hometown at considerable personal cost and risk.
4. The daughter discovered that God is really alive and able to prove His love to her in a personal way, providing her with the basis for trusting Him in reconciliation with her husband.

31

Testimony: A Marriage Miracle

. . . behold, a white horse, and He who sat upon it is called Faithful and True. (Rev. 19:11)

I had thought that if ever there was opportunity for God to demonstrate saving a marriage through godly obedience of a wife, this was it. Though it seemed that Scripture (and the evidence of my eyes) always pointed ultimately to the bridegroom as the key party to success of a marriage, I still anticipated that God had exceptions and would eventually prove it to me, if for no other reason than the fact that God is "never in a box."

In this case, the wife, Ann (not her real name), was ten years older than her husband, Patrick, and gifted spiritually. Rescued from a terrible childhood, life on the streets, drugs, and about every measure of abuse and perversion one can imagine, she had been transformed by a conversion to Jesus Christ and been given a powerful ministry for girls from similar backgrounds. She kept a group foster care home for girls, and through her God had brought many to similar conversions. Compared to her, her husband seemed a spiritual midget, barely professing a saving faith in Christ and exhibiting very little behavior that seemed to indicate it. Their home was always in strife and his favorite activity was playing Nintendo.

Patrick kept up maintenance fairly well on the home, owned by a local foster care agency, while serving at his job in the U.S.

Navy. But most of the constant conflict in their home seemed to Ann to be due to Patrick's lack of wisdom, maturity, and sensitivity to the needs of the girls. They also had a child of their own and that provided some connecting bonding for the family for a while. But eventually, the marriage broke apart. Ann, who was clearly the head of the household, threw Patrick out. After a previous such incident, this time it seemed permanent. Patrick left.

Initial efforts at counseling revealed the very shaky foundations of the marriage. Patrick came from a similar background of promiscuity, and the circumstances of their decision to marry seemed to be little more than a one-night stand. Both spouses characterized the original foundation of their marriage as extremely weak, not based on love, for convenience only, etc.. Yet they both appeared willing to work on it, so counseling ensued; sometimes with two counselors, sometimes with both spouses together. Ann was initially quite faithful to her counseling. Patrick quickly dropped off to meeting sporadically, but over a period of a couple of years built up quite a bit of time and exchange with his counselors.

It emerged that Ann was caught in a very demanding stronghold that rendered her powerless to exercise any love or respect for Patrick. Extreme spirits of scorn, ridicule, and futility toward him were resistant to prayer. Even the clarity of her spiritual eye and mind in recognizing these attitudes were wrong did not seem to aid in their renunciation through Christ. Her situation only seemed to grow worse. She placed all the blame for the marriage failure on her husband—his lack of spirituality, maturity, etc. She became convinced he was not born again in Jesus Christ and that there was no hope for the marriage.

Patrick seemed only to make inch-by-inch progress, so minute it was often discounted as illusory. Yet during all this time of living outside of the home, he continued maintaining the house and putting a considerable portion of his finances toward the work of his wife, their family, and the foster care ministry.

It was eighteen to twenty-four months before a real breakthrough seemed to take place. Without prior knowledge of the counselor, Patrick wrote a letter to Ann in which he described his shallow, shoddy motivations for marrying her and asked her forgiveness. On the surface, his words could have been considered an introduction or pretext for calling it quits and dissolving the marriage. But his words were different; evidence of Patrick's deep self-examination and repentance were apparent. Something had taken place in his heart. Patrick took full responsibility for having failed to provide the foundation of love that Ann needed. His request for her forgiveness seemed completely genuine.

Now surely, I thought, Ann will be able to respond. But I was wrong.

To my surprise and deep disappointment, this significant work of God in her husband produced no fruit in Ann. She remained as deep in bondage to her prisons as ever. Though she understood intellectually, she was still spiritually captive; her emotions and will were unmoved and unable to respond to Patrick in any way. In one of her counseling sessions, she described her own consternation when she described the Lord's having spoken personally to her, "*Ann, what are you going to do now?*" She saw in blazing clarity that she was still powerless to respond either to a changing husband or the Lord's exposure and admonishment of her helplessness. I believe that up to this point Ann had been essentially convinced of her own spiritual superiority and power over her husband, not fully comprehending her own condition. However, even with all this evidence, prayer and counseling seemed unable to break her bondage.

In the meantime, Patrick kept up his work on behalf of the family and home. He regularly took his family out and spent time with the girls, buying them treats and gifts. One day he had a particularly nasty plumbing job which required all day to complete. He finished around 10:30 P.M. Patrick was tired. Ann was extremely grateful and tried to show it.

She offered to Patrick to come to bed with her.

At this time Patrick and Ann had probably had no sexual relationship for over two years. I have no idea how he had been dealing with this situation up to then. However, I know how an average man would respond to this particular offer; without any real reconciliation in the wife's spirit, the spirit of harlotry chose this opportune time to tempt Patrick and to attempt to reclaim rule over both husband and wife.

But Patrick said, "No," and slept on the couch.

By this time over two years had passed without reconciliation of Patrick and Ann's marriage. The Christian foster care agency in charge of the home had long considered that a sound marriage was an essential criterion of establishing or continuing group home directors. Also, the agency was approaching a decision to get out of the group home business altogether. Many factors were involved, chief of which was the inordinate time and finances demanded in the business of property management and working with the state agencies involved. Also, Patrick's shore duty was coming to an end, and he was being transferred to sea duty. The situation was gradually de-stabilizing.

Another six months or so had elapsed by the time the agency made its final decision to terminate its group home foster care activity and sell the house. By this time Patrick was on the other side of the world stationed aboard a submarine. Ann was extremely threatened and nearly helpless, facing complex needs of license renewal, housing, relocation, and finances. What was she going to do? Now "her" ministry was threatened—her very lifeblood of work and fulfillment. Things most dear, certainly more important to her than her husband, were facing loss; relationships with "her" girls, "her" work for Christ, "her" gifts, "her" well-being, perhaps even "her" own child. Would God save all these seemingly precious things? If so, how would He do it?

Well, as you might anticipate, He sent her husband!

On the other side of the world, Patrick had an accident in which he broke his finger and required emergency medical leave. The Navy sent him home for placement of pins in the finger. He found himself in a position to rescue his wife, now powerless to save herself. He discussed the matter with her in terms of reconciliation of the marriage, dug deep financially, and searched out and purchased a home of their own in which she could keep her nest secure while continuing her work with abused girls.

This amazing work of God in a husband who had received almost no respect, nurture, or empowerment from his wife for many years transformed the marriage.

After some additional years, this husband and wife show a growing love and respect for each other! They support each other, vacation together (without the kids), and continue in foster care together. He is continuing to advance his career in the Navy. I anticipate (and they have confirmed an apparent calling) that as they continue to grow in Christ they will become involved in marriage counseling together. I am in awe that God could do such a thing as He did in this marriage. I think that what He did through Patrick resolved forever that Ann would know she is truly loved. How He actually did it is beyond my understanding. It is a fulfillment of God's own promise. "Now to Him who is able to do exceedingly abundantly beyond anything that we ask or think, according to the power that works within us, to Him be the glory in the Church and in Christ Jesus to all generations forever and ever. Amen" (see Eph. 3:20–21).

In this true love story, I also appreciate the manner in which God again *confirmed His ways* to me. The point, especially, where Patrick was somehow empowered to discern or resist the potentially ruinous temptation to sleep with his wife when she offered him her bed in gratitude (a most subtle expression of harlotry) was to me a sure sign of God's continued work to sanctify their marriage, after I had become convinced nothing more could be done.

Although the jury is still out as to whether God will ever use the bride to save the bridegroom, I rather think not. His way seems to be to reflect His love for the bride in some tangible way which enables her to know that God's love for her is personal and powerful. Personal because He meets her in an area of her deepest personal need. Powerful because it is usually through her hitherto unchangeable husband (who has always previously seemed to fall short) uniquely giving himself up on her behalf. This also seems always to be done in a fashion which is clearly of God and not of men in replicating the nature of Christ's death for His Bride. The husband himself is enabled to become conformed to Christ. Like Christ, he will also see the results and be satisfied.

In a much later review of this manuscript, I mentioned my admiration to Patrick for what he had done. He replied, "I was just there!" Upon further reflection, this brief word seems to me to summarize God's promise to be with us unto the end of the age. Without fanfare, without much tangible evidence of our love given in return, God keeps His promise to keep us and care for us. Patrick's self-minimizing words regarding what he did (and continues to do) for Ann seem to capture this well.

Testimony:
Facing the Serpent

Submit therefore to God. Resist the devil and he will flee from you. (James 4:7)

For months I had shared none of my concerns. In fact, my wife, Gretchen, knew nothing of the nearly pathologic fear which I had developed over rattlesnakes nor of most of the winter spent in prayerful inquiry as to this trip and the means by which I had resolved we would even continue our long-term hiking project.

We were hiking the Pacific Crest Trail (PCT) in segments, one hundred to two hundred miles a year, from Mexico to Canada. We figured it would take twenty to twenty-five years. After our two kids had grown and left home, this had seemed a good long-term project for our marriage (especially our communications!), physical fitness, and fun. We were on what was now the twelfth and last day of our second year's trip, descending from Mt. San Jacinto near West Palm Springs, California.

Our previous year, also in the spring and mostly through Southern California desert, had been uneventful regarding snakes. I'd carried a large walking staff just in case, but we'd not seen a single snake. However, during winter preparations for this next segment of trail, I'd been seized with a powerful unreasonable fear of rattlesnakes regarding our PCT project. What if we should get bitten! With great anxiety I got out my unused snakebite kit and poured over the instructions. Two or three months of prayer and meditation attempting to find direction or an understanding of my fear was unsuccessful. It eventually distilled down to this:

- The intense and irrational fear I was experiencing was (probably) spiritual attack.
- Personal risks I might be willing to take myself were unacceptable where my wife was also put at risk.
- If the project put her at risk, I would abandon it.
- I needed personal direction from God as to the risk and whether to go ahead or abandon the trip.

However, these months of inquiry had still produced no direction, and I continued in great, unexplained fear of the potential snake problem. Finally, I went to the nearby naval hospital and naively inquired about obtaining some antivenin to take with us. They had none, inasmuch as there are no poisonous snakes in the area where I live.[1] This renewed my dilemma and vigor in prayer with God. Later that day I began to "wrestle" with Him; I resolved not to proceed without definitive direction. After several intense hours of review of priorities, risks, and alternatives, it seemed that God suddenly spoke to me. *"Karl,"* He said, *"My children shall walk the earth securely."*

It is worthwhile to consider the full breadth of application of this beautiful *rhema* word of God. Over the next few days I saw that it applied not only to the snake problem but also to all of my potential issues of security—and not only to me but also to all who are God's children. It also instantly resolved the problem at hand. It seemed to me to release us for this trip, assuring complete security for both me and my wife now and forever in "walking" the earth. So we went.

But I'd also reached another conclusion. Without sharing any of the preceding concerns with Gretchen, I determined that I would always walk first. There might be a premium for alertness or consequences for failure in discerning danger, so I resolved to be "it"—the entire 105 miles. If there were to be a mistake with a rattlesnake, I would be the "bitee"! It was a considerable variation on our normal hiking patterns. Upon our arrival at Warner Springs and at the start of the hike, I merely announced that I would walk first, and Gretchen asked no questions.

By the second day, we saw snakes. Some quietly, in the middle of the trail, some nearby; most would commence rattling as we walked along or spoke. By the time we reached the snowline of the San Jacinto Mountains after six days in the desert, we'd seen nearly a half-dozen, to which we'd passed within three to five feet. Gretchen seemed to take them matter-of-factly, while I continued to do my best to avoid surprises. After we reached the high mountains, our problems turned to snow—four days of solid snow after one of the heaviest winters of the decade. But after this, a nice overnight visit to Idlewild, and a climb to the summit of Mt. San Jacinto, we emerged from the north side of the mountains and began our descent. We came down out of the snow. Our trip was now almost over.

Those with long backpacking experience know the euphoria of the last day of a good trip. Empty packs and strong bodies plus anticipation of showers, friends, and your favorite meal! It is also a time to review the good times. I began to exult in the wonderful way things had worked out. The snow camps, the water, the desert, even the snakes—plenty of them, but we'd been safe all the way. Wasn't God wonderful? Yes! He'd given us a wonderful promise of security and kept us safe.

Then, a new thought suddenly arose. *I wonder if God's promise of security assured I wouldn't be bitten or that we'd be secure even if I were bitten?!* The reader knows! It took only a moment to realize that *God's security applied regardless of whether or not we were bitten.* The time was 9:30 AM.

It was at 12:00 noon that I was bitten, while we were still seven miles from the road. The snake had been hidden in the tall spring grass by a water seep alongside the trail and had reacted without warning when I nearly stepped on it. I leaped into the air and felt nothing at first, but Gretchen, following about twenty feet behind, saw the whole thing. After first thinking it had not gotten me, I felt the first prickle of pain, saw the blood coming out of my sock, and realized I had indeed been bitten by a very large rattlesnake.[2] The pain quickly worsened.

But the surprise was only momentary. It seemed God had carefully prepared me. After waiting until the snake cleared the path for Gretchen to come ahead, we moved a few score feet further down the trail, got out my camp chair and snakebite kit. I was already thoroughly familiar with the directions, having recently nearly memorized them. Perhaps it's clear why I can say I was not surprised. It seemed so special a way in which God had prepared me. I was awed by the intensely personal nature of His attention to me. I had perfect peace. Everything was working for good in this special event for which I'd been specially chosen and prepared. We were perfectly secure. (Gretchen's was a somewhat different story. She was considerably frightened for a short while but said later that she took her cue from me. When I remained calm and assured, she did likewise.)

I treated the snakebite for an hour, considering the alternatives. We had passed nobody on the trail for over a week. It was clear we'd both have to hike out together while following instructions for periodic release of the elastic constrictor band provided in the kit. This we did for the next three-and-one-half hours, stopping every ten minutes and releasing the band for one minute. It was gradually moved up the leg as swelling and discoloration (and pain!) increased.

I continued in front, having now gotten out a tent pole section to guide my eyes over every foot of the remaining trail. I couldn't afford another bite! About two hours later, I stopped for an unknown reason, thinking perhaps I discerned a hiss or some other warning. I searched the trail with my eyes. There in the rocky shadows right in the middle of the trail was another rattlesnake, waiting to be stepped on. With some persuasion from the pole, he crawled off the trail, now rattling as he went. We reached the end of the road and Snow Creek Village at 4:30 P.M. Gretchen ran to the nearest house and placed a call to 911.

The ambulance got lost, taking an hour to find us. En route to the hospital, I chatted with the paramedic, who told of his "visit" to California from the Midwest, only to suddenly discover now that he was married with two kids. I listened attentively as he described his desire to defend his daughter from the predations of men—he got worked up enough over the subject to describe himself as a "feminist!"

After listening a while, I asked permission to ask a personal question. "If you knew your wife or daughter were to be bitten by a rattlesnake and had opportunity to spare them by taking the bite yourself, would you?"

He sat silently for a while before blowing out his breath and saying that this was an extremely difficult question. Then he added that he'd probably be willing to accept the bite himself.[3]

Comedy ensued at the hospital, where I was treated by a renowned snakebite expert and suffered a reaction of hives to the antivenin despite earlier tests which showed no reaction. I was placed in ICU overnight, still wearing all my dirty hiking clothes. I was dosed up with cortisone and Benadril and was pretty groggy when Gretchen and our waiting friends came to visit that evening. Sleep soon overcame me.

But the next morning the Lord came to visit. I began a review of the amazing events that had taken place and was drawn into extended praise and worship.

I praised God for the way in which He'd helped me to comprehend and perform my role as my wife's protector, under divine assurance. The analogy between Satan and the snake were clear and the ultimate manner in which God overcame my fear evoked my greatest amazement and gratitude. God had provided an extremely rare and exquisite moment for me to become conformed to Jesus in defense of my wife. The more I expressed praise and adoration, the more awesome and amazing it seemed to appear. I exulted in the greatness of God. His glory seemed to fill the room.

After an hour or so, God seemed to whisper, *"Karl, notice where you were bitten!"*

I considered that the bite had been received immediately above my right heel at the boot-top. It seemed even in this form of affliction, God had allowed me to share a remarkable conformance with Christ's wound on my behalf, who was "bruised in the heel, while crushing the serpent's head" (see Gen. 3:15).

I still marvel over it. What an exquisite opportunity to experience God and see Him almost nearly face-to-face. He gave me something imperishable. In Christ, I was enabled to overcome fear in serving effectually as a shield for my wife. I now also benefit from some permanent immunity to rattlesnakes. My wife, who in a few days began to hear of the events which took place prior to the trip, knows in a deeper way that she is truly loved. She sensed it in her spirit when we started out again from the scene of the bite and self-treatment. She took her place behind me on the trail with the words, "I feel so loved and protected."

Her words did not come to motivate me. They came in consequence to all the things that had already been resolved.

Applications between the natural and spiritual worlds are practically endless. I've been allowed to see God at work, to see the results and be satisfied (Isa. 53:11).

Testimony:
A Father's Preparation for Marriage

And after you have suffered for a little, the God of all grace, who called you to His eternal glory in Christ, will Himself perfect, confirm, strengthen and establish you. (1 Pet. 5:10)

This story takes a while because it was many years in the making. It required many steps in God's development of me as a father and, in the manner I experienced and recount its events, seems to have placed many of the blessings given to my daughter as consequences to actions worked by God upon me. When I responded rightly, God seemed to take the two of us to a next step.

My daughter was already eleven years old when I came to Christ in 1976. Prior to this, I had not spent significant time enhancing, endorsing, or validating the visions given to her as a little girl of an expected knight in shining armor that God had planned for her. After receiving salvation it took a few more years for me to comprehend and get rolling on this. In addition, my daughter, being a firstborn, had a lot of my own firstborn characteristics too not yet ameliorated by the Word of God. Our characteristics, unfortunately, brought us into some conflict.

By the time Suzy entered college at William and Mary in Virginia, she seemed to have a good road map regarding what was right and wrong in relationships with boys but had also accepted a lot of world values regarding dating, personal appearance, and determination of her own esteem through her peers. Her mother and I thought much of this might have come through video entertainment, to which she seemed addicted. She could stand strongly for right and wrong, as exemplified by conflicts in moral values which took place among her friends and in her college sorority (and later caused its demise), but would also occasionally take incredible risks in her dating. In these it seemed that the Lord was extremely faithful to her and to us, her parents, in exposing her folly. By the time of her college graduation I was often speaking and writing to her in attempts to enhance and confirm her vision of a special man who would be all she dreamed of in a husband, and that I was God's agent in helping her "to get where she wanted" in aiding her in the process leading to marriage to this special man. But during most of this time, my words seemed to be falling empty; she seemed to have very little, if any, response to enlisting my support.

A real crisis arose when I retired from the Navy in 1989 and left Virginia to return to the Pacific Northwest to live in an earlier home and be near my parents. It meant we would have to leave our unmarried twenty-six-year-old daughter alone in Virginia, where she had all her friends and had resolved to continue her teaching career. I prayed often over this and continued regularly over the next many years praying for her protection and for wisdom for me to serve as an effectual godly father, even from the other side of the country. Many interesting things happened.

It seemed like distance might have enhanced her communications with us as well as our ability to discern and respond to the events in her life. Chapter 11 of *Restoration of Men*, "Sovereignty: A Letter to Daughter," was an actual letter to Suzy which turned out to perfectly describe and explain events which were taking place in her life at the time by an ardent suitor (or somewhat resembling one).[1] But one thing that did not seem to ameliorate with time and distance was Suzy's concern with her "late" age and remaining unmarried. Frustration or resentment occurred when friends or cousins got married. Gretchen and I agreed this anxiety of hers was unhealthy and that a favorable attitude for marriage would probably not be resolved until she found contentment with her single status. We continued to pray.

Difficulties in her employment as a public school day care supervisor eventually resulted in her change to private school education. Although there were disciplinary aspects involved and Suzy took quite a cut in pay, it also seemed to Gretchen and me to be much more suited to her long-term welfare and personal relationships.

As I continued to pray over these matters, God would occasionally respond. One day in 1993 He reminded me again of my promise to give a special car I owned to Suzy. It was a red convertible 1965 Corsa (a turbocharged, sport model Corvair, fully restored to near "show" quality condition.) Prior to our leaving Virginia, I had promised it to Suzy, thinking that it would be appropriate to give it to her when she had a husband to care for it. Now some three or so years later, God began to uncover hidden areas of my heart.

"Karl, why haven't you given the car to Suzy yet?"

I hemmed and hawed for a while, but soon agreed that it was because she didn't yet have a husband. God probed further.

"Well, Karl, does this mean that she has less capability to take care of this car without a husband? Does it mean she does not warrant the car unless she has a husband? Does it mean she has less value, less status, less anything to you if she has no husband?"

The matter was resolved quickly. In September 1993 my wife Gretchen and I drove the Corsa across the United States to give it to Suzy. I also had new engine seals put in it, tweaked up the mechanics and some of the body trim do-dads, and the specialist who did the work soon introduced Suzy to classic auto rallies. It was a hot car and won some drag races, but the man took a shine to Suzy and she wasn't interested, so that was that. She got a garage and put the car into storage while I attempted to aid her from a distance in maintaining it.

Soon after this, God got down to more difficult work in me. Perhaps because I had been responsive to the lesson of the Corvair, God expanded a dialogue on the same general subject.

He inquired of me, *"Karl, suppose I were to decide it best for Suzy that she should never marry? Suppose I should have her remain single?"*

This caused convulsions which took two or three months to sort out. My arguments revealed I had quite a personal stake in the fulfillment of Suzy's dreams. I had been an avid source of encouragement (not quite "author") of what I had thought to be God's promises to her and to me regarding her future husband. How could I possibly relinquish such things?! How could Suzy possibly be fulfilled otherwise? It was dreadfully difficult for me to recognize my own pride, fear of loss, and interference with God's sovereignty and ownership over the little girl I had many times placed in His hands. Now it became painfully complete. I finally reached a point in my heart where I wanted only God's best for Suzy, trusted Him, and consented to it. Once this transaction was complete, I found contentment. I then shared it with my wife.

Then, at her Christmas 1993 visit, I shared my story with Suzy. Big mistake! Thinking I had abandoned her, she burst into tears, rebuked me, and declared again her full intentions of fulfilling her dream of marriage. I made another attempt the next day to clarify what I thought to be a major work of God—how He had brought me to contentment and freedom as to His purpose in Suzy's life according to His will. I don't know if I was successful or not, but it seemed to come out better the second time.

Over the next year Gretchen and I began to see definite changes in Suzy. She not only appeared to find real contentment in her work, but she also expressed it. At one point she expressed a degree of contentment in her work as a teacher and with kids which appeared to us to be supernatural. Somehow, Suzy had found fulfillment with herself just as she was, doing what she was doing.

Then God came to me again. He showed me something going on deep inside of Suzy and reminded me that years earlier I'd had the same problem, though I'd been unconscious of it. It had been so deep and unseen in me I'd have never realized it if God hadn't specifically revealed it! *Suzy felt in her subconscious that she was losing out of her time of fulfillment as wife and mother because of her being obliged to wait* upon God and His timing![2] God led me through a review of my own experience—how I had assumed that years were being "bled" out of my life with nothing to show for it. Then He refreshed me as to how He'd both revealed this sense of loss and demonstrated it to be based on a lie. God does not rob and does not owe any man! Nor can a man outgive God! Whereas I had thought I was being robbed of precious years, God had shown me how instead He had actually preserved and restored all of the time I'd sacrificed to serve His pleasure in the Navy.

After leading me through my own experience and showing me how Suzy was subliminally reliving the same difficulty through her wait for marriage, God gently said to me, *"Karl, you may tell Suzy your story, identify her concerns, and give her firm assurance that not one moment of her life has been wasted in waiting for Me. All of her years as a wife and mother, all of her fulfillment as a woman have been carefully preserved because she has waited upon Me."*

So, I did it. At Christmas 1994, I shared my story with Suzy and gave God's promise to her just as He had spoken it to me.

Three weeks later her bridegroom appeared.

Before proceeding with the marvelous story of my daughter's courtship, I wish to hover just a moment over the particulars of this story. It seems to me so beautiful of God to have given to me and my daughter something which could not have been imitated or imagined. It could have come only from the King of Kings!

After putting me to death as an advocate for my daughter's dreams and aspirations, He royally reaffirmed *everything* by resur-recting and tasking me as a messenger to her. In addition, this went far beyond my mere inner thoughts. In His words to me, God also testified of my daughter's waiting sacrificially upon Him, as I had in earlier years in my Navy career! He had equipped me to deliver to Suzy a promise in an area I had come to know personally was unbreakable! No man can outgive God!

34

Testimony:
A Bridegroom's Preparation
for Marriage

And after you have suffered for a little, the God of all grace, who
called you to His eternal glory in Christ, will Himself perfect,
confirm, strengthen and establish you. (1 Pet. 5:10)

"Dad, he's just like you! He even likes to backpack and plays
the guitar!" It didn't take Suzy long to begin to share her beautiful
reactions to Mitchell. She had actually met him briefly a year or so
earlier when he had dated one of her roommates. Now, however,
with a little "facilitation" on her part, they had attended an event
together and he began to ask her out. We knew from her very first
words that this guy and this situation were different.

Mitchell was thirty-six years old, never married, and had been
serving the Lord in the care of handicapped adults for about thirteen years. He stood about 6'1", weighed 210 pounds, and in addition to his backpacking, did a lot of work in the local weight rooms.
He sounded like an impressive guy, regardless of what my daughter thought. But it was not his appearance that began to win her. It
was the way he treated her. Like a Queen! He honored her in many
ways. He had never been skiing but took his first lessons from
her.[1] Suzy also liked to country dance, so Mitchell redirected his
swing dancing lessons toward the two-step and waltz. I began to

ask myself, *What would it have taken for me to take dancing lessons for Gretchen?! Does God really raise up guys like this? I'd really like to meet Mitchell!*

His treatment of Suzy on dates was respectful and considerate. He began to write her beautiful letters, including poetic comparisons of her beauty with women of the Greek classics! On an early date, an incident took place where Mitchell, momentarily absent, returned to find a man pressuring Suzy to dance with him. He had been abusive and rude. One glance at Mitchell and he melted into the background. Suzy shared all the details with us and was unabashed in her pleasure of feeling protected under Mitchell. I was exultant that she could have such an experience.

Perhaps the most stunning aspect of all this was the lovely openness of our daughter to sharing everything with us. We were now blessed by a daughter having no misgivings in consulting with us on all her joys, concerns, and questions. We heard of the first kiss (an early crisis; the second one was much longer in coming!) and of much of their conversations. Soon we entered into a whole new realm of counsel. It was a totally new dimension to our relationship, which exceeded anything I had ever asked or anticipated from God.

"Dad, Mitchell has asked me if I was willing to agree we would not date others. What should I do?"

While marveling at her caution and asking God for guidance, I thought aloud, "Well, honey, it sounds to me like he may be a little insecure and looking to you for encouragement. It seems he may want to take the risk out of his relationship with you. I don't know if that would be such a good idea." Then I spent some time explaining to her how important it was for guys to be able to find their way without special help, that there was no advantage to a girl for making it easy for them. Since at this time we didn't know much about Mitchell's love for Suzy or what kind of a man he was, it was especially important that he discover for himself what kind of risks he was willing to face for her. I concluded with, "Well, honey, you're free to make whatever decision you think is right, but thanks for discussing it with me. I'm grateful you wanted my opinion."

I did not hear for several months how Suzy had actually responded to Mitchell's request. What she said far exceeded any wisdom I had attempted to give her. What beautiful contentment and security in her reply, "I think you need to talk to my dad!"

Suzy was discreet but continued to share with us Mitchell's courtship, including his first love letter. What a guy! We visited Virginia, met him, and spent some time with him. I heard in considerable detail his testimony of God's work in his life, his conversion to Christ and subsequent discipleship, how God had made him a servant to others. His stories were beautiful.

Those who read this should rejoice in the beautifully open relationship Suzy had with us as her parents in the things she shared, remembering that Suzy was our responsibility, not Mitchell's. Somehow God had produced a level of openness which produced not only excellent discernment and protection for Suzy but also great enjoyment for us in participating in her courtship.

Evident from earlier testimony is the fact that Suzy routinely spent Christmas with us. However, this year some tension began to develop when Suzy delayed making airline reservations. It was obvious that she was uncertain how to plan for Christmas, which she preferred to spend with Mitchell, whose family was in the Washington, D.C. area. Around early October, she asked for some more advice and inquired if we might invite Mitchell out with her for Christmas. The conversation went somewhat along earlier lines, but because we would be the hosts if we consented, I had a bit more authority to speak. I gave a full explanation of the crucial importance of a potential husband's making his discoveries apart from the "helps" of the bride.

I first explained that Mitchell had made no commitment to her which would constitute a basis for such an invitation. Then I explained that an invitation without commitment on his part would be tacit encouragement of that type of relationship and further reduce the basis for his discovery whether he really loved her, that although we knew Mitchell was fond of her, we could not presume that he truly loved her. I explained that although women have an almost overpowering urge to assist romance with encouragement to the guys, this robs any would-be-bridegroom from absolutely crucial discoveries. A man's discovery of his love for a woman must be connected with discovery of the price he is willing to pay for her. What commitments will he make without commitment on her part? I also re-explained to her the scriptural basis for a bride to remain uncommitted until after the bridegroom has fully determined his love and committed accordingly, that it was fully impossible for a bride to know she is loved until after the bridegroom knows!

I appealed to her, "You do not want to defraud Mitchell of these things, nor yourself!" With these things in mind, we determined not to invite Mitchell out for Christmas.

As "luck" would have it, Mitchell raised an important issue with Suzy the following week. It was the most amazing conversation I think I've ever heard of in a romance. Mitchell wanted to know if Suzy loved him.

He declared again his affections for her and then asked her, "Do you love me?" Who would have guessed that she hadn't told this romantic guy she'd dated for nine months that she loved him? Who would have guessed that he was so eager to know? Her answer may be read at the end of this chapter.[2] But a result was that Mitchell soon phoned me.

"Mr. Duff. I want to ask your daughter, Suzy, to be my wife. May I please have your permission to ask her to marry me?" I gave him my permission and God's blessing, followed by a long, pleasant conversation. We reviewed some things not previously discussed that were important to his future success. In closing, he asked Gretchen and me not to reveal to Suzy that he had called. Indeed, he was not planning to propose until after our impending next visit to Virginia.

For some it would be worth almost another chapter to describe the details of our next visit to Virginia—how Gretchen had to remain silent in the face of close friends' and Suzy's discussions of her romance; how Mitchell provided the most romantic and mysterious plan for their evening on which he would propose to her; how Suzy was kept in uncertainty up to the very moment she opened the (inner) Limoges porcelain box in which rose petals and a ring were presented to her. Suzy's later consternation over our having full knowledge even of the details of the proposal evening was worth every minute we had kept silent. Both Suzy and Mitchell came out to visit with us at Christmas after all! The details were beautiful. Every bride and every bridegroom should have such stories!

Wedding plans proceeded into 1996. Suzy made plans to wear her mother's beautifully preserved wedding dress altered to fit accordingly. Through the final months Suzy kept sharing with us the preparations for meeting her bridegroom, intimate anxieties and questions that arose out of their marriage counseling. What father would not delight in his daughter so confiding in him? What bridegroom would not be blessed by a wife so able to trust first in her father, then in him? Many of these things are too rich for words. God is good.

And so came the wedding day. At the reception, I presented Mitchell with a glass tube containing Suzy's last pigtail, cut off when she was about eleven years old. It was a symbol of her fragility, innocence, and vision of a future bridegroom, her parents' love, and the value of the girl we had now entrusted to him. God would bless them!

What were the words Suzy spoke to Mitchell when he asked her if she loved him? She had thought for a moment, then replied, "I think that's just something I want to say to my husband."

Only God can raise up such security, confidence, and contentment in His daughters.

And hers is a man willing to risk asking a girl's father for permission to marry her without yet being told she loved him. Wow! Is that a man or not?

Simple Applications

Husbands, love your wives, just as Christ also loved the church and gave Himself up for her. (Eph. 5:25)

There are many false ideas prominent in marriage counseling that have little impact on improving a marriage relationship because they are contrary to God's design of gender and marriage. One of these is that husbands and wives must be *equally good listeners* and communicators to each other. In particular, it is especially often counseled that the husband (contrary to his nature) must learn to listen actively and attentively to his wife, who is known to have a strong desire to talk and relate to her husband. The popular idea is that paraphrasing and interpreting her statements give a wife's emotions and thoughts validation that is otherwise missing, especially during conflict, when she needs it most. However, a husband's mere listening and speaking is not adequate! For those who only listen and do not accomplish the works needed to perfect their love for their wives, there will be no resulting improvement to the marriage. And for husbands who do not listen well (who may even respond angrily), their marriages will do well if they submit to their wives' needs.

So, although it is helpful if husbands can be trained to speak female-ese, this is not the main point. The main point is they are being trained to die for their wives.

It has hopefully been effectually conveyed earlier in this book that women are designed for words. They are essentially verbal creatures who relate to the world through their ears. They measure their value and obtain their rewards through the praise they hear. They convey relationally through words and nurture. They are sexually stimulated through words. Words are the means by which a woman senses need, character, warning, relationships, direction, etc. and are even the means by which she ministers to herself—even unconsciously! It is instinctive for her to speak (or even dialogue) unconsciously and remember little of what's been spoken because it is not necessary for her to remember what has been spoken in order to derive value from words.

In order not to draw unnecessary offense from these characterizations, it is important to recognize that this instinctive, potentially compulsive, nature in the female corresponds to both the same nature of the male to derive things through his eyes and the much different symbolic and logic meanings of words as visual images for men, as also reviewed earlier in this book. These are just as deep and basic to a man's nature as the nature of hearing is to women.

Hence, when a wife is speaking, much of what she is saying is without expectation or ulterior motive. She is relating to her husband and ministering to herself. It is not really necessary that the husband relate to her at the same level at which she is speaking. If he attempts to do so, he will likely soon experience considerable frustration in discovering that it is nearly impossible to do this. Although she has a great need to speak and relate to him through words, it is not the husband's ability to paraphrase and play back her words that have significant value. The fact that he is within listening range and she can verbalize her thoughts is the key thing.

However, if there is a problem which needs fixing, the problem is different; the husband must be attentive to *do* what is needed to help his wife. It may be the washer, the kids, or an emotional need. It may come at the worst possible time and the husband's challenge may be to give up something else which seems more important. *But the husband needs to hear and take action if the marriage is to thrive.* Note also that the wife, although dearly desiring her husband to talk to her, is not normally particularly attentive to the basic information or logic of his words either, except with regard for its validation of their relationship and the genuine praise it may contain. Still, there is a requirement that she "respect" her husband. When there are things that need to be done by either spouse in support of the other, she must discipline all of her communications to this single commandment.

The dividing line between "the soul and the spirit" comes into play when the husband and wife exercise the Word of God (see Heb. 4:12). Until such a time, everything is of flesh and/or soul and produces death. But the Spirit produces life (see Rom. 8:5–9). The work of God to perfect a man and a marriage relationship enters when he becomes obedient to the commands of God. He is commanded to give himself up for his wife, even as Christ gave Himself up for the Church— requiring His death. When the husband exercises his accountability as the ultimate account-payer for the family, the supernatural work of God comes into play.

Who can explain it? Who can explain how God keeps and honors those whose hearts are set upon Him and who keep His word? Though not fully explainable, it can certainly be observed and reported.

Psychological research done at the University of Washington demonstrates that men who yield to the desires of their wives (i.e., "give in") have a better prospect for longer marriage than those who merely develop skills at listening and repeating back what a spouse is saying. The study of 130 newlywed couples over six years produced this finding, as well as the discovery that happily married couples do not normally use "active" listening.[1] The study also found that wives "who couched their complaints in a gentle, soothing, perhaps even humorous approach to the husband were more likely to have happy marriages than those who were more belligerent."

These findings confirm the Word of God. The husband is to give himself up for his wife and the wife is to respect her husband. Each husband who confronts something egocentric and selfish within himself and overcomes it for the sake of his wife invokes God's principles of "giving up himself" for his wife. God honors it, even if the man does not know God. It can be compared to learning math. One does not have to know the author of math in order to experience its benefits when learned and applied. The same thing is true of benevolent giving; whether one knows God or not he is assured of experiencing the blessings of one who "casts his bread upon the waters." The precepts are also true of a man who gives himself up for his wife.

Though not the centerpiece of this chapter, a wife should also be attentive to God's command that she is to respect her husband. Anger, scorn, manipulative control, and any other form of assumption that she can act as her husband's head or judge will produce only disaster. Conversely, if she is respectful and able to submit even under difficult circumstances (as did Sarah to Abraham, despite his despicable treatment of her), she will find herself and her family blessed, even if she does not yet know God.

National Role Reversal: The Age of Deborah

The Lord will sell Sisera into the hands of a woman. (Judg. 4:9)

We are living in a modern Age of Deborah. What does this mean? It means we live in an age when America (which is not alone) has its men emasculated through idolatry and sexual immorality. The large majority are consequently unable to perform their rightful functions. When this occurs, as in a marriage, role reversal takes place (see Isa. 3:9–12). Among God's children, God raises up gifted godly women to take the place of men.

Individual men lose their capacity to protect, provide, and govern when they pour out their seed as "streams of water in the street." The robbery of their vigor, strength, and hard-earned goods is ordained of God in accordance with Proverbs 5, as certain as death. All societies observe its effect on individuals. Now we see its effects on the scale of nations. This is the same thing that took place with Israel in the days of Judges.

After Joshua died, the Israelites went through a series of ups-and-downs spiritually and nationally. As they went their own way, each man doing "what was right in his own eyes" (see Judg. 17:6, 21:25), they suffered predations from the surrounding pagan nations. As they repented and turned to the Lord, they found relief from their enemies.

The root of their problems was in the worship of idols that replaced the true God of Israel.

God warned Joshua near the end of his life (as He had warned Moses before him) that Israel was not to "associate with these nations, these which remain among you, or mention the name of their gods, or make anyone swear by them, or serve them, or bow down to them" (Josh. 23:7). But this is exactly what Israel did after Joshua and the elders who survived him had died. They took to worshipping the idols and practicing the evil deeds that that worship involved. These idols require sexual immorality and child sacrifice, the very abominations which God had declared were to be wiped clean from the land He had given to Israel. (Notice these are the same spirits and practices which the United States of America embraces today with government sanction.) Listen to some of the citations from God against Israel:

- ". . . Israel did evil in the sight of the Lord and served the Baals" (Judg. 2:11).
- "So they forsook the Lord and served Baal and the Astartes" (Judg. 2:13).
- "For they played the harlot after other gods and bowed themselves down to them. They turned aside quickly from the way in which their fathers had walked in obeying the commandments of the Lord; they did not do as their fathers" (Judg. 2:17).
- They "forgot the Lord their God, and served the Baals and the Asheroth" (Judg. 3:7).
- "Then the sons of Israel again did evil in the sight of the Lord, served the Baals and the Ashtaroth, the gods of Syria, the gods of Sidon . . . Moab . . . etc." (Judg.10:6).

A study of the book of Judges reveals this cycle of God's judgment and Israel's repentance repeated many times. Each story has its own ramifications and lessons. The story of Deborah in particular reveals much about God's use of women when men are no longer fit for service to God.

We see in Judges, chapter 4, how God raised Deborah, the wife of Lapidoth and a prophetess as a judge over Israel at a time when "Israel had again done evil in the sight of the Lord." As a result, the "Lord sold them into the hand of Jabin king of Canaan, who reigned in Hazor; and the commander of his army was Sisera" (Judg. 4:1–2). When Israel cried out to God, He again sent them relief. Deborah was used to provide God's commandment to Israel as to how to respond to their oppressors.

She sent and summoned Barak the son of Abinoam from Kedesh-naphtali, and said to him, "Behold, the Lord, the God of Israel, has commanded, 'Go and march to Mount Tabor, and take with you ten thousand men from the sons of Naphtali and from the sons of Zebulun. And I will draw out to you Sisera, the commander of Jabin's army, with his chariots and his many troops to the river Kishon; and I will give him into your hand.'"(Judg. 4:6–7)

This is how Barak responded, "If you will go with me, then I will go; but if you will not go with me, I will not go" (Judg. 4:8).

Deborah's immediate response to this was, "I will surely go with you; nevertheless, the honor shall not be yours on the journey that you are about to take, for the Lord will sell Sisera into the hands of a woman" (Judg. 4:9).

This is the succinct summary of a nation ruined by idolatry being dealt with by God through a godly woman. Israel's army was represented by a commander that could not trust God in mortal combat without a woman going with him. Barak would not rise to the occasion of going without her. So God pronounced immediately that He would give the opposing enemy commander Sisera into the hands of a woman.

This seems to be a consistent in modern society also. God first gives opportunity to men to carry out their responsibilities and has given them design to be protectors of women and children. But when they use these attributes for evil, God (and the evil one, always seeking imitators and usurpers) raises up women in their place. We see today on college campuses where there are extremely few male students committed to sexual purity. We note an increasing proportion and numbers of college girls representing Christ in campus ministry. One of their marks is commitment to sexual purity. Ministry is being transferred into their hands.

Note also the squalor to which the armed forces of the United States has fallen, with sexual scandals on all hands, women serving alongside men in combat units and unmarried pregnancy rates of service women soaring while unit commanders publicly lie about it. A nation that would send its women into combat has fallen to greater depths than Israel in the days of Judges!

The story of Barak plays out as Deborah prophesied. Sisera flees the battlefield and hides in a tent under the nurture of a woman thought to be friendly. But, after he falls asleep, she drives a tent stake through his skull.

God is not limited. He is certainly not intimidated by using women!

Images are rich in the scripture recording this event. Listen to the poetry of the song Deborah and Barak sang afterwards in its phrases regarding Sisera. "Between her feet he bowed, he fell, he lay; Between her feet he bowed, he fell; Where he bowed, there he fell dead" (Judg. 5:27). Notice the emphasis on "bowing" and "falling," the man falling dead at the feet of a woman who had defeated and ruled over him. Does this not portray the type of relationship, submission, and death to which Sisera had fallen regarding women? Sisera had the same evil idols as Israel! How useless they were! What a warning against idolatry and immorality! His death was executed by a woman after his army had also been annihilated by an army led by a woman.

Isaiah speaks of a nation fallen because their "speech and actions are against the Lord," which thus has "brought evil on themselves." He says, "Their oppressors are children and women rule over them" (Isa. 3:8–12).

God works constantly to save, restore, and lift us up through relationship and trust in Him. We should not view God's hand as "shortened, that it cannot save" (see Isa. 59:1) through women as well as men. Other conditions also apply where biblical women were placed in authority over men, where they themselves were under a close male relative's authority and placed their lives at risk for the sake of others (see Esther and Priscilla). We should discern and cooperate with God in circumstances in which God is passing authority to women because men have failed to rise to the occasion.

Note the candidates for public office which God is raising up in your particular region. Are there not many women, both godly and ungodly? In 1996, in my region of the United States, it seemed most of the best political candidates were women, especially articulate godly women, many of whom publicly professed Jesus Christ as their Savior. Not all were elected, but some were, now serving in Congress or state legislative offices. Note other civic leadership in your community. Who are those who run the school boards, political parties, soup kitchens, "helplines," and charities and are least affected by scandal?

A minor note, possibly significant: In the cycle of sin and judgment which immediately preceded the above story of Deborah, Israel also had repented and called out to God. God then raised up Ehud the son of Gera. Ehud daringly and imaginatively gained access into the enemy king's palace, carrying a concealed weapon. Surrounded by enemies, he single-handedly slew the king and made a daring escape, then later led the Israeli forces which annihilated the enemy's army.

God records that after Deborah's and Barak's victory, God gave Israel peace for forty years. In Ehud's previous example of an extremely courageous man, God gave Israel peace for eighty years.

Section V: Reproduction of Seed

Reproduction of Seed

So shall My word be which goes forth from My mouth; It shall not return to Me empty, without accomplishing what I desire, and without succeeding in the matter for which I sent it. (Isa. 55:11)

It seem perhaps too obvious to point out, but the primary purpose of marriage recorded in the Word of God is to "be fruitful and multiply" (Gen. 1:28). Aside from its immense values of mutual support and physical, spiritual, and emotional intimacy, marriage is for reproduction. Yet most persons, even believers, are so centered upon themselves that they seldom get beyond seeing their problems in terms of their immediate relationship with their spouse. Their continuing responses to their marriage relationship meanwhile shape the environment in which their seed is raised. We are warned not to be deceived. "God is not mocked; for whatever a man sows, this he will also reap" (Gal. 6:7). These words apply to spiritual seed as well as physical seed.

Satan has pursued a constant war of destruction of mankind's earthly seed, especially the male. He started with Abel, the first offspring of Adam and Eve (Gen. 4:8), then extended it to the Egyptian destruction of all the male offspring of Israel (Exod. 1). The idolatry of Baal worship, an abomination to God, required the sacrificial burning of children. Later, Herod attempted to eradicate the Holy Offspring of Joseph and Mary by slaying all the male children of "Bethlehem and its environs" who were under two years of age (Matt. 2:16–18). Why does Satan do this? Why does harlotry produce a woman's willingness to sacrifice her own children? What is it about the seed bearing of men that so enrages Satan to this most awful destruction?

The book of Revelation depicts the dragon, Satan, seeking to devour the male child of the woman "clothed with the sun," in great labor and pain (see Rev. 12). Failing to accomplish this and enraged with the woman he "went off to make war with the rest of her offspring, who keep the commandments of God and hold to the testimony of Jesus" (Rev. 12:17). Satan hates God and fears the completion of history when God's reproduction of His own Seed through the dust of the earth is complete. It will mark the demise of Satan. Until then he is purposed to work within his limited knowledge of what God is about. God's strategy is the reproduction and raising up of godly seed (fruit) through the dust (ground that drinks the water; i.e., God's garden intended to bear fruit and receive blessing) of His children. Satan's tactic is to confound God's central design and strategy by limiting us to only raising up "thorns and thistles" which must be burned (see Heb. 6:7–8).[1]

The final chapters of this book are dedicated to a better understanding of what seed reproduction is all about; i.e., the real goal of restoration of marriage. We will first consider how the reproduction of mankind upon the earth models (or should model) the manner in which God reproduces His own likeness through His Son, Jesus Christ. His Seed is never wasted; it never fails; it is always brought to maturity in its own time. This discussion will support the idea already expressed that most of men's problems with sin derive from our failure to emulate God in the protection of our reproductive seed.

The second and related idea that will be explored is the link between regulation of gender relationships and reduction of sexual opportunity to the vitality of a society as a whole. This will also consider that the capacity of a society to comprehend God (the reality of the unseen world which influences our visible world) is directly shaped by the degree to which it regulates sexual relationships to be limited solely to within the marriage covenant.

Holy Seed

> Beloved, now we are children of God and it has not appeared as yet what we shall be. We know that when He appears, we shall be like Him, because we shall see Him just as He is. (1 John 3:2)

It offends some to suggest that "we shall be as God." As believers we seem to be well indoctrinated against the sin of Eve who sought to be like God and was tempted by Satan to accomplish this through eating of the fruit of the knowledge of good and evil. But it seems clear that God's replication of Himself in His own likeness is the very center of His revealed will in both His Creation and Redemption.

The Pharisees during the time of our Lord's earthly ministry also had aversion to any human being compared to the likeness of God. Yet it is important to note the scripture which Jesus quoted to them when they accused Him of blasphemy because "He, being a man, made Himself out to be God" (see John 10:33). He quoted a verse from Psalm 82 to them and said, "Has it not been written in your Law, 'I said, you are gods'? If he called them gods, to whom the word of God came (and the Scripture cannot be broken), do you say of Him, whom the Father sanctified and sent into the world, 'You are blaspheming' because I said, 'I am the Son of God'?" (John 10:34–36). Note that he not only validated this verse, but added His divine interpretation of what the verse meant. It identified those as gods *to whom the word of God came* and for emphasis declared that the word of God cannot be broken.

During the Creation, God first outlined His design for the reproduction of life. All life shall reproduce "seed" according to its own "kind" (or "species"; see Gen. 1:11–12, 24–25). Then he culminated His creation with man, "Let Us make man in Our image, according to Our likeness" (Gen. 1:26). One should see that God is not only explaining His desire and purpose, but also His design plan. It is God's plan to reproduce life according to seed. The foundation of His plan from the beginning was to reproduce Himself according to His Seed; that is, His Son. This is confirmed for us immediately after the fall of man when the Redeemer is revealed by His first title, "her seed," the Seed of woman, who will crush the head of Satan (see Gen. 3:15). We all recognize this as a declaration of Jesus' earthly virgin birth, by His Heavenly Father, through Mary.

So we see that God was not confounded at all by Satan's supposedly clever usurping of God's crowning creation of mankind but that God had a more grand design from the outset, which would produce eternal life through the exact likeness of His Son, who is the *sperma* of the Father, in Whom is the exact personification of His radiance, His glory, His nature, essence, and beauty, including all His creative and reproductive power (see John 1:1–14; Col. 1:15–17; Heb. 1:1–3; 2 Pet. 1:1–4). These depictions give us better understanding of what takes place when one is "born again" (John 3:3–8; 1 Pet. 1:3–4). New birth and saving faith are not an intellectual event at all, any more than origin in our mother's womb is. Life is created by the will of the Father. It is a new birth which takes place when the Word of God, the *sperma*, takes root in our hearts through belief in the Son of God, a power which is solely granted from the Father through the Holy Spirit.

We also should see the perfect relationship of the Son to the Father, always committed to do nothing of His own initiative but to speak and do only those things which the Father tells Him. This is part of the likeness of the Son that we should expect to be reproduced in those born again.

These portraits, framed in the death of the Son of God on our behalf, also give us some comprehension of the vast power and motivation of God to reproduce Himself. If He has such motivation, we should also expect it in ourselves since we are after His likeness. That is what we find; vast motivation and power placed into the human being, in God's likeness, to reproduce ourselves. These aspects pervade all aspects of our nature, though perverted. The desire to reproduce occupies all aspects of the human mind and flesh and produces great opportunity for Satan to make trouble.

What devastating contrast we see between human seed which is wasted nearly akin to nature, compared to God's Seed, Jesus, the Living Word, which is never wasted in even the smallest portion. God's word never returns void. It is always under the protection and power of the Father. It is always used only for righteous purpose, for creating life eternal in God's own likeness.

But man's seed is dispersed abroad, spilled like "streams of water in the streets" (Prov. 5:16). Lured away from the protection of fathers and elders, girls seek their own way to fulfill their God-given visions. They are deceived. Their visions become fantasies on how to find marriage and raise families. Boys also are lured to slaughter "as one in fetters to the discipline of a fool, until an arrow pierces through his liver; as a bird hastens to the snare, so he does not know that it will cost him his life" (Prov. 7:22–23). Fornication, adultery, and sexual perversion of every kind destroy individuals, then nations. Yet it is not the biological function that has failed. It is the spiritual function originally mandated by God. Sexual relations are for the purpose of reproducing life.

In the marriage covenant, human life can be created and brought to maturity under balanced male-female character strengths, teaching mercy and accountability, nurture and protection, and opening the door to seeing the character of God and the gospel. It is meant to mirror faithfulness and God's provision for true eternal life through His Son. Godly creation of life may seem foreign to a nonbeliever, but should not be to a believer. A believer "having a remnant of the Spirit" should be purposed to reproduce godly offspring. This is the admonition given in Malachi. "Not one" has divorced his wife, says the Lord, who is seeking godly offspring (see Mal. 2:14–17).

The promises are rich from Him into Whose likeness we are being formed:

- "For whom He foreknew, He also predestined to become conformed to the image of His Son, that He might be the firstborn among many brethren" (Rom. 8:29).
- "But like the Holy One who called you, be holy yourselves also in all behavior; because it is written, 'YOU SHALL BE HOLY, FOR I AM HOLY'" (1 Pet. 1:15–16).
- "We know that, when He appears, we shall be like Him" (1 John 3:2b).

Satan's purpose to diminish the glory of God's work is manifested by his attack upon the reproduction of godly seed. Therefore the central focus of his attack is upon the protective and life-giving faithfulness of marriage. The vow of "till death do us part" is fulfilled prior to mortal death through unfaithfulness, sexual immorality, and death; i.e., sexual relations prior to and outside the marriage covenant. Its almost certain outcome is divorce and the destruction of the next generation of seed. Failure to protect human "seed" in the fashion which God protects His is the central greatest failing causing the ruination of man and human society. Believing the lies of Satan, failure to protect our seed, and fostering the strongholds which acting out this nonbelief has established among us are the greatest single cause of ruination of marriage.

We must submit to God and His discipline of protecting human seed to be implanted only for the purpose of creating life within the marriage covenant, as He has with His Son, The Bridegroom.

Regulation of Offspring

But not one has done so who has a remnant of the Spirit. And what did that one do while he was seeking a godly offspring? Take heed then, to your spirit, and let no one deal treacherously against the wife of your youth. (Mal. 2:15)

In 1934, British author Joseph Daniel Unwin published an immense anthropological treatise, *Sex and Culture*, in which he cited data from nearly a hundred different societies relating cultural behavior to "sexual opportunity," that is, the degree to which sexual relations were restricted outside of marriage.[1] His purpose was to test what he viewed as a "startling conjecture" by analytical psychologists of the time who, noting psychological behavior and the patterns of history, theorized that "if social regulations forbid direct satisfaction of the sexual impulses the emotional conflict is expressed in another way, and that what we call 'civilization' has always been built up by compulsory sacrifices in the gratification of innate desires." He claimed that his work was conducted with "carefree open-mindedness" and in "all innocence," with no idea as to what the result would be. The conclusion of his study was remarkable and forced him to revise his personal philosophy.

Unwin's studies of uncivilized societies showed 100% correlation between the sexual opportunity afforded a society and its perceptions and practices regarding the unseen world (i.e., death, strange or mysterious events, and favor of the powers which control the world). Societies which permitted free sexual relationships from puberty onward, with little or no regard for marriage, unmarried pregnancy, adultery, divorce, etc. also proved to have little concept of an unseen world, except for regarding the departed spirits of the dead for some period. Societies which increasingly regulated sexual opportunity and provided disciplinary consequences to its practice outside of marriage always had more complete concepts and attentiveness regarding the unseen world and greater social energy evidenced in its accomplishments. Those societies that provided the strictest regulation of sexual opportunity also worshipped deity and had priests, temples, and practices to maintain relationship with the powers of the unseen world.

Unwin also studied the history of civilized societies, using additional concepts defining the degree and type of energy demonstrated by each society. They showed the same relationships on a more advanced scale. Increased prenuptial and postnuptial regulations regarding the consequences of sex outside of marriage always indicated increase of societies' power to advance themselves. Specifically, this energy was found to be in direct proportion to the degree to which a society adhered to both prenuptial chastity and postnuptial monogamy, especially among women, who have most influence on children during their formative years.

Based on his studies, Unwin was also able to defend his conclusion that the capacity, thought, and energy of a society were determined by its sexual regulations or lack thereof, not the other way round. Unwin summarized his findings in a general law: *The cultural condition of any society in any geographical environment is conditioned by its past and present methods of regulating the relations between the sexes.* Further elaboration of Unwin's supporting conclusions, as well as details of his definitions, methods, and findings are contained in Appendix C.

Why are these data important to us now? Because they provide both corroborative evidence and explanation of the same influences visible today. Rampant teenage fornication and sexual licentiousness throughout our nation are destroying not only the foundations of successful marriage but also dissipating our wealth, energy, and strength. Faith in the God of the Bible is disappearing in favor of secular values and laws. Unregulated sexual freedom is blazoned from television, magazines, public schools, newspapers, and movies. Laws against adultery, alienation of affection, and statutory rape have essentially disappeared. Parental control laws have been gutted and minimum ages of consent reduced to typical ages of thirteen or fourteen years of age. There is essentially no societal regulation of relations between the sexes except for what little parents may still provide. If there is to be a future for our children and nation, it is crucial that regulatory reduction of sexual opportunity, especially prenuptial opportunity among youth, be reasserted.

There is additional persuasive data which suggests that parental involvement and regulation have dramatic influence on sexual practices and outcomes for their children. Following is a summary of data relating to sex education and regulations for dating among American youth from studies of the late 1980's.[2]

1. Delay of dating reduces likelihood that girls will become involved sexually as teens. Girls that commence dating at age twelve were nearly six times (over 90%) as likely to become involved in sexual intercourse as teenagers than those who did not date until age sixteen (16%). Those who commenced dating at age thirteen were three-and-one-half times (54%) more likely to become involved sexually. Those who waited until age seventeen to date had least likelihood of becoming involved (under 13%).

2. Girls having had "moderately strict" numbers of rules about dating were found to have low probability of premarital sexual intercourse (13%) compared to those having "no rules" (52%), "few rules" (41%), or "moderate rules" (27%). The same trends were reflected in the strictness of discipline as well as the numbers of rules for both girls and boys.[3]

3. A *strong belief that premarital intercourse is usually or always wrong* is a contributor to adolescent virginity.

4. Adolescents living with both parents have the least permissive views of premarital sex, followed by those living with a parent who has remarried.

Overall it has been found that sexual activity and pregnancy rates have increased in relationship to public spending on all value-free "family planning"[4] sex education programs. This trend was also noted to have commenced in Sweden when such education was commenced there in 1956. In Sweden the illegitimate birth rates immediately increased in all age categories of youth except the older youth for which such sex education was not provided. This finding is consistent across all federal and state programs, the only claimed exceptions having easily been proven to have neglected such important factors as shrinking overall school populations or numbers of pregnancies ended by abortion. Many experts have concluded that the boldness of liberal sex education and contraceptive information in public education desensitizes youth to natural restraints in intragender relationships, inclining them to become more permissive and promoting sexual activity.

In contrast to the sex education programs typical of Planned Parenthood and other liberal organizations promoting sexual knowledge, pregnancy prevention, and safety rather than regulation of intragender relationships, value-based abstinence training programs show sharply opposite results. A particularly startling outcome resulted from the *Fertility Appreciation for Families* program, demonstrated in four test centers from 1983 to 1987 to more than 3,678 adolescents and 2,478 parents. The pregnancy rate of girls questioned one year after participation was 4 per thousand. This compares with 113 per thousand for girls in a Planned Parenthood Clinic and 96 per thousand reported by the Alan Guttmacher Institute program during the same period, both liberal programs.

Children should normally learn at an early age that decisions and actions bring about related consequences. Misery and grief result from bad decisions, whereas blessing and fulfillment result from good decisions. The Bible warns of this over and over (see

Deut. 28, 30). Why should something as important as reproduction of the human race be any different? By the time a child becomes an adolescent he or she should be well grounded in the values related to human sexuality. These should obviously be biblically based, but do not have to be restricted to this. Information related to disease, support or ruination of relationships, death of the unborn, poverty, education and other long-term life consequences should all be taught as potential outcomes dependent upon abstinence from sexual relations until marriage.

There is no reason in Christ that those of a previous generation repentant from sexual sin need to see their own sins reproduced in their offspring. The blood of Christ and the name of Christ have power to deliver us from generational sin, to release us from the bondage of slavery and into the freedom of the glory of the sons of God (see Rom. 8:21). Parents, be bold in addressing these issues in Christ with your children. Do not let your past sins hold you in shame and bondage. Remember that the primary fruit of your marriage is your children. Do not neglect your seed or your stewardship for God's offspring entrusted to your care. Just as you would give your life to see your children spared from physical mayhem or death, so you can and should effectually work to avoid the grievous wounds and life-long torments which will come to your children if they succumb to the evils of premarital sex.

What could be stronger parent motivation than desiring to spare your children the grief and torment of your own or previous generations? Not only the mortal lives of our children are at stake but also national survival as well. Nations which fail to regulate relationships between the sexes become weak, succumbing easily to forces which devour their people and fruits. "Do not be deceived. Your sins will surely overtake you." Consider Korah, Dathan, and Abiram (see Num. 16). Consider Achan (see Josh. 7) and all the other biblical examples whose sin caused the destruction of entire families! Consider Ahab (see 1 Kings 17–22). Consider the actions of God, Moses, and Phinehas against those who joined themselves to the Midianites in harlotry, even to the execution of Zimri and Cozbi when they pursued their fornication in the midst of a grieving nation under judgment (see Num. 25). As individuals who spill their seed on the ground "as streams of water in the street" will perish with their seed, there is also a destructive curse upon nations that do likewise and fail to change their ways.

Yet it must be admitted that most marriages in danger of dissolution have brought one or more spouse to the point where the welfare of their offspring is not sufficient to motivate them to seek the salvation of Christ for themselves, their spouse, or their seed, much less for their nation. They are locked upon themselves at the expense of all others. They need deliverance, but have thus far refused to seek the only Source, the only Person Who can set them free and preserve all that should be dear to them. Rules and formulas won't do. Procedures, acting, and cosmetic coverings won't do. Efforts to change your spouse won't do. "There is a way which seems right to a man, but its end is the way of death" (Prov. 16:25). All the ways of man result in death.

40

Death

Who will set me free from the body of this death? (Rom. 7:24)

To what degree can death be explained to a child? Of what value could it be? Or how could Romans, chapter 7, possibly aid one who has not already observed and been confounded by sin and death working through his own members? Help must generally apply to a known problem; otherwise, aid is wasted. That is why the Bible is of little effect to those not yet convicted of their sins and of their great need for a Deliverer. Hopefully, most readers know they have a sin and death problem and are seeking help because it is devouring their marriage. But even if not, the law of sin and death is working inexorably their lives, your life, and mine.

Perhaps you are over age forty and have noticed you don't have the vigor of twenty years ago. You can't run as fast; your reflexes are slower. Perhaps you are over fifty; your fingers fumble a bit more with the car keys. It's more difficult to get something into or out of a wallet, purse, pocket, or plastic bag. Soon, if not already, you will notice memory lapses, yours or those of your spouse. How long will it be before you need aids to walk or bathe? How do you feel about palsy or paralysis or dementia in yourself or your spouse? Are you prepared to bath your invalid spouse? Thomas Jefferson, near the age of eighty-five, listed in a letter to John Adams the many decays he had experienced after the age of sixty-five, stating he would not voluntarily choose to live this portion of his life over again.

Have you yet experienced the aging and death of a parent—or one of their contemporaries? Did you notice that dissolution of their bodies and personalities tended to go hand-in-hand? Strength and coordination fail. Plans and activities diminish. Communications fade. Bad habits get worse. Death pervades all. Connecting relationships with others as well as temperance, reasoning, and cooperation drop away like leaves as the faculties of the aging person disintegrate. People become more childlike, self-centered, and demanding. Bad behavior once under a veneer becomes more overt. Anger, frustration, and isolation tend to increase. This is the death process. It is the same process that enters into marriage, driving the husband and wife apart, deeper into anger, frustration, and isolation. They are dying because sin and death are inexorably working through them as it does in all of us in accordance with God's law of sin and death.

The process also intensifies with time. Things unnoticed at the time of marriage (perhaps ten to twenty years ago?) first become noticeable; ten years later they become irritants, then frustrations. We would like to remove them, but can't. Why do these things bother us now if once upon a time they weren't noticed? Perhaps it is a control issue; do we prefer to control rather than the other way round? Were we ever really in control or merely unconscious and tolerant? Perhaps young life was more of an illusion. Jesus said to Simon Peter, "When you were younger, you used to gird yourself, and walk wherever you wished; but when you grow old, you will stretch out your hands, and someone else will gird you, and bring you where you do not wish to go" (John 21:18).

What Jesus said to Peter is a divine summary of aging and death, a crucifixion we must all face with Peter.

Possibly what is really happening is loss of flexibility. Like young saplings and tree limbs we used to bend with adversity and grow strong in the process. Then we lose our ability with age to bend with circumstances. Change becomes viewed as adversity. We become brittle and resistant to the same forces which previously produced life and strength. As we lose flexibility, we resist being pruned by the True Vinedresser and are eventually "thrown away and burned" (see John 15:6).

Have you become stiff necked? Are you fed up with the same old problems again and again between you and your spouse? Consider what happened to Pharaoh with Moses and take warning. After many opportunities to keep his promises and yet repeatedly breaking them, "God hardened his heart" (see Exod. 6–14). He and the nation for which he was responsible, including all its first born sons, were destroyed. Like an old tree limb, "A man who hardens his neck after much reproof will suddenly be broken beyond remedy" (Prov. 29:1). Perhaps Pharaoh resented the pain and destruction he saw as his nation disintegrated. Perhaps he resented his powerlessness. Perhaps he was angry with God for not accommodating to *his* rulership (listen husbands!), *his* desires and needs (listen wives!), *his* "knowing" what was right, *his* responsibilities, *his* reputation (listen all!). Perhaps when he was asked to change his mind and ways he did not believe Moses was really speaking from the true and living God.

Do we foolishly respond as Pharaoh did?

What promises have you made? (Don't rush on; consider them.) Have you kept them or broken them? Are you becoming hard of heart? Have your members become obedient to God or enslaved as "instruments of unrighteousness" (see Rom. 6:13–16)? Have sin and its strongholds become master over you? Would you rather work things out God's way or your way? Do you know yet that your ways only produce death? Would you rather have life?

In your own power you will never get your spouse to stop spending, eat more or eat less, stop drinking, gambling, listen to you, agree with you, change their nasty habits, give up adultery, pornography, anger, foolishness, etc. You are being overtaken by the law of sin and death. You cannot overpower it, cheat it, or escape it. God has ordained that those of us born in sin will live by the law of sin and death—and die by it. So will your children.

Is there any escape?

41

Deliverance, Part I

There is no savior besides Me. (Isa. 43:11)

Two difficulties vastly reduce prospects for recovery of failed marriages. The first of these is that the marriage is frequently dead before either spouse is awakened or motivated to seek help. Selfish lusts and presumptions have blinded them to the death taking place. The protecting word of God has been stolen away by deceiving spirits, leaving one or both spouses to follow voices of destruction. Ensnared by a lover and the soulish intoxication of new "romance," at least one spouse has frequently already completed their death and mourning process. The second difficulty is that motivation for counseling is frequently for wrong reasons; a spouse merely wants to get their husband or wife back or wants to "save the marriage." The feeling of failure is great, but there is no purpose of becoming pleasing to God or aiding the other spouse. The agony of pain motivates solely to seek to relieve personal pain; it presumes merely to restore the status quo and return to control of the environment (i.e., the other spouse). Marriage counselors purposing to bring people closer to God find themselves frequently under attempted manipulation to obtain desired response in the other spouse.[1] This narrow and generally futile hope is always exposed in due time.

"What is the source of quarrels and conflicts among you? Is not the source your pleasures that wage war in your members? You lust and do not have; so you commit murder. And you are envious and cannot obtain; so you fight and quarrel. You do not have because you do not ask. You ask and do not receive, because you ask with wrong motives, so that you may spend it on your pleasures" (James 4:1–3).

We are not speaking merely of the flesh; these wars of the soul involve our intellectual, emotional, and willful desires to be like God, to act like God, to usurp God and take His place, lusts which have been with us since Eve.

Husband, you are provoked when your wife jeopardizes your finances. You don't like the way she distracts your purposes, diverts your activities, requires your deep attention to understand her or your children, pulling you away from what you want to do instead. Her actions are something you cannot *control*! Wife, you are dismayed when your husband acts "foolishly" to jeopardize your visions and desires! You exhaust every means of getting him to behave the way you want him to! You are both in the *control* game. Failing to control or manipulate, you turn to your own way at the expense of your spouse. But you are entertaining death. You are joined together. In your behavior you are denying God in the crucial matters of life. You are not trusting Him. You are providing residence in your flesh for wars to rage, leading only to more frustration and despair. You must realize you will not see God work on your behalf while you are insisting on your own power and *control as your means of deliverance*! You must seek God and His righteousness first (see Matt. 6:33). He knows you have legitimate needs. But you must seek Him first before God's promises to you can be fulfilled. God and His doing of things (in His righteous way) must come before life can follow. "But put on the Lord Jesus Christ, and make no provision for the flesh in regard to its lusts" (Rom 13:14).

There is only one Deliverer. Neither can anyone else deliver out of His hand. Idols cannot deliver. Satisfying your lusts and bitterness cannot deliver. Lying spirits cannot deliver. Emotions cannot deliver. Material possessions and reasonings cannot deliver.

God has taken great pains to help us understand that our deliverance from all things that threaten us is from Him alone.

- "Do not fear! Stand by and see the salvation of the LORD which He will accomplish for you today" (Exod. 14:13a).
- "Many are the afflictions of the righteous; But the Lord delivers him out of them all" (Ps. 34:19).
- "The salvation of the righteous is from the Lord; He is their strength in time of trouble. And the Lord helps them, and delivers them; He delivers them from the wicked, and saves them. Because they take refuge in Him" (Ps. 37:39–40).

Listen carefully to God's assurances:

Because he has loved Me, therefore I will deliver him; I will set him securely on high, because he has known My name. He will call upon Me, and I will answer him; I will be with him in trouble; I will rescue him, and honor him. With a long life I will satisfy him, and let him behold My salvation. (Ps. 91:14–16)

These scriptures only scratch the surface. We are addressing the deepest, most profound aspect of God's nature and power. *God's very essence is Salvation. His very name is Salvation.*

The "name which is above every name" (Phil. 2:9) establishes without dispute the attribute of God more important than any other. It is His power and purpose to deliver, to rescue, to save, to lift us from miry clay onto solid rock. This name is *Jesus!* The name of *Jesus* (in Greek) is *Yehoshua* in Hebrew. This literally means "Jehovah (the true and living God of Israel) is Salvation." [2] His name points literally and personally to God, the God of the Bible, as the exclusive deliverance for all things in human affairs.

But how can anyone trust God and see His deliverance while bound up in lust, bitterness, and fear, attempting to have one's own way? How can we be set free of the lies and destructive power of satanic strongholds? We must give up attempting to usurp God, to be our own deliverer, trying to fix our spouses instead of dealing with God. We must deal responsively to God with our own sin, our own behavior. We must cease trying to take the splinter out of our spouse's eyes while we are blinded to the log that is in our own. We must stop this and give it up to God, even if total exhaustion is the only means by which God can bring us to do it!

Would it not be preferable to trust God's promises and instructions before desperation leaves no alternative? But our hardness and unbelief often give God no other way to teach us the Way of Salvation. If one's knowledge of God's Word, instructions, and promises is too weak, exhaustion is the only thing that can prevail. Eventually, whether by ignorance or hardness of heart, we will always be brought to ruin trying to do things any other way.

Dear brother and sister in Christ, is this what is happening to you? What evil are you holding onto that keeps the Lord out of your relationship with your spouse? How can you possibly know our wonderful God acting on your behalf while clinging to your idols? Is it bitterness? You must forgive in Christ and close all accounts in heaven and earth—forever! Is it deceit? You must give up exaggeration, deception, secrets, and lies and come to love the truth. Is it lewdness, immorality, evil thoughts, or imaginings? You must repudiate these before witnesses in the name of Christ and cleanse your temple by the Word of God. You must stop grieving the Holy Spirit and put away factions, anger, and all the other uncleanness that defiles you. Repent; turn from your evil ways. Seek and trust God for your safekeeping; accept the loss of all you covet, if that is God's purpose. Flee to God. Become surrounded, contained in, filled, and protected within and without by the Word of God.

Dear brother or sister, yield everything dear to you up to God just as Jesus did to the Father. Give up your prerogatives. *Give up your controls,* and cast yourself upon Him who cares for you. Yield to the possibility that all your precious things may fall to the ground and be ruined. Give them to God! Don't take them back! Again, "Put on the Lord Jesus Christ and make no provision for the flesh in regard to its lusts" (Rom. 13:14).

God has promises to those eager to see the goodness of the Lord in the land of the living. He will save from despair. "Wait for the Lord; Be strong, and let your heart take courage; Yes, wait for the Lord" (Ps. 27 13–14). Wait upon the Lord. Serve Him. Let Him decide to do and to save as He chooses. His arm is not short that He cannot save. He will not fail you.

"Those who wait for the Lord will gain new strength; They will mount up with wings like eagles. They will run and not get tired. They will walk and not become weary" (Isa. 40:31). Trust Him and you will surely see the deliverance of the Lord. "Offer to God a sacrifice of thanksgiving, and pay your vows to the Most High; Call upon Me in the day of trouble; I shall rescue you, and you will honor Me" (Ps. 50:14–15).

How does one "put on" the Lord Jesus Christ? Many people, even those who have professed Christ, are ignorant of how God has provided for us to "be found" in Him. For those with a heart to hear and obey, a short biblical summary follows.

Deliverance, Part II

For you who fear My name the sun of righteousness will rise with healing in its wings. (Mal. 4:2)

Jesus Christ is the Word of God. Despite many statements of this, including the statements of John, chapter 1, many view the Bible as something separate from the Son of God and falsely believe they can have a relationship with Jesus without reading, digesting, memorizing, meditating, and acting upon the Bible as the Word of God. But this cannot be done. "Man shall not live on bread alone, but on every word that proceeds out of the mouth of God" (Matt. 4:4).

"In the beginning was the Word, and the Word was with God, and the Word was God" (John 1:1). "The Word became flesh and dwelt among us, and we beheld His glory, glory as of the only begotten from the Father, full of grace and truth" (John 1:14). The very radiance of the glory of God and the "exact representation of His nature" are imprinted in the Word of God, Jesus Christ made flesh (Heb. 1:3).

Many do not realize that Christ as a living Person must be eaten in order for them to live. As the children of Israel had to eat of the sacrificed Passover Lamb to have strength to walk out of their slavery in Egypt, so God's children must eat of Christ to have strength to escape and subsequently resist the evil one. Lack of spiritual comprehension made this thought seem offensive and drove many to leave Christ during His work on earth and does so likewise today (see John 6). As with all food given for the life of those who eat it, God also required the actual death of Jesus' human flesh for our sins. Because His death was accomplished "once for all" and He is now resurrected; we now live by consuming Him through the Bible, while representing the actual consumption of His flesh and blood in the sacraments of Holy Communion. This is the beginning of understanding of the mystery of Jesus' oft-repeated commandment to His true disciples that we are to be found "in Him" and He "in us."

The second crucial aspect of being found "in Christ" is in obeying His commandments.

We are not here speaking of salvation. We are speaking of the fruit bearing of those who so "prove to be His disciples" (John 15:8). According to Scripture, there are many saved who bear no fruit. This is forewarned in the parable of the seeds (Luke 8:1–15). Only the first of four categories of seed sowed by the sower fails to sprout and produce new life. This is the category that applies to the devil's coming and taking "away the word from their heart, *so that they may not believe and be saved*" (Luke 8:12, emphasis added). The remaining three categories of seeds spread by the sower all sprout into new life, *but only one of the three bears fruit*. As Jesus describes, the other two categories either (1) "have no firm root; they believe for a while, and in time of temptation fall away" (Luke 8:13) or (2) "are choked with worries and riches and pleasures of this life, and bring no fruit to maturity" (Luke 8:14).

In fact, by analogy we recognize that all seeds which sprout in the earth eventually die. The distinction is whether or not they bear reproductive fruit!

I believe these two categories failing to reproduce seed apply to many professing Christ, but who are nevertheless undergoing the destruction of their lives, offspring, and marriages through divorce. It may be that one or more spouse once believed in Christ unto salvation, but they failed as disciples of Christ. They may attend church and act out a form of piety, but are no longer connected to the Vine. As they do not bear fruit they are taken away by the Vinedresser, are thrown away as a branch and are dried up. Their judgment is in John 15:6. They are "cast into the fire and burned" (John 15:6).

This judgment sounds nondoctrinal to many who have falsely believed that once saved all the issues of their lives in Jesus Christ have been resolved. They have confused positional salvation with the working out of their salvation, which remains to be done (see Phil. 1:6, 2:12). They have confused birth, which is determined solely by the father, with discipleship as children in a mutual relationship. They have neglected to hear or respond to the doctrine of sanctification (setting themselves apart for Christ) which applies to the rest of their lives. Assured of eternal salvation, they may have no further heart for serving Jesus out of love. But Jesus assures us, regardless of how we came to salvation, that such a love is the only criteria sufficient to keep us in Him. "If you love Me, you will keep my commandments" (John 14:15; see also John 14:21, 14:23–24, 15:10).

Again, the issue is not salvation. It is fruit bearing. Other warnings are found in the prophecies of judgment by fire of all men's works separating those founded in Christ and those which are not. "If any man's work which He has built upon (Christ) remains, he shall receive a reward. If any man's work is burned up, he shall suffer loss; but he himself shall be saved, yet so as through fire" (1 Cor. 3:14–15). This destruction by fire of all fruit not in Christ is further seen in the judgement by fire of the seedbed ground described in Hebrews, chapter 6:

> For ground that drinks the rain which often falls upon it and brings forth vegetation useful to those for whose sake it is also tilled, receives a blessing from God; but if it yields thorns and thistles, it is worthless and close to being cursed and it ends up being burned (Heb. 6:7–8).

When burned, the ground, i.e., the seedbed of the dust of the earth watered by God, is not destroyed, though "close to being cursed." It is its fruit which is burned up.

Other scriptures indicate that disciples of Christ may be "disqualified" and that rewards of service are based upon completion of the race (1 Cor. 9:23–27; Gal. 2:2; Heb. 12:1). Still others emphasize that "overcoming" the temptations, worries, and pleasures of this life are key to receiving the richest rewards of God's Kingdom (Rev. 2:7, 2:17, 2:26, 3:5, 3:12, 3:21).

Those whose lives are being devoured *should not presume they are in a discipling relationship with Christ*, if indeed they ever were. Divorce is not even the issue. They may not be born again into new life. Or, if they indeed were once truly born again and have tasted the beauty and power of Christ, it is possible that they have fallen away and cannot again be won to Christ. According to the Bible, these who once were "...enlightened and have tasted of the heavenly gift and have been made partakers of the Holy Spirit, and have tasted the good word of God and the powers of the age to come, and then have fallen away, it is impossible to renew them again to repentance, since they again crucify to themselves the Son of God, and put Him to open shame" (Heb. 6:4–6).

Those with reverent fear that the above may be true or who are concerned with having a relationship with Christ in which their lives can ever again bear fruit in this world should prayerfully turn to God and seek the only Salvation, the only safe place, Jesus Christ. God's impregnable Fortress is Jesus Christ! No assault by the enemy, no destruction can reach us when we are in Him! (see Ps. 91).

What are God's provisions for being found within the Stronghold who prevails against all other strongholds? How may we be "in Him" and He "in us"? We must be willing to follow Christ's example of His love and obedience to the Father. The following teachings are not metaphors or euphemisms. We must serve Christ as Christ served the Father, unto death.

Jesus gave His disciples strong teaching following the Last Supper just before His death, then went out into the night and completed his demonstration of all He had taught. He addressed the central issues over which His disciples were confounded and did not yet comprehend. Upon what did Jesus focus? His disciples (1) did not comprehend serving others with their lives (John 13). They (2) did not comprehend that He was going away or why, and (3) they did not comprehend the same issue we face, the issue of Jesus being "in the Father" and the Father "in Him" (see John 14:1–11). In John 13 through 17 are Jesus' concentrated instructions regarding *His example of love, obedience, and death,* as a condition for resolving the above issues. It is through living in Christ in the same manner that He dwelt in the Father that we may dwell (abide) in Him. Christ's instructions are summarized below:

- "A new commandment I give to you, that you love one another, even as I have loved you, that you also love one another" (John 13:34).
- "If you love Me, you will keep My commandments" (John 14:15).
- "He who has My commandments and keeps them, he it is who loves Me; and he who loves Me shall be loved by My Father, and I will love him, and will disclose Myself to him" (John 14:21).
- "If anyone loves Me, he will keep My word; and My Father will love him, and We will come to him, and make Our abode with him" (John 14:23).
- "He who does not love Me does not keep My words; and the word which you hear is not Mine, but the Father's who sent Me" (John 14:24).
- "But that the world may know that I love the Father and as the Father gave Me commandment, even so I do. Arise, let us go from here" (John 14:31).[1]
- "Every branch in Me that does not bear fruit, He takes away; every branch that bears fruit, He prunes it, that it may bear more fruit" (John 15:2).
- "Abide in Me, and I in you. As the branch cannot bear fruit of itself, unless it abides in the vine, so neither can you, unless you abide in Me. I am the vine, you are the branches;

he who abides in Me, and I in him, he bears much fruit; for apart from Me you can do nothing" (John 15:4–5).

- "Just as the Father has loved Me, I have also loved you; abide in my love. If you keep my commandments, you will abide in My love; just as I have kept My Father's commandments, and abide in His love" (John 15:9–10).
- "This is My commandment, that you love one another, just as I have loved you. Greater love has no one than this, that one lay down his life for his friends" (John 15:12–13).
- "You are My friends, if you do what I command you" (John 15:14).
- "This I command you, that you love one another" (John 15:17).

Why would Jesus have given commandment to love if love is merely an emotion? Isn't love actually a right response in supporting life in others?[2] These instructions contain the secret of how to put on and live in Christ. We obey Him! We keep His word. His own actions and prayer to the Father in John, chapter 17, conclude of Jesus' provisions for His disciples to live in and be glorified in Him. Then He illustrates! Jesus goes to His death, for our sake, because He loved us and the Father.

Those struggling with discipleship and with loving their spouse would do well to memorize all the above chapters and to seek to lay hold of the love that Jesus had for His Father in laying down His life for us when we hated Him.

Apart from Christ, we can do nothing. Why should we attempt saving our marriage or any marriage if we are not in Christ? It will all be without fruit and destroyed by fire anyway. All of Christ's promises of His future presence, answer to prayer, and revelation in the lives of His disciples just prior to His death consummate in the question of whether or not we will bear the fruit of Christ. If we love Him we will seek to keep His commandment — to love one another just as He loved us. We cannot run from our failure to keep his commandment by attempting to persuade God that it is just too hard. We must instead identify and remove the iniquity in our hearts that makes war against our souls and prevents us from loving God and our spouse as Jesus loved us. Witnesses and helpers can assist us to do this, but it must start with our purpose to be clean in the Word of God and to be right with Him. This requires "confession" (i.e., agreement with God on what the truth is) so we can be cleansed from our unrighteousness and forgiven for our sins (1 John 1:9).

The Word of God also tells us that God is a "rewarder of those who seek Him" (Heb. 11:6), that the effective "prayer of a righteous man can accomplish much" (James 5:16), that iniquity or wrong motives can block the answers to prayer (see Ps. 66:18; James 4:3). Dealing harshly with a wife can cut a husband off from answers to prayer (see 1 Pet. 3:7). We must be humbled in the presence of God as a condition of receiving His grace (James 4:6; 1 Pet. 5:5). One beautiful and effectual means of humbling ourselves before God is to express gratitude, to sing His praise and give thanks for what great things He has done for us. The Lord inhabits the praises of His people. Many believers refuse to do this, being too proud, therefore finding themselves disagreeing with the truth and cutting themselves off from God.

Do you see dear brothers and sisters that the manner of our salvation does not define our response to Jesus Christ? We may have come to Christ through fear of hell, intellectual conviction, signs and wonders, or teaching and indoctrination running back as far as childhood. All these have nothing to do with discipleship! Discipleship has only to do with whether or not we love God to desire to please Him. If our response to salvation is only to gain for ourselves (what we selfishly covet) then we can bear no fruit. If we are unable to respond in love to what He has done for us, all the new life He has given to us will be wasted and choked out. Like Pharaoh, we will be useful only as examples of those who hardened their hearts against God, that others might not do the same! You must make a solid, truthful appraisal of your responses to God regarding the above scriptures.

Spend time seeking God. Many would not think of cutting themselves off from fellowship with their employer or friends and yet they spend no quality time with God. How would you determine the instructions of your employers without spending time with them? How could your children discover your intentions without doing likewise? Seek to find out God's will in order to do it, to bring the Lord pleasure and to imitate Him (Matt. 7:24–27; Rom. 12:1–2; 2 Cor. 5:9; Eph. 5:1). Those who think they know God but do not seek to please Him are trying to deal with Him in the abstract, according to their own imaginings rather than reality. They neither know Him nor love Him because they do not dwell in His Word.

Yet God is merciful. He is our Deliverer because He is of that nature and purpose, not because we are able to smoothly and skillfully handle our appeals to Him. He seeks broken and contrite hearts. He will not turn away those who are broken in spirit, who seek cleansing in the Lord (see Ps. 51). His righteousness is our Salvation.

How can two walk together unless they be agreed? (see Amos 3:3). Would God agree that your mate is too difficult to love? Would He agree you have humbly sought His aid and power to love? Would He agree you have been honest about your weaknesses, sins, and even your true intentions?

Who puts on a yoke unless they trust their yoke mate?

Section VI: Strength
and Encouragement

Propitiation

If God is for us, who is against us? (Rom. 8:31)

There is a popular lie that pervades the Church, indistinguishable from that which also pervades the unbelieving world—which knows no true God. Until this lie is destroyed, it will always prevent obedience to God's Word in the area most critical to receiving the fullness of His power and in carrying out the precepts of this book in healing marriage. The lie is that God's forgiveness (and hence, our forgiveness which is to be in His likeness) creates *neutrality* toward the person being forgiven. But this is not true at all. It is a lie about God and a lie about what He is reproducing in us.

To a large extent this same lie is reproduced in other ways, too. For instance, it is a popular belief that there are three dominions: God's, man's, and Satan's. There is the false idea that one can avoid God or Satan and merely go one's own way. But this is not what the Bible says, is it? The Bible says there only two masters and you must either serve one or the other. It also says, "You are the slaves of the one whom you obey, either of sin resulting in death, or obedience (to God) resulting in righteousness" (Rom. 6:16). The whole idea of a "neutral zone" is preposterously against the nature of God and of His creation.

So where do we get off track? Part of the difficulty is that in learning of God's forgiveness, we grasp only part of what He has done for us in the blood sacrifice of the Son of God. We are taught that God through Christ "takes away our sins" (John 1:29), "cleanses us from all sin" (1 John 1:7), has "put away sin" (Heb. 9:26), etc., but we are not as clearly taught that He has reversed the power and effects of sin upon us. We are taught that sin is *expiated* (rubbed out, made to "vanish") but not that it is *propitiated* (used for propitious favor in our lives). But this is the whole truth: God does not merely remove sin and its effects from us in Christ (which would be great and wonderful enough!), but reverses the whole scenario of our sin and its outplaying in our lives to work gloriously *in our favor*; to shape us into the wonderful image of Jesus Christ. Forgiveness of sin has taken us from God's wrath to God's unrestrained and full outpouring of favor on our behalf. There is no neutral zone.

Another part of the problem is that the word *propitiation* is seldom used anymore. In English, because of its unmistakable prefix, it is clearly a positive, favorable word, much like *promise, provide, promote, prosper* or even *proton* (denoting the positively charged subatomic particle as opposed to its mate, the *neutron* which is neutral). Many modern Bible translations have dropped the word *propitiation* and substitute instead words less clear.[1] To gain better understanding of the true biblical meaning of God's character of *reversing the effects of evil*, it is useful to consider the evil actions of Joseph's brothers and Joseph's own summary of it. "And as for you, you meant evil against me, but God meant it for good in order to bring about this present result, to preserve many people alive" (Gen. 50:20). The outcome of the story of Job, the Exodus, the Babylonian captivity, the lives of David, Saul of Tarsus, and others in the history of the Bible, as well as our own lives all illustrate how God is able to transform evil into something gloriously good beyond our wildest imaginations (see Eph. 3:20).[2] Doctrinally, Paul reviews it all thoroughly in Romans, summarizing with Romans 8:28 ("And we know that God causes all things to work together for good to those who love God, to those who are called according to His purpose") and concluding the chapter by explaining its stupendous meaning.

Think for a moment of how immeasurably greater is a God who does not merely erase our sinful actions (either their effects or our memories, as we well know) but who maintains masterful sovereignty over each sordid event meant for evil and uses it for good instead! A God who accomplishes the former is great indeed, but One Who, moment by moment, for every event in our lives (and in all those around us who believe, as well, simultaneously), is committed, wise, and powerful to mold us all into righteousness, keeping our memories intact to observe all this and praise Him for it is immensely greater than one who erases! It is one of God's great self-attributes that He uses all things to reveal His glory and that He uses evil to shape us into the image of His Son.

Where we get into trouble is in attempting to forgive others in a totally different way than God does. We attempt to find a neutral zone, where our emotions and thoughts can be left alone and where we can similarly leave the person who has wronged us alone also. How self-centered and disconnected from people that leaves us! We seek to be content just to have our anger, pain, or bitterness removed or reduced to the point where we can merely tolerate thoughts of the other person, while "going on with the rest of our lives." But, the idea of working in favor of the person usually never occurs to us.

Yet it is crucial to joy in Christ to pass through neutral and undertake attitudes of favor for those who wrong us. As with a horse drawing a wagon, it is not satisfactory to merely find a place where we can stand slack in the traces where the wagon does not draw us backward. We must pull positively on the traces to move the wagon forward. There is no neutral zone.

Anyone who has been grievously hurt by the intentional or thoughtless wound of a relative or friend knows of the failure to find peace and freedom in merely "forgiving," where forgiveness means only "letting go." It may provide a few minutes or hours of peace, but soon returns with a flood of mental turmoil and stomach acid nearly as fresh and painful as the initial wound. This is especially true when prayers of forgiveness include some assumption or provision that "God take care of the other person." This will not work, because God demands our favor for the other person and has clearly spelled it out in the gospels as well as portray it in His own nature.

"Whatever you bind on earth shall have been bound in heaven; and whatever you loose on earth shall have been loosed in heaven" (Matt. 18:18). "If you forgive the sins of any, their sins have been forgiven them; if you retain the sins of any, they have been retained" (John 20:23). If there is any thought that God expects us to fall short of His perfection and standard, it is removed in these words:

> You have heard that it was said, 'You shall love your neighbor, and hate your enemy.' But I say to you, love your enemies, and pray for those who persecute you in order that you may be sons of your Father who is in heaven; for He causes His sun to rise on the evil and the good, and sends rain on the righteous and the unrighteous. For if you love those who love you, what reward have you? Do not even the taxgatherers do the same? And if you greet your brothers only what do you do more than others? Do not even the Gentiles do the same? Therefore you are to be perfect, as your heavenly Father is perfect. (Matt. 5:43–48)[3]

Human attempts to find neutrality fall short of the grace of God; they may in time produce scabs of outer normalcy but will conceal roots of bitterness (Heb. 12:15). Nor can they ever produce the true fruit of the kingdom of God, which is Christ in us, the hope of glory. This is the real pay dirt of God's economy, reproducing Christ in us. Since God has propitiated our sins, we are to do likewise with others who do evil against us, using them for good in their lives. It is the sure proof that we are children of God.

Husbands are warned against becoming embittered against their wives (Col. 3:19). Wives are asked to do their husbands good and not evil all the days of their lives (Prov. 31:12). These things are impossible without true forgiveness, where the heart of the spouse continues to always work in favor of the partner. For those who have entered marriage with abuse, sexual sins, and damaged relationships that have never been reconciled, it is essential that Christ be given full obedience in making propitiation for those who have caused the destruction. Go to work in prayer, intercession, and activity on their behalf. Get down to business and don't just talk about it. Write it out, fast and pray, and work with witnesses, if necessary, but do not leave this crucial work of Christ undone. If He Who is the Seed lives in us, His fruit will propitiate sin through us and be unmistakably different from the so-called forgiveness which the world produces, which is more akin to *forgetfulness*.

Ultimately, an ability to forgive and propitiate is far superior to an ability to "forgive and forget." In the demonic warfare which takes place among sinful and damaged spouses, it is the key to demolishing Satan's strongholds. "Love never fails" (1 Cor. 13:8). "Do not be overcome by evil, but overcome evil with good" (Rom. 12:21).

An Aspect of Grace

For by grace you have been saved through faith; and that not of yourselves, it is the gift of God; not as a result of works, that no one should boast. (Eph. 2:8–9)

Strong attempts have been made by the Protestant Church to clarify and resolve the doctrinal paradox of salvation's elements of "choice" by God (of the elect) on the one hand and "choice" by man of Jesus Christ on the other, whereby His atoning sacrifice as God's personal solution for his sin is accepted and one's adoption into the family of God is resolved. There nevertheless arises constant confusion over the position and role of the will of man in salvation.

Perhaps the most noteworthy historic event on this subject was the Synod of Dort in 1618–19, in which the Reformation Church of Holland, with representatives from England, Scotland, Germany, and Switzerland, dealt at length with the doctrine of Arminianism, which held that God's offer of grace to man was universal rather than limited to the elect and that man by his free will could accept or reject God's provision for salvation. After over six months of debate, the Reformation Church ruled that Arminianism was heretical to true biblical doctrine. It reaffirmed its belief in Calvinist doctrine which holds that God has predestined His elect, the Church of Jesus Christ, to their calling in Christ and that His grace is provided for the empowerment of their response to His revelation and offer of salvation.

Though the Arminian view was rejected and its remonstrators removed from church office, the view was later published and by 1630 its followers received religious toleration. Later, in 1795, it received official Netherlands recognition.

Today, the Arminian view is well implanted in evangelical and pentecostal churches and tends to quickly arise in any aspect of discussion regarding issues of man's obedience to God, either in response to salvation or subsequent growth in discipleship in Jesus Christ. Statements such as, "God will never overrule man's will" or "Man always has free will to choose as he desires, including rejecting Christ" are continually put forward in attempts to explain relationships of men and God, as though these views are really a fundamental doctrine of the Bible. The history of the Synod of Dort, alone, ought to illustrate that this is an extremely questionable view.

The Bible is filled with statements quite contrary to the idea that man's will can successfully resist God's. These include clearly stated precepts that God chooses whom He wishes (Deut. 7:6–7, 14:2, 18:5; 1 Sam. 10:24, 16:8, 9, 10; Ps. 89:3; John 6:37, 44, 15:16), hardens and softens the hearts of those He wishes (Exod. 7:3, 7:22, 8:32, 9:7, 9:12, 9:35, 10:1, 10:27; Josh. 11:20; John 12:40; Rom. 9:18), and loves some and rejects others (Exod. 33:19; Hos. 1:10, 2:23; Mal. 1:2–3; Rom. 9:19–24). It extends from one extreme of the futility of resisting God's judgment to the extreme that His love can overcome all things (1 Cor. 13:7–8; John 16:33). The idea that man's will can somehow confound and frustrate God in His desire for us one way or the other has been characterized as another of the many self-exaltations of man for himself, who continually constructs false idols or ideas not correctly portraying God's character, purpose and power, or His relationships with men.

The Bible also reveals that response to the gospel, even in its repudiation by unbelievers, is according to the precept that all those appointed to eternal life believe (Acts 13:46–48) and that those appointed were predestined from before the foundation of the world (Rom. 8:29; Eph. 1:4–6).

God also gives us a most outstanding specific example of His capacity to transform the heart of one hardened toward Him, if He so chooses. This example involves, historically, the most stiff-necked, murderous, and vicious enemy of Christ recorded in the Bible, in whom education, lineage, reputation, self-righteousness, zeal, and all the other attributes of position and influence which support a hardened heart must exceed any other character described in its pages. This is Saul of Tarsus.

Saul of Tarsus was as bound as any man in spiritual blindness, traditions, and the law of Moses and perhaps more deceived in believing that his persecution of the Church was serving God's righteousness. Yet, in a moment of time, in a face-to-face appearing of the Lord Jesus Christ, all of this vanished. From the instant of his confrontation and the identification of Whom he was facing, Saul responded in complete obedience to the same Lord he had previously denied (Acts 9:1–8). Where is the will of man to be found in the account of Saul's conversion? Was it not overwhelmed and subordinated to the awesome presence of Christ? Whose will prevailed? If even Saul could not resist such revelation, how could any other man to whom God should choose to reveal Himself in such a fashion?

And yet one can always point to the other Pharisees not ultimately reached and the outstanding example of Judas Iscariot who spent three years in the company of Jesus Christ. He was exposed to His personality, character, miracles, and teaching as well as many other signs of love and endearment which Jesus proffered upon him personally (including the washing of his feet and offering of the sop at the last supper, the night he betrayed Him). Yet he was unable to respond to Jesus' love and to attain to a saving relationship with His Savior, the Messiah. Why did his heart remain hardened?

We have many other examples also, where it appears some people were enabled to choose God (Joseph, Rahab, Joshua, Ruth, Nebuchadnezzar, etc.) and others were not (Korah, Dathan, and Abiram, Achan, various kings of Judah and Israel, etc.). Scripture records that the decisions and attitudes were made by the people involved; ". . . choose for yourselves today whom you will serve . . . but as for me and my house, we will serve the LORD" (Josh. 24:15). But were these individuals really acting on their own; i.e., independent of God? Scripture also says that the hearts of kings are as rivers of water, that God turns them wherever He wishes (see Prov. 21:1). He says that Scripture, itself, serves as "examples," "shadows," and "patterns" of truth given for our instruction (1 Cor. 10:6; Heb. 4:11, 8:5; James 5:10; 1 Pet. 2:21; Jude 7) and that all Scripture is "profitable...for training in righteousness" (2 Tim. 3:16). God has given us these histories for our instruction as children of God!

Jesus Himself said clearly that He did not have power or authority to call everyone to Himself, but rather, "No one can come to Me, unless the Father who sent Me draws him" (John 6:44). We see, therefore, that the revelation of Christ Himself to Judas was not sufficient to change his hardened heart. The Father did not draw Judas.

Paul himself, the murderer of Tarsus, seems to have comprehended the means by which God chooses men by His sovereign will, enabling them to respond to His purposes. It is by *grace*. Without God's grace we are left unable to see God or respond to our helplessness. We remain lost in our sins, subject to the prince of this world, lost to his deceptions and the futile lusts of the mind and the flesh which are his dominion among the lost (Eph. 2:1–3). But by grace, God enables the saved (Eph. 2:8) to believe and receive life! More than any other person, Paul seems to have comprehended this and he repeats, over and over, the *means* by which God called him and granted him faith in Christ.

- "But when He who had set me apart, even from my mother's womb, and called me through His grace, was pleased to reveal His Son in me. . . ." (Gal. 1:15).
- ". . . to the praise and glory of His grace, which He freely bestowed on us in the Beloved...the forgiveness of our trespasses, according to the riches of His grace, which He lavished upon us" (Eph. 1:6–8).

- "... according to the gift of God's grace which was given to me according to the working of His power. To me, the very least of all saints, this grace was given, to preach to the Gentiles the unfathomable riches of Christ" (Eph. 3:7–8).

Moreover, Paul invokes and teaches grace consistently and repeatedly through all of his writings. Of 128 references to *grace* made in the New Testament, Paul authors 89 of them. He also exhibits a consistent pattern in its invocation in his writings, which no other author employs. That is, he invokes it at both in the opening and closing of *all* of his writings![1] Why does he do this?

Perhaps realizing that his salvation rested solely on God's grace sovereignly granted to Him, Paul also recognized that his own ministry would be futile unless God's grace was also granted to those to whom he in turn apostled. Paul thus refers to the "stewardship of God's grace" (Eph. 3:2) which was given to him for those to whom he ministered. Hence, he invoked grace upon the readers of all of his letters at their opening and he closed with the invocation of enabling grace upon the responses of those he touched. Here is something we should remember in our prayers.

As a final example for our contemplation, there is yet another object of God's affection whom God has hardened—temporarily. That is Israel, whom he has shut up in hardness until the "fullness of the Gentiles has come in" (see Rom. 11:7–25). Then God promises to transform the entire nation, the entire remnant of which has been saved for that day. And *He promises to do it in a single day!* How can even God possibly do such a thing in a single day?

We read in Zechariah the following words:

And it will come about in that day that I will set about to destroy all the nations that come against Jerusalem. And I will pour out on the house of David and on the inhabitants of Jerusalem, the Spirit of grace and supplication, so that they will look on Me whom they have pierced; and they will mourn for Him, as one mourns for an only son, and they will weep bitterly over Him, like the bitter weeping over a firstborn. In that day there will be great mourning in Jerusalem…and the land will mourn . . . by themselves; all the families that remain, every family by itself, and their wives by themselves. (Zech. 12:9–14)

We see it again! Grace is an Old Testament promise! It is the grace of God that melts hardened hearts, even to the extent of calling an entire nation in a single day!

Where then is the "will of man," either individually or collectively? It is explicitly ruled out regarding birth, on earth and in Heaven. Only the will of God is involved (see John 1:12–13). It may indeed remain sovereign in the soul of man to resist all evidences of God's reality and provision, including His divine Word, lacking God's grace. But when God's grace is bestowed, man's will is swallowed up in the will of God. A bride's doubtful heart may be overcome and her will melted by a revelation of her lover's true love, some certain proof of her value to him and his heart for her. So can our hearts be won by God's own revelation of His love for us. God Himself is the enabler of the human heart, providing the power to believe.

Now is the time of God's grace. "To you it has been granted for Christ's sake…to believe in Him…." (Phil. 1:29). It is the time of the purification of His bride.

May the fullest measure of God's grace be given to those who read these pages, who purpose to be the complete men and women of God to which our Father has called them, to hunger and thirst after His righteousness, and to seek His face diligently. God, grant us grace to be enabled by Your great power to hear Your voice and respond to Your work of building Your kingdom in our lives and our seed. To the glory forevermore of Him who redeemed us, Jesus Christ. Amen.

Epilogue

Allegory of Death for Wives

> This mystery is great; but I am speaking with reference to Christ and the church. (Eph. 5:32)

Mortar concussions shake the earth, methodically coming closer to the soldier. He is face down, pressed as close to the ground as possible. Bullets fly overhead. Nearby, other men are dying, their moans and calls for "Medic!" going unanswered as the enemy fire pins them down. Critical help is not available. Reinforcements are already committed. Medics are committed. Rescue is not possible. Mothers and wives are thousands of miles away.

Enemy fire is reducing their ranks, but a response is required. The mortars are coming closer. To remain immobilized means death. A decision to move against the enemy means potentially the same thing. What is to be done? Others are dying around him or paralyzed with fear. The soldier is impressed with the need for action and his last previous orders to advance against the enemy. He rises up, firing his weapon as he runs toward them. He is hit and falls to the ground. He lies there wounded, his life ebbing away. He dies alone, without comfort, in a place far from his loved ones, sharing death with the others around him.

This story is not merely a story of death, which always bears similarities of senselessness and futility regardless of where or how death occurs (see Luke 13:1–5). It is also a specific portrait of combat over the past forty or fifty centuries. It is a *type* of all death of most men killed in conflict over issues for which they've been obligated to defend with their lives. Whether in defense of families or entire nations, soldiers are seldom in company with the precious ones they are defending. While men face a common fate, they each die alone. Regardless of their attitudes, they all face death, either paralyzed with fear or obeying their orders. Death itself is ultimately inescapable. It is the fate of men.

This is by God's design. Death is a unique function for which men are designed in their conduct of defense of wives and little ones. It is the function of a shield to take the mortal blows intended for those it protects. Men instinctively recognize this as their responsibility. It comes with their turf; i.e., their territory. *Territory rightfully belongs only to those willing to die in rightfully defending it.* It is the mark of a true shepherd, one who lays down his life for his sheep. He does not attempt to transfer the job to a hireling for wages (John 10:11–14).

It is the manner and the position in which the Son of God carried out His successful defense of mankind, interceding for our lives with His life and setting for us an example. "For you have been called for this purpose, since Christ also suffered for you, leaving you an example for you to follow in His steps" (1 Pet. 2:21). He did it alone, with only the shallowest support from his three closest disciples before all twelve abandoned Him (Mark 14:50). It is the manner in which all men are called to live and die for their wives (Eph. 5:25–33). A successful man stands and dies alone, isolated from all except the Lord. Jesus died without even the fellowship of His Father.

The advanced destruction of American society is now well marked by the strident call to authorize armed combat in the armed forces by women, called for by enemy spirits who would have women defend our men and little ones! Where are our men? They are busy indulging their flesh and fleeing their responsibilities! Manhood is dead in a nation that sends its daughters to combat!

There is a deep-seated desire by all men to cling to life and to gain recognition for their good deeds. Both of these are put to death in the unique manner in which a man is called to die for his wife. Others close by can scarcely see the things in which a man yields his life for her sake. The invisible sword of God, working through his wife, her methods, habits, and fallen nature constantly cuts away at his secret places, exposing his strongholds and confronting him with decisions for which there are no real witnesses except the eye of God. A man can attain fellowship and counsel, but there will be little specific understanding or vicarious support from other men having other wives, men who are not tasked with dying for *his* wife.

His wife is also blind to it, a natural situation which seems to produce many difficulties for a husband. A man would like to have recognition for his sacrifices and receive understanding appreciation from his wife as to what he does for her. However, what kind of sacrifice would it be if a man were being praised while being crucified? As pointed out in the chapter on Affirmation, men are not designed or purposed to receive affirmation or fulfillment through the praise of their wives. They are designed to find fulfillment through their eyes, as with Moses, Boaz, and Jesus, in seeing the results of their efforts on behalf of their wife, building a fulfilled, free woman (Isa. 53:11). Therefore, though the flesh cries for vindication, it is not to be. Wives are designed to provide men with nourishment and healing, not praise. Men must find resolve and capacity to do what is right through some other source.

So how does a man successfully resolve this mystery of death on behalf of his wife? What is his life worth? He who clings to his life shall lose it. Is a wife worth dying for? Can his life be preserved through slavery to the fear of dying? It is to be free of this slavery for which Jesus came (see Heb. 2:14–15)! It is time for men to make decisions in Christ!

Is the love of Jesus for you greater than yours for your wife? Undoubtedly so. But whom else has He placed upon the earth to be His instrument of love and protection for your wife, and what does His love of you require? To him whom much is given, much is required. We must remember Jesus' words:

- "Greater love has no one than this, that one lay down his life for his friends. You are My friends, if you do what I command you" (John 15:13–14).
- "For whoever wishes to save his life shall lose it; but whoever loses his life for My sake shall find it" (Matt. 16:25).
- "Husbands, love your wives, just as Christ also loved the church and gave Himself up for her" (Eph. 5:25).

On the basis of relationship with God a man is brought into life-giving obedience unto death. Through the death of men, wives and little ones live! It is a mystery, as Paul says! But there is no doubt that it is true (Phil. 3:7–11; Eph. 5:25–33).

This is accomplished in those who live in Christ. It is the Light of Christ which reveals a man's strongholds. It is the living Word Who encircles enemy strongholds in us with His power to tear them down. His Lordship brings every thought and action captive. His blood provides the scarlet seal of ransom which sets captives free from destruction. The enemy is to be destroyed by the sword of truth, and in this we become free indeed!

So, as Paul points out graphically, we are indeed being baptized as men into the death of Christ, in order that as He "was raised from the dead through the glory of the Father, so we too might walk in newness of life" (Rom. 6:3–4). Here is the hope of the dead in Christ! He is calling us to resurrection Life!

He is drawing each man everywhere to rise to the occasion, to walk, to occupy, to face the dreaded consequences, to taste resurrection life in his marriage and in the raising of godly seed.

We must pursue and lay hold of the Truth, Jesus Christ. It is decision time between each man and Christ. We have a choice of how we die—of remaining paralyzed or getting up and advancing against the enemy. His words to us are, "Get up and walk—with Me!"

Appendices

Appendix A

A Summary of Technical, Medical, and Political Information Relating to Homosexuality

Alfred Kinsey's 1948 claim that 5% to 10% of the American population was homosexual has proved untrue. Many aspects of Kinsey's work, including survey population, methods of obtaining information, and definition of *homosexuality* are now discredited within the medical community, though many of his false claims became popular and some sources still quote them.

More recent surveys in France, Britain, the United States, Canada, Norway, and Denmark show actual numbers of persons exclusively homosexual is under 1%. In the United States about 1.2% have had any homosexual experience in the past year. *Within the past 5 years, about 1.5% of males have had any homosexual experience.* Over lifetime, those who have had any homosexual experience at all ranges from about 2.7% (Denmark) to 4.7% (U.S.) to 6.1% (Britain).[1]

Male homosexuality has been shown to be closely linked to broken or damaged father relationships, especially during the child's age of six months to three years (see below). Based upon this it is possible to anticipate that the increasing failure rate of American families will cause an increase in the number of homosexuals in our population.

Many therapists report that *for those who wish to leave their homosexual lifestyle*, statistics of success range from 60% to 95% (far superior to those for alcoholism or drug abuse.) Most of these statistics are not journal published since they either involve religious counseling methods or are otherwise not supported within the medical community. However, one published work involving purely secular methods is the work of Schwartz and Masters. Using the intensive two-week sexual therapy methods of Masters and Johnson, they produced 79% success in enabling men to adopt an exclusively heterosexual lifestyle, which remained 71% persistent after five years.

The Schwartz and Masters method involves intensive daily counseling as well as immediately available on-call counseling twenty-four hours a day, primarily focused upon one thing: *to modify the behavioral anxiety of the male resulting from goal-oriented relationships with women.* The goal of the therapy is to remove anxiety by removing the goal (or anticipated need) for sexual intercourse and performance. In effect, the therapy seeks to redirect the focus of the male toward satisfaction in *process-oriented activity* rather than achievement of an end goal.[2]

In addition, other data has demonstrated that, even among psychologists who do not believe homosexual behavior to have adverse social or moral ramifications and who do not support therapy as a means of changing sexual orientation, reasonable success rates in therapy occur nonetheless.[3] It seems apparent that a sizeable proportion of the population of male homosexuals can be easily treated to produce a satisfied heterosexual lifestyle, if they have desire to do so.

However, the same sources indicate that approximately one-third of the homosexual community is highly resistant to effectual therapy, producing continued behavior dangerous to themselves and others. Published data shows average life expectancy of a male homosexual to be 41 years of age. AIDS shortens this by only a year or so. Women homosexuals live only two or three years longer. Why? Because the homosexual lifestyle is filled with self-destructive behavior and the spread of life-shortening disease, including hepatitis A, hepatitis B, a variety of venereal diseases, depression, risk taking, violence, and suicide. [4]

"Normalization" of homosexual behavior is generally promoted by the media as a political-ideological issue. This has also reached unprecedented levels in the medical community and has tended to curtail information available to medical professionals or the public. The rapid progress in de-pathologizing deviant behavior is seen in the actions of the American Psychiatric Association, which recently (1995) modified its Diagnostic and Statistical Manual (DSM-IV) to redefine pedophilia as non-pathologic unless it is also accompanied by feelings of guilt or functional impairment. Hence, the new medical definition of the behavior of child molestation is no longer considered a disorder unless it produces distress in the offender; i.e., if there is no feeling of guilt there is no sociopathic problem! The same type of change in definition has also been introduced for sadomasochism. These two are now commencing the same de-pathologizing progression as homosexual behavior did in the 1960s (being listed as sociopathic in the original 1952 DSM and being removed in 1968 in DSM II).[5] Unless effectual means are taken to reverse this trend, we could reasonably expect current citizens' concerns over health and safety of our youth to be coerced to accept forms of pedophilia as "normal" sexual orientation provided it produces no distress in the offender. This is currently being actively promoted by some homosexual groups and publications.

Statistics show men molested as youth (98% of the time by a male homosexual) to be eight times more likely than average to molest a girl and twenty times more likely than average to molest a boy, demonstrating that this behavior tends to reproduce multiplied damaged children in later generations.[6] Although child molestation is certainly not limited to the homosexual community, it is disproportionate; one-third of U.S. child molestation cases are committed by homosexuals, despite their only making up about 1.5% of the American population (homosexual incidence within the past five years per the data presented above.)[7]

As stated in the main text, the common factor in male homosexuality in nearly all studies of the past century is (a) an absent or ineffectual father or (b) traumatic experience(s) with the father.

Dr. Elizabeth Moberly, a psychologist who specialized for many years in gender identity research, has proposed a model of homosexual behavior which is based upon repressed love-need of the young child which may be reactivated in later years. According to her model, every child receives its gender identity through the love of the same-sex parent during its childhood growth, especially during its first three years of life.[8] Failure to receive this love-need leaves the child incomplete in gender identity until the need is met. If the removal of the love-need is through a traumatic, hurtful experience, it may also cause a defensive detachment on the part of the child to protect against recurrence of pain. This detachment, which can also become repressed along with the original trauma, will effectually block receiving love from the father (or any other substitute same-sex love source) for as long as it is repressed and unrecognized. Hence, reestablishment of even inadvertently painful relationships (such as when military service calls a father into a prolonged absence) may be unable to restore the same-sex source of love which the child needs to grow into his gender identity. In later years, in a fashion similar to lessening of other types of repression, the repression of both the need for a same sex love source and the defensive detachment which has prevented receiving it will dissipate, and the boy (or later, man) will attempt to satisfy his unmet need by seeking a male source of love.

As stated in the main text, Dr. Moberly presents persuasively the idea that the need for the same-sex source of love is essential for therapy and natural in terms of the completion of gender identity. She advocates that it should not be thwarted but provided in an appropriate therapeutic manner leading to the man's security in a loving relationship which helps him complete his gender identity. *Lacking gender identity, he will never achieve interest in or capacity to love a woman and find the greater level of personal fulfillment in a stable heterosexual relationship.*

Homosexuals can change. However, much traditional counseling has neglected dealing with the underlying psychological issues of homosexuality. Although heterosexual behavior, even persistent heterosexual behavior, can be achieved by some methods of counseling, including that cited above by Schwartz and Masters, it does not necessarily mean that the change in behavior is indicative of cure. Where underlying injury and repressed barriers against receiving love have been established and persisted for long periods in a person, those involved in complete healing must recognize that appropriately long periods of therapy, love, and work by God may also be required.

Appendix B

To My Friend

I remember how you liked to go mushroom hunting
    and had an expectant look in your eye.
And when you found some, how eager you were to come home
    to clean and cook your prize.
A simple country-like girl in love with animals, birds and trees;
    serenity found in God's natural gifts to her—
Not taking anything—but just enjoying the simple beauty
    that comes from being one with God and nature.
    These are the quiet things I love about Holly.

She is able to discern different plants,
    and name them with a soft affection for each one,
    as if she were reflecting;
"What it would be like to be that plant or bird?"—
    clothed with its splendor—
    being blown by the wind and gently rained upon,
    or softly being moved by the freedom of a breeze
    or a bird flying free in God's heavens.
It makes my heart soar when she smiles. It is like
    the sun has come out and her blue eyes dance with delight.
    And they are filled with compassion.
Her face has happiness lines on it that come from a joy from a
    pure heart, bounding energy to do good for others,
    With little regard for her infirmities.
She has a quiet unspeaking knowledge of what truth is
    She is the reflection of mercy and nourishment
And healing is in her touch.

When she walks, there is bounce and determination to her
step.
    and her hair is like spun gold,
    Bouncing softly around her shoulders and face.
When she listens she is intent on meanings
    When she speaks it is from her heart.
    And when she whispers it is an enticing aroma
That kindles fire from my heart and makes tears well up.
    These are the quiet things I love about Holly.

Appendix C

A Synopsis of Anthropological and Historical
Findings Regarding the Energy of Societies and
Regulation of Sexual Relations Between Genders,[1]
by Joseph Daniel Unwin

1. Study covered eighty uncivilized and sixteen civilized soci-
    eties throughout the world over approximately three thou-
    sand years to determine if there might be any corroborative
    evidence to the theories that subconscious repression of hu-
    man desires must always manifest in symptomatic behavior.
    Since one of the most powerful human instincts is sexual,
    Unwin thought he might look for the symptomatic behavior
    of societies as a function of the degree to which they repressed
    sexual freedom. He called this "sexual opportunity" accord-
    ing to the extent to which sexual continence was required
    before marriage and monogamy required during marriage.
2. Studies of uncivilized societies were based on actual *prac-
    tices* recorded by explorers and missionaries, in addition to
    language used for describing the unseen.[2] The two *prac-
    tices* studied were:

    *   sexual regulations placed upon the society, both pren-
        uptial and postnuptial;
    *   the language and practice rites of the society regarding
        the powers of the unseen world interacting with their
        visible world (i.e., treatment of the dead, the powerful
        dead, strange or unusual events, propitiation of spirits,
        priesthood and temple worship, etc.).

3. Unwin found that each uncivilized society could be placed into one of three cultural conditions. Determination was made through consideration of "steps taken to maintain a right relation with the powers in the universe." These categorize into three levels of conception, as follows:

- the *zoastic* condition: Neither temples nor post-funeral attention to the dead is given. These societies were considered to be at a "dead" level of conception.
- the *manistic* condition: Temples are not built, but post-funeral "tendence" and payments were made to powerful men (cults) after they died, seeking help in warding off danger or sickness. Rites were conducted in places of "unusual" historical events which were decorated. The attempts to deal thusly with unseen powers were felt to reflect a higher level of thought, reflection, and energy.
- the *diestic* condition: Rites and offerings were made in specially erected temples and through the agency of priests. Memory of ancient "unusual" events and powerful men were longer than in manistic societies; also exhibited other types of energy.

4. Representative issues addressed in the last two societies included weather, health afflictions, and treatment of ghosts/spirits either through priests or magicians. Unwin set voluminous rigorous definitions and standards for all determinations (or nondeterminations) that he made from the literature.

Unwin also established three definitions for degree of sexual opportunity:

- those which allowed complete prenuptial sexual freedom;

- those which had adopted such regulations as compelled an irregular or occasional continence, both prenuptially (as during betrothal) or postnuptially (as in restricting divorce or relations outside of certain designated individuals);
- those which insisted on prenuptial chastity.

5. Unwin found 100% correlation that cultural condition was always a reflection of the degree to which sexual opportunity was restricted, both across categories and within categories to the degree that variations of each existed within categories.

6. A few civilized societies could include a fourth possible cultural condition, the *rationalistic* condition. Higher levels of reflection and energy included characteristics of *societal expansion* and *productive expansion* and were found to always correlate with those societies which insisted on prenuptial chastity as well as postnuptial monogamy.

Endnotes

PREFACE

1. Drafted long prior to the disclosures of 1998 that have confirmed our nation elected a president that accurately reflects our morality.

CHAPTER 4

1. Includes fathers, uncles (see Mordecai and Esther in the Book of Esther), and mothers-in-law (see Naomi and Ruth in the Book of Ruth).
2. The only exception being harlotry by the wife. This is also the only situation in which God makes a case for Himself in His estrangement from Israel, harlotry being essentially indistinguishable from idolatry. See the Book of Hosea and Ezekiel, chapters 16 and 23.

CHAPTER 6

1. Shepherding includes both nurturing tasks and mortal defense tasks, producing a unique combination of character and attitudes of both the shield and breast; i.e. result-oriented tasks and never-ending processes. Combining all these functions and more, God's most frequent portrait of Christ is as the Shepherd of His people.
2. This important design feature is of utmost importance in the rearing of daughters in preparation for marriage. Once a daughter is convinced that her father is her agent (God's agent) for guiding her and enhancing her preparation for marriage to the man of her dreams, she will gladly submit to this process and is much less likely to go off on her own "doing what is right in her own sight."

CHAPTER 7

1. A mystery little fathomed for which many candidate theories have been offered. Possibly a portion of the fear of death men now have is a propitiating correction to Adam's foolishness or bravado in deciding to "stick with" Eve because of his great love for her. Perhaps also Adam's non-deceived deliberate act presages the death of the Bridegroom on behalf of His bride, but failed to correctly see the necessity for substitution in her

place rather than joining her disobedience. Certainly it marks the susceptibility of men to accept nurture from women that is attractive to the eye
but forbidden by God.

2. Institute in Basic Youth Conflicts: 1976–77 Curriculum Lecture Notes.

3. Note that Genesis 3:7 indicates Eve did not herself realize she was deceived
when she first gave the fruit to her husband, Adam, to eat, but only when
his eyes were opened did she see the deception.

4. To the chagrin of many millions of women over centuries, a facsimile of this
evocative power of words has been used by unrighteous men to play to
their weakness for deception. It tends to disappear after marriage and be
replaced by "rule." Yet, most women would love to hear their husbands
touch them with such words.

CHAPTER 14

1. There may also be prophetic significance regarding relationships with principalities of nations as to the basic means by which God will accomplish
the release of grace to Judah in order to convert and transform the entire
remnant nation of Israel (i.e., the house of Judah) in a single day as prophesied in Zechariah, chapter 12, and Isaiah, chapter 66.

CHAPTER 15

1. See *Restoration of Men*, chapters 1 through 11. This review of the biblical
design of men and women includes explanation of how men and women
are bonded and the deception under which women falsely believe sex will
bond a man to them in the same fashion as it does the woman to the man.
Men are bonded only through ransom and fire. Men are always able to
leave a sexual relationship and will in fact be driven to do so by a woman's
demands/manipulations/appetite for a deeper, more secure relationship,
unless the man is previously bonded by fire that leads to a covenant relationship (*Restoration of Men*, Destiny Image Publishing, 1990). Differences
in the urges for reproduction as well as the lies which work in the male
and female to lead toward sexual immorality are reviewed in detail suit-
able for teenagers in the author's book *Teens, Sex and Happiness* (Destiny
Image Publishers, 1994).

2. When Susan Smith's 1995 South Carolina murder of her two children was
first announced in national news, this characteristic was applied to predict
to a men's prayer fellowship that she certainly had a lover that had refused
to marry her because of her children. This information emerged in the newspapers several days later.

Chapter 16

1. Francis Frangipane, *The Three Battlegrounds* (Advancing Church Publications, 1989). Joyce Strader, "The Jezebel Spirit" (*Ministries Today Magazine* September/October 1990).
2. Frangipane, *The Three Battlegrounds*.
3. Ibid.
4. Strader, "The Jezebel Spirit."

Chapter 17

1. See also *Section V, Reproduction of Seed*, in this book.
2. Examples include the following pathologies for youth from single parent families: 63% of all youth suicides, 70% of all teenage pregnancies, 71% of all adolescent chemical/substance abuse, 80% of all prison inmates, 90% of all homeless and runaway children. Youths from fatherless homes are twenty times more likely than youths from two-parent homes to be incarcerated in juvenile dentention. Source: Dave Garrod and Bob Burk; compiled from various State of Georgia, Texas Dept. of Corrections (1992), and U.S. Census Bureau figures, plus other sources. *15 Oct. 1994, burk@MV.MV.COM*
3. Dr. Elizabeth R. Moberly, *Psychogenesis: The Early Development of Gender Identity* (London: Routledge and Kegan Paul Limited, 1979).

Chapter 19

1. *Restoration of Men*, Chapter 5, or *Teens, Sex and Happiness*, Chapter 14.
2. Note elements of this pattern also in Revelation, chapter 6, where Christ breaks the seals of judgment. Between the sixth and the seventh seals there comes to the "kings of the earth and the great men and the commanders and the rich and the strong and every slave and free man" the knowledge of the wrath of God in final judgment. They say to the mountains and to the rocks, "Fall on us and hide us from the presence of Him who sits on the throne, and from the wrath of the Lamb; for the great day of their wrath has come; and who is able to stand?" (Rev. 6:15–17). Their hearts melt, as did those of the inhabitants of Jericho. Wrath falls with the breaking of the seventh seal and the successive blasts of seven trumpets, as also in the case of Jericho.

   The same prescription also provides deliverance of God's people. The stronghold is removed with the blast of trumpet and a great shout. The interior city is opened to its conqueror. In the return of Christ for His Church and preceding His judgment of the world, these signs will be a joy to those who know God and shattering to those who do not (See I Cor. 15:51–53, I Thess. 4:15–17).

3. Note that her encircled stronghold was indistinguishable by the world from the other enemy strongholds of death throughout Jericho and would have served only as an instrument of death had she not identified it with the "cord of scarlet thread in the window." This scarlet thread, representing the *propitiating* blood of Jesus Christ, is the critical transforming agent between death and life in the judgment of a stronghold; that is, in redeeming life out of a stronghold of death.

CHAPTER 21

1. The same lack of realization is true of women also, but one of the main tenets of this book, reviewed scripturally in *Restoration of Men*, is that the primary responsibility for seeking wisdom and accepting sacrificial death through right actions for the success of a marriage (indeed, also, the freeing and healing of many women) is with the husband and is only possible in relationship with Jesus Christ.

2. See Chapter on Harlotry.

CHAPTER 22

1. That is, men willing to commit to the risks of carrying out one's assigned task and trusting God for the results.

2. Hebrews, chapter 11, warns us that many of the faithful died without yet receiving the promises.

3. He was won to Christ by a miraculous, providential intervention the week after his ex-wife agreed to remarry him without further conditions. Both were therefore in Christ when they remarried. This story is recounted in some detail in the author's *Still the Master of the Sea,* This family had three more children by the second marriage and are close friends of the author and his wife.

4. In one instance, after eighteen months of weekly counseling, what I thought to be significant changes in a man's financial and other attitudes began to take place. He gave up many of his "rights" and began to sincerely seek peace with his ex-wife with a number of relinquishments that moved me to weeping. Only a few weeks later he complained bitterly that a "so-called" Christian man (whom I soon realized I knew personally) had begun to date his wife. I prayerfully inquired of the Christian man if he realized that the woman's husband was seeking reconciliation. He said he hadn't and stopped dating her. At this time the counselee stopped coming. Within six weeks of this I was informed through a third party that the counselee had been dat-

ing another woman and had announced his engagement to marry her! When I inquired of him, he angrily accused me of meddling in his affairs, including the call to the Christian friend who had been dating his wife.

CHAPTER 23

1. There is much to note here about the power of Sarai's righteous submission to her husband and the opportunity it afforded God to work on her behalf because she obeyed "with a gentle and quiet spirit, precious in the sight of God" (1 Pet. 3:4). It is obvious that it also benefited her husband Abraham, even when his actions and motives were ungodly.

CHAPTER 27

1. See *Restoration of Men*, Chapters 10 and 12, plus its Part II, "Accountability."

CHAPTER 29

1. During this time, Gary had experienced a considerable burning irritation on his hand in the corresponding vicinity where her cyst was located, but the cyst never appeared on his body.

CHAPTER 30

1. This may be the most difficult time in the father-daughter relationship, including counseling surrogate daughters. The father must be as encouraging and informative as possible to persuade the daughter to enjoy her place of protection with him until God's work in the bridegroom is completed. Keeping in mind, though, that he usually explains things in facts and linear forms of logic and that she is persuaded by her inner heart, this is very difficult. God seems to determine if or when the girl in this kind of difficulty will "bolt" her protection to return to her lover (who begins to "come around") and whether or not the work with him has been adequate for a secure future.

CHAPTER 32

1. It also requires refrigeration and is unsuitable for use by a layman in the field.

2. The snake was about four feet long and as thick as a man's forearm. The fang marks were 3/4" apart.
3. I used this exchange to later write him a letter showing how Jesus Christ delivered us from sin in the same fashion.

CHAPTER 33

1. When Suzy testified of this and that she was sharing the letter with her friends, it was decided to include the letter as a general letter to daughters through that book.
2. In my situation some years earlier, I had been led to recognize that my Navy career held nothing more for me and at the very moment of acting to submit my retirement had been asked by the Lord, *"Karl, what if I asked you to stay in?"* After some thought, I responded that I would do so provided I could find fulfillment in Him alone, with the evidence that He was with me and bearing fruit through me. As a result, I stayed in the Navy for another seven years in work that was frustrating, futile, and unfulfilling, though God provided ample fulfillment in seeing His presence and beauty. However, a subliminal resentment which I carried throughout that period was that I was being robbed of more important "other" things, including the years of my life so devoted to this otherwise pointless Naval work. He later revealed both my resentment and its false premises when, after retirement, he surrounded me with incredible and gifted godly friends, all of whom were seven years younger than I!

CHAPTER 34

1. Mitchell's immediate observation on her first two hours of patient instruction to him was that Suzy "had a true servant's heart." Little did he know that he was being lured into her web of romance!
2. In reviewing this manuscript, Suzy and Mitchell did not recall his asking for a confirmation of her feelings for him. Now Gretchen and I question our memory on this! Did we just dream it up? In the review, however, Suzy confirmed that though she knew that Mitchell truly loved and was committed to her, she never told Mitchell she loved him until his proposal of marriage.

CHAPTER 35

1. Thomas H. Mauch II, "Hubby's Key to Happy Home: Try 'Yes, Dear,'" (originally appeared in *Los Angeles Times*) *Tacoma News-Tribune*, 21 February 1998. Refers to study by psychologist John Gottman, University of Washington.

Chapter 37

1. Note that this applies only to the children of God and not to the unsaved world, since the ground itself is referred to as only "close" to being cursed. Still it is possible for all its fruit not in Christ to be destroyed.

Chapter 39

1. Joseph Daniel Unwin, *Sex and Culture* (Oxford University Press, 1935). Originally published as the abstract "Sexual Regulations and Human Behavior" (Messrs. Williams and Norgate, Ltd., 1933). Unwin's published treatise and findings are summarized in Appendix C.
2. Dinah Richard, Ph.D., "Has Sex Education Failed Our Teenagers?" (Colorado Springs, CO: Focus on the Family Publishing, 1990). This report has a wealth of study references included for each of its many topics discussed.
3. However, extremely strict rules were also related to some increase in likelihood of sexual involvement.
4. That is, family planning, school-based clinics and contraceptive sex education.

Chapter 41

1. An illustrative response comes frequently from women who, in discussion of their actions and attitudes toward their husbands, make the statement, "I tried that, and it didn't work." Further discussion unfailingly confirms that these words mean that their husbands did not change, thereby unwittingly revealing that the underlying motivation (and measure of success) of their efforts to become godly women is to achieve change in the behaviors of their husbands. Needless to say, their efforts have been in vain because their actions are not primarily purposed to become pleasing to God and to look to God for both their personal affirmation and need.
2. Jesus: Greek *Iesous* (Strong's #2424) of Hebrew *Yehoshua* (Strong's #3091), constructed of *Jehova* (Strong's #3068) and *Yasha* (Strong's #3467) meaning to avenge, deliver, defend, help, preserve, save, etc. (Note the distinction between this specific name and the more general "Jeshua" which means "He saves.")

Chapter 42

1. It is important to note that this remarkable summary of Jesus' motivation for His going to His death comes immediately after He explains that Satan is

coming to have his way, even though having nothing in Jesus. That is, even though Satan has no claim on Jesus, Jesus is going to His death out of love for the Father and is *keeping the Father's commandment in doing so!* How might this compare with our keeping His commandment not to divorce?

2. It seems clearly explained in Genesis 4:6–7 that emotions are in response to actions and that right actions produce good emotions. Possibly "love" can be explained as an emotion in these terms. See also I Cor. 13.

CHAPTER 43

1. For example, the NIV uses the phrase *atoning sacrifice*. Today's English Version translates it as "the means by which people's sins are forgiven." The Jerusalem Bible uses a host of interchangeable phrases, including "win reconciliation through faith" (Rom. 3:23), "atone for human sins" (Heb. 2:17), and "sacrifice that takes our sins away" (1 John 2:2, 4:10), all of which capture *expiation* but completely lose the idea of reversal of God's wrath to His completely unlimited favor.

2. This is all summarized and given its most glorious example in the crucifixion of Christ, which was the culmination of the work of all evil in history to take the life of the Son of God, but which was reversed by God in Christ's resurrection and all its consequences for our lives, both in this age and in the one to come.

3. It is interesting that Matthew, the forgiven tax collector, seems to have captured this in his gospel more clearly than all the others, just as Paul, the ex-Pharisee and persecutor of the Church, seems to have grasped understanding of "grace" more clearly than any other. "From anyone who has been given much shall much be required" (Luke 12:48).

CHAPTER 44

1. A possible clue that Paul did not write the book of Hebrews.

APPENDIX A

1. Dr. J. Gordon Muir, *Kinsey, Sex and Fraud* (Huntington House Publishers, 1990) and *The Wallstreet Journal*, 31 March 1993.

2. Mark F. Schwartz and William H. Masters, *"The Masters and Johnson Treatment Program for Dissatisfied Homosexual Men,"* American Journal of Psychiatry 141 (1984): 173–181. (Some will recognize this difficulty as a general cause of problems in many male-female relationships; i.e., the male tendency to orient toward sexual intercourse and climax interferes with the female goal

of extended close personal intimacy with the male in which she finds much of her greatest fulfillment. This general tendency of women to be process-oriented while men tend to be goal-oriented is also discussed in chapter 6.

3. One group of 285 such psychoanalysts who had treated 1215 homosexual patients reported that 23% of their patients changed to heterosexuality, while 84% received significant therapeutic benefit. See Houston MacIntosh, M.D., "Attitudes and Experiences of Psychoanalysts in Analyzing Homosexual Patients," *Journal of the American Psychoanalytic Association* 42, no. 4: 1183–1207.

   A bibliography of twenty-five resources that report treatment success of homosexuality is contained in the *National Association for Research and Treatment of Homosexuality (NARTH) Bulletin* (July 1993).

4. P. Cameron, W.L. Playfair and S. Wellum, "The Longevity of Homosexuals: Before and After the AIDS Epidemic," *OMEGA Journal of Death and Dying* 29, no. 3 (1994).

5. J. Nicolosi, "Pedophilia Not Always a Disorder?" *National Association of Research and Therapy of Homosexuality (NARTH) Bulletin* (April 1995).

6. Various surveys involve both "interest in" and "actual contact." The most conservative figures (shown in text) are "interest in" by those who have been sexually molested. Actual contact figures are about twice as high. See P. Cameron, *Family Research Institute Report* (September-October 1994).

7. P. Cameron, W. Coburn, Jr. et al, "Child Molestation and Homosexuality," *Psychological Reports* 58 (1986): 327–337.

8. Moberly, *Psychogenesis: The Early Development of Gender Identity* (London: Routledge and Kegan Paul Limited, 1979).

APPENDIX C

1. Joseph Daniel Unwin, *Sex and Culture* (Oxford University Press, 1935).

2. In contrast to *beliefs*, which proved subject to considerable misrecording or misinterpretation by historians, causing elimination of a number of societies from the data base.

Books by Karl Duff

- *Restoration of Men (God's Rescue of Women and Children):* God provides healing, restoration, and protective accountability for men who find themselves ineffectual as husbands and fathers.
- *Lord and Scoutmaster:* The author relates humorous as well as educational true life adventures he had as a Scout and then as a Scoutmaster.
- *Leader's Guide for High Adventure:* This is a booklet of practical tips for leading Scouts or youth groups on extended backpacking or canoeing trips, based upon three decades of experience.
- *Still the Master of the Sea:* With signs and wonders God intervened in a modern hydrofoil warship program and changed a prideful naval officer. A remarkable testimony of miracles.
- *Teens, Sex, and Happiness:* God's design of male-female relationships is an important part of His plan for our lives. Youth must obey God's plan to find happiness and fulfillment. Includes discussion questions.

To order additional books, contact the author at:

Karl Duff
6112 Wynn Jones Road East
Port Orchard, WA 98366
206.871.1265

Place this order form in an envelope along with your check or money order.

Quantity	Description	Unit Price	Total Price
	Restoration of Marriage	$13.95	
	Restoration of Men	$9.95	
	Lord and Scoutmaster	$8.95	
	Leader's Guide for High Adventure	$3.00	
	Still the Master of the Sea	$10.95	
	Teens, Sex, and Happiness	$9.95	

Ship. (quant.) 1–2   3–5   6–9   10–14   15–19   20–25
Ship. Cost $2.50   4.00   6.50   10.50   13.25   16.00

Subtotal	
Less Discount	
Plus Shipping	
TOTAL DUE	

Name: _____

Address: _____

City/State/Zip: _____   Phone #: _____

Signature: _____   Date: _____

20% Discount for 5 or more copies